CiTY·SMaRT™
GUIDEBOOK

Milwaukee

Second Edition

Nathan Guequierre

John Muir Publications
Santa Fe, New Mexico

John Muir Publications, P. O. Box 613, Santa Fe, New Mexico 87504

Copyright © 1999 by John Muir Publications
Cover and maps copyright © 1999 by John Muir Publications
All rights reserved.

Second edition. First printing August 1999.
Printed in the United States of America.

ISBN 1-56261-442-8
ISSN 1093-0825

Editors: Peg Goldstein, Chris Hayhurst
Graphics Editor: Bunny Wong
Production: Rebecca Cook
Design: Janine Lehmann
Cover Design: Suzanne Rush
Typesetting: Diane Rigoli
Maps: Julie Fenton
Printer: Publishers Press
Front cover photo: © Andre Jenny/Unicorn Stock Photos—Downtown Milwaukee
Back cover photo: © Eric R. Berni/Unicorn Stock Photos—The domes at Mitchell Park

Distributed to the book trade by
Publishers Group West
Berkeley, California

*While every effort has been made to provide accurate, up-to-date information,
the author and publisher accept no responsibility for loss, injury, or inconvenience
sustained by any person using this book.*

CONTENTS

See Milwaukee the City•Smart™ Way   v

1 Welcome to Milwaukee   1
Getting to Know Milwaukee 2 • Milwaukee History 4 • The People of Milwaukee 8 • Weather 9 • Dressing in Milwaukee 10 • When to Visit 11 • Calendar of Events 12 • Business and Economy 14 • Housing 15 • Schools 16

2 Getting Around Milwaukee   17
City Layout 17 • Public Transit 19 • Driving in Milwaukee 22 • Bicycling in Milwaukee 23 • Air Travel in Milwaukee 24 • Rail Service 25 • Bus Service 26

3 Where to Stay   27
Downtown 29 • East Side 34 • North Side 37 • South Side 39 • West Side 45 • Waukesha County 48

4 Where to Eat   51
Downtown 53 • East Side 61 • North Side 67 • South Side 70 • West Side 76 • Waukesha County 78

5 Sights and Attractions   80
Downtown 81 • East Side 88 • North Side 92 • South Side 93 • West Side 99 • Waukesha County 101 • City Tours 102

6 Museums and Galleries   105
Art Museums 106 • History and Science Museums 108 • Other Museums 109 • Galleries 110 • Public Art 113

7 Kids' Stuff   114
Animals and Nature 114 • Museums and Libraries 116 • Children's Theater 117 • Stores Kids Love 118 • Places to Play 120

8 Parks and Gardens   123

9 Shopping   132
Shopping Districts 133 • Bookstores and Newsstands 137 • Other Stores of Note 139 • Department Stores 144 • Shopping Malls 145 • Outlet Stores 147

10 Sports and Recreation   148
Professional Sports 149 • Amateur Sports 151 • Recreation 152

11 Performing Arts   165
Theater 166 • Music and Opera 168 • Dance 171 • Concert Venues 172

12 Nightlife   176
Dance Clubs 177 • Jazz Clubs 177 • Blues Clubs 178 • Rock Clubs 178 • Country Music Clubs 180 • Other Music Clubs 180 • Pubs and Bars 181 • Comedy Clubs 185 • Dinner Theater 186 • Movie Houses 186

13 Day Trips from Milwaukee 188
The East Shore 188 • Frank Lloyd Wright's Taliesin 191 • Kettle Moraine North 193 • Cambridge 194 • Cedarburg 195

Appendix: City•Smart Basics 197
Emergency Phone Numbers 197 • Major Hospitals 197 • Recorded Information 197 • Visitor Information 197 • City Tours 198 • Post Offices 198 • Public Transit 198 • Car Rental 198 • Multicultural Resources 198 • Other Community Organizations 198 • Child-care Referral 199 • Newspapers 199 • Magazines 199 • Bookstores 200 • AM Radio Stations 200 • FM Radio Stations 200 • Television Stations 201

Index 202

MAP CONTENTS

Milwaukee Zones vi–vii

3 Where to Stay
Downtown Milwaukee 28
Greater Milwaukee 36
South Side 40

4 Where to Eat
Downtown Milwaukee 55
East Side 60
Greater Milwaukee 64
South Side 71

5 Sights and Attractions
Downtown Milwaukee 83
Greater Milwaukee 90
South Side 94

13 Day Trips
Milwaukee Region 189

See Milwaukee the CiTY·SMaRT™ Way

The Guide for Milwaukee Natives, New Residents, and Visitors
In *City•Smart Guidebook: Milwaukee*, local author Nathan Guequierre tells it like it is. Residents will learn things they never knew about their city, new residents will get an insider's view of their new hometown, and visitors will be guided to the very best Milwaukee has to offer—whether they're on a weekend getaway or staying a week or more.

Opinionated Recommendations Save You Time and Money
From shopping to nightlife to museums, the author is opinionated about what he likes and dislikes. You'll learn the great and the not-so-great things about Milwaukee's sights, restaurants, and accommodations. So you can decide what's worth your time and what's not; which hotel is worth the splurge and which is the best choice for budget travelers.

Easy-to-Use Format Makes Planning Your Trip a Cinch
City•Smart Guidebook: Milwaukee is user-friendly—you'll quickly find exactly what you're looking for. Chapters are organized by travelers' interests or needs, from Where to Stay and Where to Eat, to Sights and Attractions, Kids' Stuff, Sports and Recreation, and even Day Trips from Milwaukee.

Includes Maps and Quick Location-Finding Features
Every listing in this book is accompanied by a geographic zone designation (see the next page for zone details) that helps you immediately find each location. Staying on Old World Third Street and wondering about nearby sights and restaurants? Look for the Downtown label in the listings, and you'll know which little-seen statue or great café is not far away. Or maybe you're looking for the Harley-Davidson Factory. Along with its address, you'll see a North Side label, so you'll know just where to find it.

All That and Fun to Read, Too!
Every City•Smart chapter includes fun-to-read (and fun-to-use) tips to help you get more out of Milwaukee, trivia (did you know there are more taverns per capita here than in any other American city?), and illuminating sidebars (for the best frozen custard stands, see page 66). And well-known local residents provide their personal "Top Ten" lists, guiding readers to the city's best architectural jewels and more.

GREATER MILWAUKEE ZONES

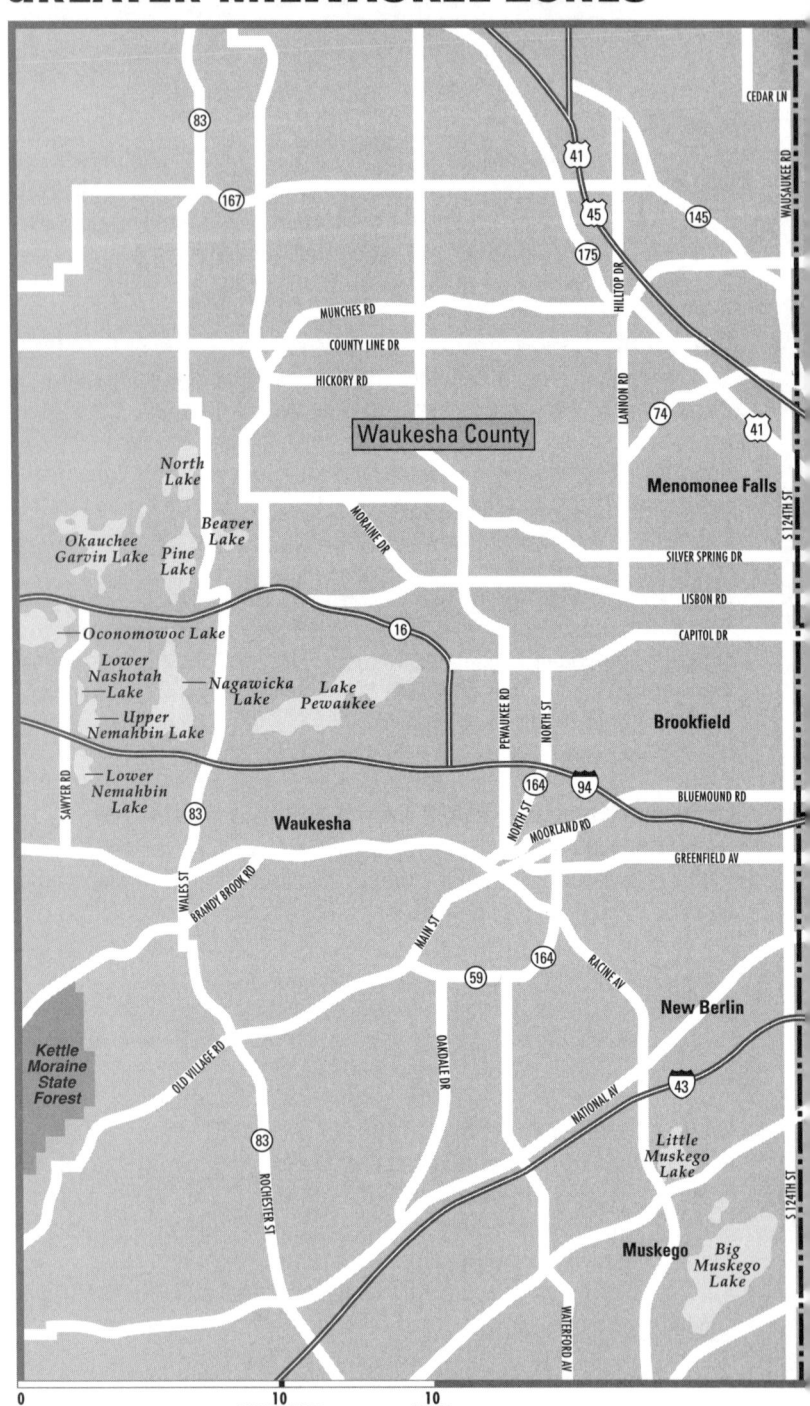

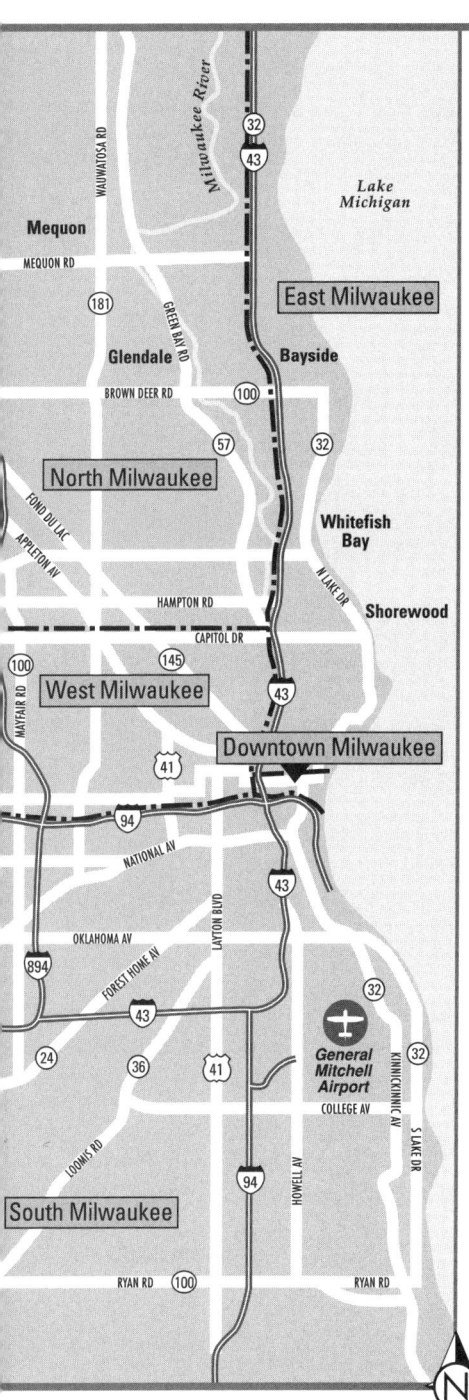

MILWAUKEE ZONES

Downtown (D)
Bordered by Lake Michigan on the east, West Vliet and East Lyon Streets on the north, North 27th Street on the west, and the Menomonee River Valley on the south.

East Side (ES)
Lies north of downtown Milwaukee, with the lake on the east and the Milwaukee River and I-43 on the west. Includes Shorewood, White-fish Bay, Fox Point, and the eastern part of Mequon.

North Side (NS)
Bordered by the Milwaukee River and I-43 on the east, the zone extends northwest on the north side of West Lisbon Avenue and West Capitol Drive.

South Side (SS)
Extends from Lake Michigan to Waukesha County south of the Menomonee River Valley and I-94. Includes Mitchell International Airport, Bayview, West Allis, and Greendale and part of the sprawling South Side.

West Side (WS)
Bounded by North 27th and North 108th Streets, the Menomonee River Valley, West Lisbon Street, and West Walnut Street, the West Side includes Wisconsin State Fair Park, the VA Hospital, and County Stadium.

Waukesha County (WC)
Includes the cities of Brookfield, Elm Grove, New Berlin, and Waukesha and extends west to the south unit of the Kettle Moraine State Forest.

1
WELCOME TO MILWAUKEE

In other cities, the local joke runs, "the Three Bs" stand for Bach, Beethoven, and Brahms. In Milwaukee, the epicenter of oompah German America, they stand for Beer, Bratwurst, and Bowling. While that *Laverne and Shirley* stereotype no longer rings true, Milwaukee is still firmly grounded in a strong ethnic and working-class heritage.

Milwaukee is a city that prides itself on stability. The industries on which the city's wealth was founded—brewing (think Miller High Life), manufacturing (think Harley-Davidson), printing, and transportation—remain the cornerstones of a booming regional economy. And with that boom has come a strengthening of the city's neighborhoods, the real soul of Milwaukee.

A city of immigrants, Milwaukee has strong enclaves of Poles and Serbs, Italians and Latvians, Germans (of course), and new immigrants from Central America, Russia, and Southeast Asia. Because Milwaukeeans love a party, they celebrate that diverse heritage in shops, taverns, and restaurants, street fairs, and enormous lakefront festivals throughout the year.

What does all of this mean for visitors? It means, quite simply, that Milwaukee is a great town to visit. With miles of Lake Michigan shoreline, stunning parks, a bustling downtown, distinctive neighborhoods, and a strong art, music, and theater scene, Milwaukee offers visitors beer, bratwurst, and much more. From polka taverns to the world's largest outdoor pop-music festival, from hasenpfeffer to phad Thai, from Second Empire office blocks to Miller Park—the new Brewers baseball stadium—visitors to Milwaukee can take in the best of the past and see the outlines of the future.

Getting to Know Milwaukee

Milwaukee is a lot like other mid-size American cities. It has factories and concert halls, vertical office towers and sprawling suburbs, expressways and flower-lined avenues, specialty shops and huge shopping malls. Still, Milwaukee has a flavor all its own—from the Lake Michigan shoreline that defines its eastern edge to the glacial moraines that rise along the metropolitan area's western border.

Geographically, for a metropolitan area with just over 1.5 million people, greater Milwaukee is relatively compact. Downtown Milwaukee, set near the point where the Milwaukee, Menomonee, and Kinnickinnic Rivers join to flow into Lake Michigan, is the financial and commercial center of the region. It is also the focus of much of Milwaukee's artistic and civic energy—site of the Milwaukee Art Museum, the Marcus Center for the Performing Arts, and the Bradley Center sports arena. The southeast section of downtown, the Historic Third Ward, is a neighborhood of century-old warehouses turned to lofts and condos, tony shops, art galleries, and upscale restaurants.

Radiating outward from downtown along major thoroughfares are the city's residential districts, neighborhoods with characters all their own. North along the lakefront is the young and hip east side and the gracious North Shore, with classy shopping areas and large, well-maintained lakefront mansions. Farther north are rapidly growing suburbs, complete with enormous homes on huge lots and fancy shopping malls. South along the lakeshore lies Bayview, a quaint working-class neighborhood of modest Victorian homes. Beyond that, Milwaukee's South Shore continues in much the same vein, with neat middle-class homes and stunning lakefront parks.

Milwaukee's North Shore

Greater Milwaukee Conv. and Visitors Bureau

> **TRIVIA**
>
> ## City Planning
> One of three sites chosen for the New Deal "greenbelt" project, the city of Greendale was built from scratch on Milwaukee's southwest side in the 1930s. Planned on the scale and model of a New England village, Greendale featured a central city square, a system of pedestrian and bicycle paths, and residents selected for their willingness to participate in community activities.

On the west side of downtown, along Wisconsin Avenue, stands Marquette University, with its old cathedrals and new apartment developments. Beyond that is an area of faded glory—struggling to regain some of it former grandeur—where fabulous 19th–century houses commingle with soup kitchens. Also on the west side are stable, lovely neighborhoods like Washington Heights, its streets lined with "Milwaukee Bungalows," and the charming old suburb of Wauwatosa, along with Miller Brewing, the County Zoo, and the baseball stadium. Beyond the zoo, rapidly growing municipalities like Brookfield and Waukesha spread into the glacial moraines.

To the south and southwest of downtown is the real beating heart of ethnic Milwaukee. Walker's Point, across the Menomonee River from the city center, has historically been home to the city's most recent immigrants. National and Forest Home Avenues cut through poor but bustling Hispanic and Asian neighborhoods, past the small, neat bungalows and "Polish Flats" of the south side and industrial West Allis, and into the suburbs beyond Whitnall Park.

To the north of downtown is an area remarkable mostly for its fall from grace during the 1960s and '70s. The near north side struggled in those decades as the original German residents moved out and the city's booming African American population moved in. As the new residents worked to establish a foothold, the area was beset by race riots and failing schools. Bright spots are now emerging, however—crime is declining, housing is improving, and Martin Luther King Drive (North Third Street) is slowly becoming a vibrant shopping district once again. Beyond the near north side is a sprawling region of middle-class residential areas, from Sherman Park with its stately old houses to the village-turned-suburb of Menomonee Falls.

Wherever your travels take you in the area, you'll find one constant. The people of Milwaukee are friendly and outgoing. The city has been called "America's biggest small town." You can strike up a conversation just about anywhere—on the bus or in the checkout line. Milwaukeeans are proud of their city and want you to enjoy it as much as they do. And they'll go out of their way to make you feel at home.

Milwaukee History

The story of Milwaukee's development and growth is one of fortuitous location and hard work. Long before French explorer and missionary Père Jacques Marquette first entered Milwaukee Bay in 1673, Sauk and Potowatomi people called the place Mahn–ah–wauk, roughly construed to mean "gathering place by the water." With three water highways leading in from the north, northwest, and southwest, it was the ideal site for council grounds and meetings among nations.

Those water routes also made Milwaukee a natural fur-trading center. Throughout the 18th century, as European fashion demanded more and more beaver pelts, Milwaukee Bay thrived as a seasonal home for trappers and traders. In 1795 Jacques Vieau established the city's first permanent residence, as well as a trading post on the south bank of the Menomonee River.

In 1813 the future arrived in Milwaukee in the person of French-Canadian entrepreneur Solomon Juneau, who established the American Fur Company in the heart of today's downtown. In 1834 Milwaukee's two other founding fathers arrived. The genial Virginian George Walker settled south of the Menomonee's mouth, and Byron Kilbourn, a cantankerous

Ten Milwaukeeans Who Shaped the World

1. **Golda Meir**—prime minister of Israel
2. **Brooks Stevens**—pioneering industrial designer
3. **Major Henry Roberts**—author of *Roberts' Rules of Order*, standard parliamentary procedure
4. **General Douglas MacArthur**—commander of U.S. Pacific forces in World War II
5. **Lydia Ely Hewitt**—a creator of the National Soldier's Home system, which later became the Veteran's Administration
6. **Ole Evinrude**—inventor of the outboard motor in 1910
7. **Christopher Latham Sholes**—inventor of the typewriter in 1868
8. **Increase A. Lapham**—naturalist and founder of the U.S. Weather Bureau
9. **Warren Johnson**—inventor of the thermostat
10. **Mathilde Franszika Anneke**—founder of the first women's suffrage newspaper

Milwaukee Admirals game

Yankee with a dream of founding a city, built a house on the river's west bank.

The race to control the city's development was on. Each founding father was mistrustful of the other two, with a particular animosity between Juneau and Kilbourn. The results of this rivalry are evident today in downtown streets, which each settler purposely built not to match with the rival's streets across the rivers. Consequently, bridges had to be built at oblique angles to the roadways, a difficulty that precipitated the Bridge War of 1845 (see sidebar on page 11). In 1846, after a decade of haggling, the three men put aside their differences and joined forces to incorporate the City of Milwaukee.

"The Cream City," so called for its buildings' distinctive cream-colored brick made from local clay, grew rapidly through the 19th century, largely due to an influx of Irish laborers and German "48ers," intellectual proto-Socialists who left Europe after the failed revolution of 1848. Industrious and committed to social justice, the German immigrants left an indelible mark on the city. So great was their influence that in the mid-19th century, four of the city's seven newspapers were written in German. Germans also began the city's famous breweries and established musical and athletic societies and professional theaters.

As Milwaukee grew, it became the region's commercial center. By the time the Civil War ended, Milwaukee was the leading grain-shipping port in the West, exporting more than 60 million bushels of wheat during the war years. The 1890 census rated Milwaukee as the "most foreign city" in the United States, with 72 percent of its population of Germanic origin. Milwaukee capped off its glorious century of growth with the construction, in 1896, of a new city hall. Rising 393 feet above Water Street, the Flemish Renaissance–style building perfectly embodied Milwaukee as a city that faced the future by embracing the past.

Around the turn of the twentieth century, with the Industrial Revolution in full swing, Milwaukee was well on its way to becoming "America's Workshop." New waves of immigrants from Germany and Eastern Europe fueled the industrial economy with a heavy influx of labor.

They also helped inaugurate the socialist era in Milwaukee politics. In 1910 Emil Seidel was elected Milwaukee's first socialist mayor (the last, Frank Zeidler, would step down in 1960). The poet Carl Sandburg, who then lived on Milwaukee's upper east side, was Mayor Seidel's secretary.

MILWAUKEE TIME LINE

pre-1670	Potowatomi, Fox, and Mascouten Indians inhabit the Milwaukee area.
1673	Father Jacques Marquette stops in Milwaukee as he explores Lake Michigan.
1779	The British send the HMS *Felicity* into Milwaukee Bay to discourage Indians from siding with the colonists in the Revolutionary War.
1795	Jacques Vieau establishes a Northwest Company fur-trading post.
1818	Solomon Juneau arrives from Canada, establishing an American Fur Company post on the present site of downtown Milwaukee.
1834	George Walker and Byron Kilbourn arrive.
1839	The first Irish and German immigrants arrive in large numbers.
1844	Jacob Best founds the brewery that will become Pabst Brewing.
1846	Kilbourn, Juneau, and Walker set aside their differences to incorporate the City of Milwaukee. Juneau is elected mayor.
1852	The forerunner of the Milwaukee Public Library is founded.
1854	An abolitionist mob frees fugitive slave Joshua Glover from the county jail and sends him to Canada.
1860	The Cream City Club, Milwaukee's first professional baseball team, is organized. The *Lady Elgin* sinks, with the loss of 400 lives.
1870	Increase Lapham founds the forerunner of the U.S. Weather Bureau.
1872	Milwaukee breweries ship much of their product to Chicago, whose residents are thirsty after the Great Fire.
1884	The Milwaukee Public Museum opens.
1892	The Third Ward burns, leaving 2,000 people homeless.
1895	Milwaukee's present City Hall is opened.
1906	Edna Ferber becomes a *Milwaukee Journal* reporter.
1910	Emil Seidel is the first socialist mayor of Milwaukee.
1919	Prohibition forces breweries to close.
1920	Goldie Myerson leaves Milwaukee for Palestine, where she eventually becomes Prime Minister Golda Meir of Israel.
1932	Pabst is the first brewery to distribute canned beer nationwide.

Fifty-seven Milwaukee factories produce parts for the atomic bomb.	1945
Hillside Terrace, the city's first public housing project, opens.	1948
The Boston Braves become the Milwaukee Braves.	1953
The Braves win the World Series, with Hank Aaron voted MVP.	1957
The Saint Lawrence Seaway opens, giving Milwaukee shippers ocean access.	1959
Braves leave Milwaukee for Atlanta.	1966
Race riots paralyze the city. Father James Groppi leads open housing marches.	1967
Summerfest begins.	1968
The Milwaukee Brewers are formed, bringing baseball back to Milwaukee.	1970
Public schools are ordered to integrate by the federal courts.	1976
The Bradley Center sports arena is completed.	1988
The Midwest Express Convention Center opens.	1998

The socialist legacy is clearly evident in modern Milwaukee, with its fine park system, abundance of affordable housing, and neat system of service alleys that keep the public faces of commercial and residential buildings tidy.

Because much of its economy was based on the manufacturing of durable goods, Milwaukee fared better during the Great Depression than did many other American cities. In fact, news of employment opportunities in the Cream City caused signficant migration from other parts of the country during the early 1930s. When economic collapse did arrive, however, it arrived with a vengeance. In addition to a fall-off in industrial employment, Prohibition had destroyed the city's thriving breweries.

With the wartime economy, manufacturing soon boomed again. By the end of the Second World War, Milwaukee was a manufacturing heavyweight. Meanwhile, new housing patterns were established, as African Americans moved to the central city, displacing the old German population on the north side, who moved into the burgeoning suburbs. In the late 1960s, Milwaukee suffered race riots and found an unlikely Civil Rights hero in James Groppi, a Jesuit priest from working-class Bayview who led open-housing marches across the Sixth Street viaduct into the heart of the white south side.

In the 1970s and early 1980s, Milwaukee, along with many other

Henry W. Maier Festival Park

industrial midwestern cities, vied for the title of "Rusty Buckle on the Rust Belt." As the economy faltered, well-paying industrial jobs went south. In the name of "urban renewal," expressways replaced decaying neighborhoods and historic buildings were torn down. Milwaukee had bottomed out. Crime increased, wages dropped, and more than 55,000 jobs were lost.

But the picture has brightened considerably since those dark days, and Milwaukee is currently riding a decade-long boom. The city's economy is leaner and more diverse than at any time in the past, and unemployment rates are at their lowest in decades. Like many cities, Milwaukee underwent a building boom in the 1980s, with a half-dozen new office towers rising above downtown.

Now, at the end of the century, Milwaukee is enjoying another wave of construction. This time the projects tend to be more horizontal than vertical, symbols not of corporate achievement but of community spirit. The first phase of the Midwest Express Convention Center opened to national acclaim in 1998. The new millennium will see the completion of the Riverwalk, water-level pedestrian thoroughfares along the Milwaukee River, complete with boat landings and water taxis, outdoor cafés, and contemporary sculpture; completion of a spectacular addition to the Milwaukee Art Museum; and an expansion of Mitchell International Airport. Finally, Miller Park, the new home of the Milwaukee Brewers, will host its first baseball-happy crowds under a massive retractable roof on Opening Day 2000.

The People of Milwaukee

Walker's Point or Greendale? Cambridge Heights or Washington Heights? Whitefish Bay or Bayview? Each of Milwaukee's distinctive neighborhoods carries with it connotations of ethnic background, occupation and avocation, economic status, and personal values. If you grew up in Lincoln Village, it's likely that your family is Polish. If you grew up on Brady Street, there's a good chance you're of Italian extraction. If you live in Riverwest you may be artsy. If you live in Brookfield you may likely have a young family and commute to an office tower downtown.

The earliest white settlers to the city were Yankees and French Canadians, followed by Irish, German, and Norwegian immigrants. At the end of the 19th century, great waves of Catholic immigrants from Eastern Europe, Ireland, and Italy built many of the city's most pleasant neighborhoods and created that most enduring of Milwaukee social institutions, the Friday night fish fry.

The 20th century has seen new waves of immigration, from southern African Americans after World War II to more recent Hispanic and southeast Asian immigrants, centered on the city's near south and west sides. Most recently, a large number of Russian Jews have built a thriving community on the upper east side.

There is a grimmer side, however, to Milwaukee's status as an immigrant mecca: hyper-segregation. According to the U.S. Census Bureau, Milwaukee is the least integrated city in the United States. The reasons for this phenomenon include the tendency of immigrants to settle in small geographic areas and an embarrassing track record of institutionalized racism in bank lending patterns. So entrenched are the divisions that George Wallace, recalcitrant anti-integrationist, once remarked, "If I had to leave Alabama, I'd want to live on the south side of Milwaukee." There are exceptions to the rule: the Riverwest, Walker's Point, Sherman Park, and Washington Heights neighborhoods are relatively well integrated, as is much of the near west side.

Weather

Milwaukee lies in the middle of the temperate zone. In practical terms, that means that the city enjoys four distinct seasons and that temperatures fall within tolerable ranges all year long. Milwaukee also experiences the "Cooler by the Lake" phenomenon: Within six or seven miles of Lake

TRIVIA

Milwaukee hasn't led the country in beer production in decades, yet Milwaukeeans still take their beer seriously. There are more taverns per capita here than in any other American city, and Milwaukeeans, as a whole, drink more beer and brandy than anyone else.

Michigan, temperatures are five degrees cooler in summer and warmer in winter than in the city's farther western reaches.

Every season, however, brings with it a few days of extreme temperatures. Four or five summer days each year top 100 degrees, and winters have been known to feature weeklong sub-zero stretches. White Christmases are not uncommon. Winters tend to be cloudy, spring and fall are rainy, and summers are sunny and pleasant, particularly when Lake Michigan warms up enough for swimming, usually around the end of June.

Dressing in Milwaukee

As befits a town proud of its working-class roots and easygoing attitude, Milwaukeeans are casual yet conservative dressers. Jeans, shorts, T shirts, and sweatshirts are all you'll see at Summerfest or at most Friday-night fish fries. Office buildings downtown are populated by conservative suits, and, in general, the farther you go from the older neighborhoods, particularly up the North Shore or into Waukesha County, the more expensively tailored the citizens become. Sport coats and dresses are *almost* required at big cultural events like the symphony or opera, and Milwaukeeans tend to dress up at nice restaurants. There are pockets, too, of the hip and the chic. Anything goes—from vinyl to bell-bottoms and platform shoes—on Brady Street, for instance.

The weather certainly comes into play when choosing your wardrobe

Average Monthly Temperature

	Ave. High Temps (°F)	Ave. Low Temps (°F)
January	26	11
February	30	16
March	39	25
April	54	36
May	65	45
June	75	55
July	80	61
August	78	60
September	71	53
October	60	42
November	45	30
December	32	18

here. You'll want to bring a sweater to the lakefront any time but midsummer. Winters require warm clothes: an overcoat, hat, boots, scarf, and gloves.

When To Visit

Milwaukee has a lot going for it any time of year, but because winters are long and cold, the city really comes out of its shell in summer. There are more sporting events and festivals than you can count, parks are full of picnickers, sidewalk cafés sprout like garden flowers, and the lakefront is packed with swimmers, bicyclists, in-line skaters, anglers, walkers, and boaters from sunrise to sunset.

But while summer gets top billing, autumn is perhaps the most spectacular time of year in Milwaukee, particularly in the many lake- and riverfront parks, as the warm days give way to chilly evenings, and the trees put on their annual spectacle of color. Winter, too, has its joys: ice-skating downtown and in many county parks and plenty of sledding, snowshoeing,

---

A Bridge Too Far

As rival settlements struggled to control Milwaukee's destiny, bridges became the focus of a rancorous dispute between east side and west in the beginning of the 19th century. Newcomers arriving by land couldn't get to the east side of the river, where the land office stood; those arriving by boat couldn't get to the interior, where the resources lay.

Questions of who would benefit from bridges, who was going to pay for them, and who was going to maintain them eventually led to Milwaukee's 1845 "Bridge War." On May 7, the west side town board passed a resolution calling the Juneau Avenue bridge a "menace to river navigation," and the following morning crews began dismantling it. Tempers flared across the river as eastsiders brandished firearms and even dragged a canon to the river's edge. Fortunately, no cannonballs could be found, and destruction was averted. Realizing that hanging together is better than hanging separately, Milwaukeeans put aside their differences and incorporated the city the next year.

TRIVIA

A 1998 census of school-age children, completed by the Milwaukee Public Schools, concluded that slightly over 50 percent of that population is non-white, for the first time in the city's history. This statistic might put pressure on Milwaukee's historic tendency toward segregation, perhaps slowly erasing the lines that divide white from black from brown.

and skiing. Indoors, winter is the height of the cultural season, with art galleries, the opera, ballet, symphony, and theater companies in full swing.

Calendar of Events

January
Polar Bear Club Lake Michigan Swim, Bradford Beach
U.S. International Snowsculpting Competition, Marcus Center for the Performing Arts

February
International Arts Festival Milwaukee, various locations
Greater Milwaukee Boat Show, Midwest Express Center
Greater Milwaukee Auto Show, Midwest Express Center

March
Milwaukee Journal–Sentinel Sports Show, Midwest Express Center
St. Patrick's Day Parade, downtown
Midwinter Pow-wow, Wisconsin State Fair Park

April
Craft Fair USA, Wisconsin State Fair Park
Milwaukee Public Museum Dinosaur Dash, downtown
Milwaukee Brewers season opener, County Stadium/Miller Park

May
Cinco de Mayo Festival, Mitchell Park
Grape Lakes Food and Wine Festival, Milwaukee Art Museum
PPG CART Series Auto Racing Miller 200, Milwaukee Mile Speedway

June
RiverSplash! Music Festival, downtown

Milwaukee Highland Games, Old Heidelberg Park
Miller Lite Ride for the Arts, Summerfest Grounds
Rainbow Summer begins, Marcus Center for the Performing Arts
Rose Festival, Boerner Botanical Gardens
Lakefront Festival of the Arts, Milwaukee Art Museum
Summerfest begins, Summerfest grounds at the lakefront

July
Firstar Fireworks, Veteran's Park
Great Circus Parade Week, downtown/Veteran's Park
South Shore Water Frolics, South Shore Park
International Cycling Classic pro bicycle races, various locations
Bastille Days, Cathedral Square

August
GenCon Gaming Fair, Midwest Express Center
Wisconsin State Fair, State Fair Park
Bradley Sculpture Garden Party
Greater Milwaukee Open pro golf tournament, Brown Deer Park
PrideFest gay and lesbian festival, Summerfest grounds

September
Oktoberfest, Schwabenhof
Al's Run and Walk, lakefront
Cedarburg Wine and Harvest Festival, Cedarburg
Kite Festival, Veteran's Park

Villa Terrace Decorative Arts Museum

October
Milwaukee County Historical Society Antiques Show and Sale,
 Grain Exchange Room
Milwaukee Admirals hockey season begins, Bradley Center

November
City Holiday Tree Lighting Celebration, Red Arrow Square
Holiday Folk Fair, Midwest Express Center
Christmas Parade, downtown

December
Holliday at the Allis, Charles Allis Art Museum
Firstar Eve Celebration, various locations

Business and Economy

Milwaukee is called "the city that works"—and works hard. A diversified manufacturing center, Milwaukeeans make engines and motorcycles, beer and mining equipment, auto chassis and the bulk of the world's X-ray equipment, the yeast that makes your bread rise and, very likely, the magazines to which you subscribe.

A number of major corporations are headquartered or have significant operations here. Harley–Davidson sends panheads, fatboys, and motorcycle culture to the world from Milwaukee; A. O. Smith makes structural components for vehicles, and Bucyrus Erie makes earth movers; Allen-Bradley makes industrial control equipment in its enormous Walker's Point factory; Siemens makes gigantic gas turbines in West Allis, and Harnish-pfeger makes mining machinery.

In addition, G.E. Medical, Master Lock, Miller Brewing—which ships millions of barrels of beer annually from its State Street brewery—and Quad/Graphics, an enormous magazine printer, are headquartered in the metropolitan area. Northwestern Mutual Life Insurance Company, one of the world's largest insurers, has been tied to Milwaukee since 1859. The company's East Wisconsin Avenue headquarters, a colonnaded Greek Revival affair, is among the city's most impressive structures.

Metro Milwaukee's unemployment rate is among the lowest in

Marquette Golden Eagles mascot

the country, and the recent demand for workers has led to increasing salaries, even for entry-level positions. The single sore point in the last several years has been the raiding of Pabst Brewing by its California owner. A Milwaukee fixture since 1845, the brewery ceased operations here in 1997 after an acrimonious battle with labor. Many Milwaukee taverns, out of respect for the workers, now refuse to carry Pabst products.

With its history of socialist government, organized labor, and high level of city services, Milwaukee is not the cheapest place in the country to do business. But while property taxes are relatively high—around $37 per $1,000 of assessed value in the city—sales taxes remain a fairly low 5.6 percent in the metropolitan area. Wisconsin corporations are taxed at a rate of 7.9 percent.

Milwaukee's cost of living is just slightly above the national average and downright cheap compared to coastal cities. In general, Milwaukee is a remarkably affordable place to live or visit. The following average costs reflect this affordability:

> Five-mile taxi ride: $9
> Double hotel room: $80
> Dinner for two: $25
> Movie ticket: $7
> Daily newspaper: 50¢
> Friday fish fry: $7.50
> Six-pack of Miller High Life: $3.75
> Four-pack of Lakefront Brewing Cream City Pale Ale: $5

Housing

A unique expression of regional architecture, Milwaukee Bungalows are common in many city and suburban neighborhoods built during the 1910s through the 1950s. Based on Arts and Crafts prototypes, these bungalows are small, well-designed, solidly built two-story houses. Their abundance is due to socialist city-government zoning regulations that favored owner-occupied houses over apartment buildings. Charming, bright, and

TRIVIA

The Polish Flat is a Milwaukee housing phenomenon common on the south side. The flats are duplexes featuring basement-level apartments whose windows peek above grade level by four or five feet. Eastern European immigrants built and lived in the basement apartments first, with makeshift roofs popping out of the ground. As residents saved money, they eventually built the upper two floors of their houses.

> **TRIVIA**
>
> For the last five years, Milwaukee has been at the center of the national debate over "school choice," a system by which children attend private schools with taxpayers subsidizing the cost. The city is, in fact, the crucible in which school choice theories are being tested, with the nation's first fully implemented program. Although much political capital is riding on Milwaukee's experiment, no conclusive data is yet available to prove its success or failure.

surprisingly spacious, they sell for $35,000 to $135,000, depending on the neighborhood.

Otherwise, housing in the Milwaukee area runs the gamut from $20,000 fixer-uppers in Riverwest to million-dollar mansions on North Lake Drive. The city's northern and western suburbs have seen the building of ever bigger and more expensive houses, as big as 7,000 square feet and costing $700,000 or more.

Downtown Milwaukee has also seen a housing boom in the last five years, particularly along the riverfront, where older office buildings are being renovated into luxury condominiums at a spectacular rate. Costing from $115,000 to $275,000, these new units feature many creature comforts—like riverside balconies—not to mention an exciting location near great restaurants, museums, and performing-arts venues.

Schools

Milwaukee's school system faces problems common to big-city schools: overcrowding, lack of parental involvement, fairly high dropout rates, and internal squabbles about resource disbursement. Unfortunately, many MPS successes are overlooked in the sometimes acrimonious debate over the district's future. Most notably, the system runs outstanding magnet schools (with long waiting lists) focusing on foreign languages, college prep, technical education, and the arts. The metropolitan area is home to numerous outstanding private schools, and several North Shore public school districts—Shorewood and Whitefish Bay—consistently rate as the best performing public schools in Wisconsin.

The metropolitan area is also home to a dozen colleges and universities, from the basketball powerhouse Marquette University to the University of Wisconsin–Milwaukee and Alverno College, a highly regarded, innovative women's school. The Milwaukee School of Engineering is consistently ranked as one of the finest engineering colleges in the nation.

2
GETTING AROUND MILWAUKEE

The Milwaukee metropolitan area has just over 1.5 million inhabitants, nearly half of whom live within city limits. In all, four counties comprise the metropolitan area. Milwaukee County has the bulk of the population. Waukesha to the west is the second largest county, while Ozaukee to the northeast and Washington to the northwest are less densely populated.

One of Milwaukee's greatest assets for visitors is that it doesn't sprawl across the countryside as much as do many similarly sized cities. It's more urban that suburban, and that means fewer twisty-turny streets and dead-end subdivisions. Sure, there are suburbs (this is the United States, after all), but in much smaller proportion than in many other cities.

Milwaukee sits on the western shore of Lake Michigan, and that shoreline is the city's defining feature. If you know where the lake is—some think the sky looks different over the water—you know where east lies. The lake can also be the benchmark for your wanderings around the city's regular checkerboard of streets.

In general, elevation increases as you travel away from the lake, until you reach the terminal moraines of central Waukesha and Washington Counties. These landforms, a line of hills several hundred feet high, mark the point where the Wisconsin Glacier receded in the last ice age.

City Layout

Thanks to its fairly compact size, utterly reasonable house- and street-numbering system, and a set of fixed landmarks, Milwaukee's geography

Finding your way around downtown Milwaukee just got a lot easier. So did finding the perfect restaurant, a secret parking space, and even your hotel. Area businesses have established a corps of "Downtown Ambassadors" to aid visitors and residents alike. They walk and bike around downtown in black-and-white uniforms, armed with maps, information about downtown attractions, loads of local knowledge, and decidely extroverted personalities. If you have a question—any question—don't hesitate to ask.

and physical layout are fairly easy to comprehend. That's good news for visitors and newcomers to the area.

Although Milwaukee's regular grid system of streets makes finding your way around fairly easy, it wasn't always so. Rivalries between the city's founders led to their intentionally misalining streets where they should have joined at downtown rivers. Bridges could not be built at oblique angles with mid-19th-century technology. Even when bridges were built, streets had different names on the east and west sides of the river—East Wisconsin and West Grand Avenues were the same street—until the city's street-naming system was regularized in the 1920s.

Today, Milwaukee doesn't prove too difficult for visitors to navigate. The Milwaukee River parallels the lakefront north of downtown about one and a half miles inland, and the Menomonee River flows into downtown from the west roughly following I-94. Ground zero for street orientation is found at the confluence of the two rivers in the Third Ward, at the south edge of downtown, just before they flow into Lake Michigan.

In the naming of streets north or south, the dividing line follows the east-west segment of I-94/I-794. East-west streets are marked E. or W. depending on their relationship to the Milwaukee River. North-south streets east of the river are named, and are numbered west of the river. Moving away from the river, numbers increase, at increments of 100 per block. In other words, 5600 North 39th Street is 56 blocks north of I-94 and 39 blocks west of the Milwaukee River.

Once beyond the county line, though the numbering system remains largely intact, the efficient grid of streets breaks down. The city of Waukesha, on the western edge of the metro area, is particularly difficult to navigate, even for natives. Fortunately, Milwaukeeans are a friendly lot, and you can always ask directions.

Major expressways transect the metropolitan area. I-94 runs north from Chicago into downtown Milwaukee, where it turns abruptly to the west and runs to Waukesha County and Madison. At the point of its turn, I-43 runs north to Green Bay, 100 miles distant. The place where the two roads merge, the Marquette Interchange in the center of downtown, is a monstrous high-rise cloverleaf and the site of major traffic jams, accidents, and delays. Mitchell International Airport is located six miles south of downtown, just to the east of I-94.

On the western edge of the county, U.S. 45, a limited-access expressway, runs north from I-94 to Menomonee Falls and Fond du Lac, while I-894 loops south and eastward to form an east-west bypass from the airport to Waukesha County. The southern leg of I-43 runs southwest from I-894 in the extreme southwestern corner of Milwaukee County toward Beloit. I-794, a spur, runs east from the Marquette Interchange through the Third Ward to the lakefront, where it swings south and crosses the harbor on the Daniel Webster Hoan Bridge, a graceful high-rise suspension bridge. It should be noted that there is no east-west expressway connection on the northern edge of the metropolitan area, a fact that leads to congestion on major roads like West Brown Deer and West Good Hope.

Public Transit

Milwaukee's public transit system is in the throes of major change these days. The western suburbs want more expressways, the mayor of Milwaukee wants rapid transit, and the Wisconsin governor wants to use mass-transit money to rebuild the Marquette Interchange. There is currently no end in sight to the debate.

Although Milwaukee County has an excellent bus system—consistently rated as one of the nation's best—transit in the suburbs remains a hit-or-miss proposition. If your travels take you outside central Milwaukee or the east side, your best transportation bet, by far, is to rent a car.

Badger Coaches Bus, p. 26

> **TRIVIA**
>
> The Park East Freeway, an elevated spur that runs from I-43 to North Jackson Street on the north edge of downtown, is part of a 1960s lakefront expressway project that was, fortunately, aborted before Milwaukee's stunning lakeshore could be paved over. Milwaukee's mayor intends to have the little-used road removed eastward from North Fourth Street. A boulevard will probably take its place in the next few years.

Bus Service

Milwaukee's highly efficient bus system serves many thousands of people each day, and 90 percent of all county households are within four or five blocks of a bus route. Planning a trip by bus is a simple proposition. Routes and buses are well marked, bus drivers are more than happy to answer questions, and downtown bus shelters have transit-system maps and fare information. If you are unsure of what routes serve your destination, call the 24-hour transit hot line at 414/344-6711. Fare is $1.35 for adults, 65 cents for children; exact change is required. Major downtown bus routes frequently used by visitors include:

- Route 30—running east and west on Wisconsin Avenue, turning north near Lake Michigan to ascend Prospect Avenue and the east side, and continuing to the University of Wisconsin-Milwaukee. This route takes you within easy walking distance of the lakefront, Milwaukee Art Museum, Betty Brinn Children's Museum, Summerfest, Central Library, Marquette University, and Historic Brady Street, as well as all downtown museums, the convention center, and major hotels.
- Route 15—travels north and south on Water Street, past the Center for the Performing Arts, the Water Street Entertainment District, Historic Brady Street, and the Historic Third Ward.
- Route 80—travels south on Sixth Street downtown to Mitchell International Airport.

Special bus service is provided—often with discounted fares—to all major summer events, including Summerfest and the ethnic festivals, the Wisconsin State Fair, the lakefront fireworks, Milwaukee Brewers home games, and the Great Circus Parade. It is advisable to use public transit to the fireworks and Summerfest, as parking downtown is nearly impossible (not to mention very pricey) during these events. In an effort to curb drunken driving, bus travel is free on New Year's Eve and St. Patrick's Day.

Downtown Loop

Inaugurated in 1997, the Milwaukee County Transit System's Downtown Loop service has proved very popular with tourists and locals who want to explore the treasures of the lakefront, lower east side, and downtown.

From May to September, bright red trolley-shaped buses run a 40-minute route past many of the city's major attractions and through several historic and eclectic shopping neighborhoods. The fare of $1 allows unlimited rides all day, with buses arriving at each stop on the route every 20 minutes.

The Downtown Loop visits the Museum Center, Central Library, Grand Avenue Mall, Riverwalk, the Third Ward, Cathedral Square and tony Jefferson Street, the Milwaukee Art Museum, Veteran's Park, McKinley Marina and Government Pier, Charles Allis Art Museum, Brady Street, Old World Third Street, Marquette Park, and the Bradley Center. Look for Downtown Loop signs at bus stops downtown, or call the MCTS hot line at 414/344-6711 for information.

Taxi Service

As Milwaukee sits in the part of the country that is outside New York, don't expect to step onto the street and hail a cab very easily. Unless you're at the airport, bus station, train station, or a major downtown hotel, it's best to call ahead to schedule pickup. A taxi-ride consolidation center is found at Mitchell Airport, at the Transit Center just outside of baggage pickup. There, two or more travelers heading to the same side of town can be paired up to share rides and save on fares.

The major cab companies in Milwaukee providing 24-hour service are American United (414/220-5000), Brew City Cab (414/442-2739), City Veteran (414/291-8080), and Yellow Cab (414/271-1800). Most cab companies accept plastic.

Commuter Rail

In the summer of 1998, a commuter rail link was established from downtown Milwaukee to the western suburbs, the city's first active commuter rail line in 30 years. Though the service was only a test run, the response was so positive that some permanent version of the trains will likely be put in place soon. The Hiawatha Extension, as the service was called, ran through Wauwatosa, Elm Grove, Oconomowoc, Pewaukee, and Watertown and was timed to link up with Amtrak's popular Hiawatha commuter service to and from Chicago.

The Marquette Interchange, the enormous cloverleaf where I-94, I-43, and I-794 converge in downtown Milwaukee, is scheduled to undergo a complete rebuilding after the turn of the century. The project will take several years to complete and should snarl traffic for miles around. Whenever possible it will be best to avoid the interchange altogether once construction starts.

Milwaukee International Airport, p. 24

Driving in Milwaukee

A decade ago, driving in Milwaukee was a snap. People were friendly, traffic was relatively light, and the whole system of expressways and surface streets flowed smoothly. While commuting is still relatively hassle-free in the Brew City, things have changed as traffic density and tension have risen. In 1998 Milwaukee was awarded a federal grant to reduce incidents of "road rage," hazardous and aggressive driving, and even violence, brought about by stress in traffic.

Still, car travel in Milwaukee tends to be efficient and, in many parts of the metro area, the only realistic transit option. MONITOR, a system of traffic-measurement devices and roadside messages alerting motorists to construction and traffic jams, has been in place for a couple of years. Traffic engineers hope that system will eventually ease congestion by as much as 30 percent. Dangerous interchanges have been rebuilt, and much of the interstate system has been resurfaced in the last half-decade.

Rush hour, though it does cause significant delays, could be worse. Major jam points include the Marquette Interchange, where I-94, I-43, and I-794 meet downtown; northbound I-43 at Silver Spring Drive; and the Zoo Interchange, the confluence of I-94, U.S. 45, and I-894 on the west side.

Driving downtown has been made both easier and safer by the city's project to eliminate one-way streets downtown by the turn of the century. Recent studies have proved that drivers travel more slowly on two-way streets, thus two-way traffic is safer for drivers and pedestrians. Two-way streets also take drivers more efficiently and directly from one place to the next, thus reducing unneccessary driving. Most of downtown's many one-way streets have already been divided.

As the suburbs have grown, certain roads in the metropolitan area have become very congested. Bluemound Road in Brookfield is the worst, with its eight or more lanes of endless traffic entering and exiting strip malls and fast-food restaurants. Port Washington and Mequon Roads in Mequon probably run a close second, as does Brown Deer Road on the city's northwest side.

Parking

Concerned with a landscape that in places seemed dominated by vacant lots, a decade ago Milwaukee's mayor declared a moratorium on the creation of new surface parking lots downtown. Since then, many lots have given way to office buildings. However, since most office buildings are required to provide parking structures, it is unclear whether there has been a net loss or gain in parking spaces. What is clear is that parking prices have risen—downtown parking meters now cost $1 per hour and are very well monitored.

Special event parking downtown costs between $4 and $11, depending on how close you park to the Bradley or Marcus Centers, Theater District, or other attractions. Most downtown street parking is free on Saturday and after six on weekday evenings, but check parking-restriction signs carefully. If you double-park for very long, expect to get a ticket. Parking at businesses in the suburbs is ample and free.

Bicycling in Milwaukee

While bicycling is not always the best transportation option in Milwaukee—it's hard to imaging suiting up for a ride when howling winter winds are telling you that the best move would be to drink another hot chocolate in front of the fireplace—things aren't bad for both recreational cyclists and bike commuters. With 141 miles of designated bike routes and 35 miles of safe off-street routes, Milwaukee's bicycle system is already fairly large.

The city has also made a commitment to increase the number of bicycle commuters by improving bike trails, building bike lanes, and installing improved bicycle racks and even lockers around the city. Major improvements will include bike-only lanes on the formerly dangerous 27th Street Viaduct, which crosses the Menomonee River Valley near the Mitchell Park Domes, and at the Locust Street Bridge, which joins the upper east

The parking structure behind the Grand Avenue Mall downtown offers special pricing for weekend parkers—only $1.25 all day Saturday or Sunday. It's perfect for a day of museum and gallery hopping. Enter from North Plankinton Avenue (one block west of the Milwaukee River) just south of West Wisconsin Avenue.

The Lady Sinks

Milwaukee's greatest transportation disaster befell the steamship Lady Elgin *in 1860. Returning from a pleasure excursion to Chicago, the ship's 225 passengers were drinking, dancing, and making merry into the wee hours, when a sudden fog blew up along the nearshore. In the thick of it, the* Lady Elgin's *captain never saw a lake schooner glide up out of the mist. It was already too late to maneuver for safety, and the vessels collided.*

The Lady Elgin *sank with almost all hands lost. The sinking was the worst disaster in Milwaukee history. Most of the passengers were Irish immigrants from the Third Ward. It is speculated that the city's Irish population was so decimated, and so many of its prominent citizens lost, that the ethnic group never regained power in city politics, which was taken over by Germans.*

side (and the University of Wisconsin-Milwaukee) with Riverwest. In addition, an off-street trail now joins Riverwest with Schlitz Park on the north side of downtown, and an off-street connection between the Third Ward and Bayview, south of the harbor, will eliminate a treacherous ride through the industrialized areas around the Port of Milwaukee.

Air Travel in Milwaukee

Mitchell International Airport (414/747-4525), located six miles south of downtown Milwaukee just east of I-94, is Milwaukee County's chief passenger and air-cargo facility. In many ways, Mitchell is among the nicest big airports in the country: It's relaxed and well appointed, not wholly unpleasant architecturally, and with adequate and (relative to other airports) inexpensive parking facilities. In reality, Mitchell International isn't all that big, and many local travelers use Chicago's O'Hare Field instead.

Mitchell International contains all the facilities one expects from an airport: post office, gift and specialty shops, coffeehouses, restaurants and taverns, traveler's information, car-rental agencies. It also houses one extraordinary store, Renaissance Books (see Chapter 9: "Shop-ping"), and one extraordinary airline, Midwest Express.

Midwest Express Airlines started as the private jet of the Kimberly Clark

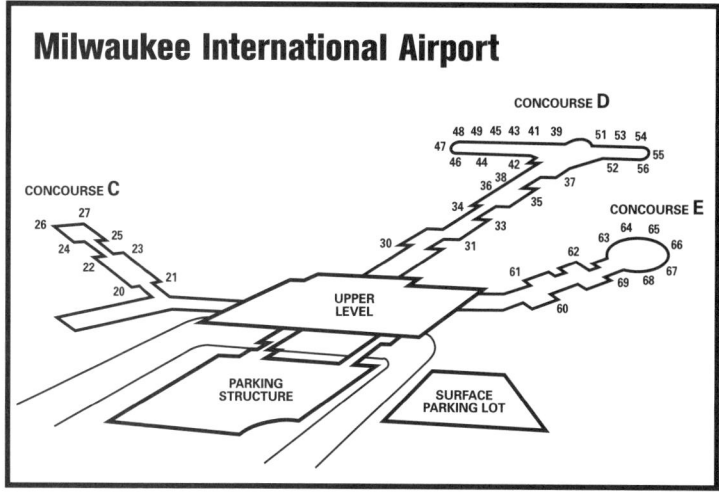

Corporation, a paper manufacturer based in the Fox River Valley. In 1984 the airline incorporated, basing its operations on the belief that service counts. Since then, from its Milwaukee and Omaha hubs, Midwest Express has been providing "the best care in the air" to hundreds of thousands of passengers annually. All flights are first class, with wide leather seats, complimentary champagne and wine, and simply the best food in the airline business, served on real china with real silverware—all for the same price as flights on other airlines.

Commercial Airlines Serving Milwaukee

Air Canada	800/776-3000
America West	800/235-9292
American Trans Air	800/435-9282
American Airlines	800/433-7300
Continental Airlines	800/523-3273
Delta/Comair	800/221-1212
Midwest Express	800/452-2022
Northwest Airlines	800/225-2525
TWA	800/221-2000
United Airlines	800/241-6522
US Air	800/428-4322

Rail Service

Amtrak serves Milwaukee with seven departures daily to Chicago and one to Minneapolis-St. Paul and points northwest. The Chicago service is popular among commuters (I-94 is very busy between the two cities), and some

TIP: Recent statistics show that running red lights is the fastest growing cause of car crashes in Milwaukee County. Be especially wary at the most dangerous intersections: West Silver Spring Drive and U.S. 45, West National Avenue and South Sixth Street, East Locust Street and North Oakland Avenue, West National and South Second Street, and West Townsend and North 27th Streets.

trains have standing room only, particularly during Summerfest and the holidays. Tickets may be purchased by phone, through a travel agent, or at the station before departure.

Increased rail service in the Midwest corridor should become a reality in the near future, as Wisconsin's governor, who is keen on trains, is now heading up the Amtrak board of directors. Milwaukee Mayor John Norquist, an unabashed rail supporter, has also been appointed to the train service's Midwest advisory council. Highest priorities on the list: re-establishing rail service between Milwaukee and Green Bay and Milwaukee and Madison, and further study of a high-speed rail link between Chicago, Milwaukee, and the Twin Cities.

Milwaukee's train station is located at 433 West St. Paul Avenue downtown. Call 800/USA-RAIL for train information and reservations. Call 414/271-0840 for station information.

Bus Service

Greyhound Bus Lines operates a passenger station at 606 North Seventh Street downtown, providing service to Chicago, Minneapolis, and many cities in Wisconsin and Michigan's Upper Peninsula. Call 800/231-2222 for schedules and fares, or call the station at 414/272-2259.

Directly across the street from the Greyhound station is the Badger Bus depot, at 635 North Seventh Street. Badger Bus runs many connections daily between Milwaukee and Madison, at very reasonable prices. The frequency of service, high-quality buses, and friendly staff make the 75-mile commute nearly effortless for businesspeople and University of Wisconsin students. Buses stop at Marquette University, Mitchell Airport, and several suburban and rural locations between the two cities. Call 414/276-7490 for schedules and information.

Finally, Wisconsin Coach Lines is the primary means of commuting between Milwaukee and suburban Waukesha County. Wisconsin Coach buses pick up and drop off at a variety of locations around downtown, the University of Wisconsin-Milwaukee, Mitchell International, and several places in Waukesha. Call 262/544-6503 for more information.

3
WHERE TO STAY

Whether you crave 19th-century grandeur or just a pillow on which to lay your head, it's all available in Milwaukee. As are boutique hotels in historic buildings, suite hotels catering to long-term visits, European-style inns, and motels that go easy on the pocketbook.

Lodging in Milwaukee tends to be clustered around the major business districts: downtown, the airport, the Mayfair area on the west side, and along the North Shore. For the most part, Milwaukee is a practical-minded and level-headed town, and Milwaukeeans are people who crave value for their money. For that reason, there are a lot of mid-range chain hotels around town that offer decent lodging at decent prices.

With the opening of the Midwest Express Convention Center last year, some fear that downtown Milwaukee might not have enough hotel rooms to accommodate convention-goers and casual travelers. However, several new hotels are under construction downtown, and many hotels in the metropolitan area are upgrading to meet increased demand. Just to be safe, make a reservation ahead of time. Rooms fill quickly during big summertime events, and if you wait until the last minute, you may have a long drive to the Summerfest grounds at the lakefront.

The following price guidelines—for a room for two with one bed—reflect an average. Actual prices vary.

Price-rating symbols:
$ Under $50
$$ $51 to $75
$$$ $76 to $125
$$$$ $125 and up

DOWNTOWN MILWAUKEE

Where to Stay in Downtown Milwaukee

1. Astor Hotel
2. Best Western Inn Towne Hotel
3. County Clare
4. Holiday Inn Milwaukee City Centre
5. Hotel Metro
6. Hotel Wisconsin
7. Hyatt Regency Milwaukee
8. Knickerbocker Hotel
9. Hilton Milwaukee City Center
10. Park East Hotel
11. Pfister Hotel
12. Plaza Hotel
13. Ramada Inn Downtown
14. Wyndham Milwaukee Center

DOWNTOWN

ASTOR HOTEL
924 E. Juneau Ave.
Milwaukee
414/271-4220
$$$

Yankee Hill is a quiet neighborhood of stately brick homes, turn-of-the-century apartment buildings, and still-older churches. Located on the east end of downtown Milwaukee and hugging Lake Michigan, the neighborhood is close to parks, the art museum, and Summerfest. The Astor, built in 1918, is a classic residence hotel listed on the National Register of Historic Buildings. It offers 69 guest rooms and an equal number of apartments, largely occupied by senior citizens. The muted colors, quiet hallways, septuagenerian residents, and very slightly frayed graciousness of the Astor lobby are comforting. The rooms are clean, large, and tastefully appointed, with the little architectural quirks of the era before pre-fab and poured concrete. There are good views and a well-regarded if not overly imaginative restaurant. Guests receive member privileges at the Bally health club a few blocks away. ♿ (Downtown)

BEST WESTERN INN TOWNE HOTEL
710 N. Old World Third St.
Milwaukee
414/224-8400 or 800/528-1234
www.bestwestern.com
$$$

In 1998, the 80-year-old Straus office building was converted into a mid-range hotel. The architecturally interesting exterior loses some of its charm on the inside, but the Inn Towne's price and proximity to downtown attractions—it's a few steps from the Grand Avenue Mall and a quick walk from museums, restaurants, and theaters—make it a great choice for budget-conscious travelers who want a four-star location but don't need four-star amenities. The rooms are small but tidy, and the views, especially on the upper floors, are impressive. Across the street from Reuss Federal Plaza, the Inn Towne often has young soldiers and sailors in residence, but they are a quiet and well-behaved lot. Parking is available nearby for $7 a day. ♿ (Downtown)

COUNTY CLARE
1234 N. Astor St.
Milwaukee
414/272-5273
$$$

Welcome to Ireland! Perhaps the most amazing thing about this amazing hotel is the fact the building is new. But it looks like it's been there forever (or transported beam by beam from Europe), with its mansard roof, salmon-colored stucco, and green trim. The County Clare's 31 guest rooms are possibly the nicest in the whole city and among the very few that don't seem to have come out of a can. They feature four-poster beds and *en suite* bathrooms with double whirlpool baths and separate showers. The rooms have individual phone lines, and the County Clare is complete with a delightful pub, fireplace and all. This is a great hotel, relatively affordable for downtown, and is highly recommended. Best of all,

Wyndham Garden Hotel, p. 49

it's snuggled in a quiet Yankee Hill street within a quick walk of downtown skyscrapers, the lakefront, and great east side restaurants. ♿ (Downtown)

HILTON MILWAUKEE CITY CENTER
509 W. Wisconsin Ave.
Milwaukee
414/271-7250
or 800-HILTONS
www.hilton.com
$$$$
Opened in 1928, the Hilton Milwaukee is grand in every sense of the word. The marble floors and gold leaf of the lobby bespeak the powerful elegance of industrial capitalism. The furniture is graceful, the chandeliers sparkly, the wrought iron magnificent. The Hilton is . . . the Hilton, and there's no hotel in town like it.

A recent renovation of all 500 rooms and public spaces updated the hotel's facilites while restoring the original deco style. Everything you would expect is here: a big staff, bright cafés, softly lighted lounges, and a grand ballroom that holds 1,000 people. The Hilton is currently building another 250 rooms in an enormous addition, set to open in August 2000. It will include a huge indoor water park with a Jamaican theme and a real sand beach. ♿ (Downtown)

HOLIDAY INN MILWAUKEE CITY CENTRE
611 W. Wisconsin Ave.
Milwaukee
414/273-2950 or 800/HOLIDAY
$$$
From the outside, you'd hardly know it's there, so unobtrusive and bland is the Holiday Inn City Centre. Inside, however, is another story: All 245 rooms have been remodeled in the last couple of years, and the lobby has been completely rebuilt t o provide a serene environment along a busy stretch of Wisconsin Avenue. It's a Holiday Inn, so the rooms are nice without making a statement, and the facilities are

considerable—including a rooftop pool for summer use. Business travelers will find their needs met with voice mail, ironing boards, and space for meetings of all sizes. Kitty-corner from the Midwest Express Convention Center, this hotel provides indoor valet parking. ♿ (Downtown)

HOTEL METRO
411 E. Mason St.
Milwaukee
414/272-1937 or 800/448-8355
www.hotelmetro.com
$$$$
Step through the curved glass foyer and into the lobby of this refurbished art-deco office building and . . . hey! Isn't that Nick and Nora Charles over there, sipping martinis in the lounge? Downtown Milwaukee's newest hotel, and one of the most elegant around, the Hotel Metro brings the streamlined age into the 21st century. The remarkable lobby—with gorgeous rugs, period furniture, and multilingual desk staff—gives way to 65 suites that interpret the 1930s with all the contemporary amenities. Down comforters, CD players, in-room safes, and the most gorgeous custom-made glass sinks you've ever seen grace all the suites, while some feature fireplaces and conference space as well. There is a highly regarded restaurant in the hotel, valet parking, and bicycles available for guest use. The Hotel Metro, in short, is fantastic. ♿ (Downtown)

HOTEL WISCONSIN
720 N. Old World Third St.
Milwaukee
414/271-4900
$$
In the early 1900s, the Hotel Wisconsin's skyscraper-cum-Flemish-Renaissance architecture perfectly embodied the modern metropolis with Old World roots. Once glamorous, the Wisconsin degenerated into a residence hotel for weirdos, shell-shocked vets, and recovering junkies. Now, it's the hotel that is slowly recovering. Under new ownership, the Wisconsin is supposed to undergo a complete rebuilding and room reconfiguration. A fitness center, indoor pool, and meeting rooms are planned, along with a chain affiliation. However, those plans were made in early 1998, and no work has begun, leaving the project's status in doubt. The Hotel Wisconsin is open, however, and though the quality of its rooms is anybody's guess, its location and prices are unbelievably good. If you don't mind a few . . . uh . . . quirks in your hotel experience, this place isn't an altogether bad choice. (Downtown)

HYATT REGENCY MILWAUKEE
333 W. Kilbourn Ave.
Milwaukee
414/276-1234 or 800/233-1234
www.hyatt.com
$$$$
Impeccable service, awe-inspiring interior architecture, and a great location are the hallmarks of the Hyatt Regency Milwaukee. The hotel's 484 rooms are arranged around a remarkable 18-story atrium that looks like a 1970s fantasy of the hanging gardens of Babylon: Plants drape over balconies, staff scurry along walkways, and guests chat quietly in the ground-floor lounges. Cater-

ing to conventioneers, high-caliber business travelers, and vacationing families who want to be in the heart of the action and are willing to pay for it, the Hyatt offers every amenity imaginable. There are several restaurants in the building, including Polaris, a revolving rooftop restaurant and lounge providing perhaps the best views of the city anywhere. The hotel is connected to the city's skywalk system, a nice feature when winter winds are howling. ♿ (Downtown)

KNICKERBOCKER HOTEL
1028 E. Juneau Ave.
Milwaukee
414/276-8500
$$$
Another National Register of Historic Places property in Yankee Hill, the Knickerbocker is unique among Milwaukee hotels in that all the 184 units are privately owned condominiums. One hundred of these are rented to guests. That means that each of the rooms—which range from efficiencies to one-bedroom apartments—is unique (although all must conform to quality standards). The jazz-age Knickerbocker features a marble-floored lobby, spa, laundry room, kitchenettes in all units, and a wonderful location near the lake and downtown Milwaukee. The Osteria del Mondo, one of the city's more exciting restaurants, is in the same building (see Chapter 4: "Where to Eat"). Offering a monthly rental discount, the Knickerbocker is ideal for long-term visitors to Milwaukee who need a quiet and tasteful home base in a quiet and tasteful neighborhood. ♿ (Downtown)

PARK EAST HOTEL
916 E. State St.
Milwaukee
414/276-8800 or 800/328-7575
$$$
Offering many of the amenities of downtown hotels that are half-again as expensive, and located as close to Lake Michigan and the festival grounds as a hotel can get, the Park East is equally favored by business travelers and vacationers. The 159 rooms have a clean and contemporary, but not particularly distinctive, look. What is distinctive are the views of the lake and skyline, the fairly high level of service—including a concierge—and the spectacular rooftop deck, a great place for a summer-evening cocktail. Complimentary breakfast in the hotel's atrium restaurant is included in the room rate, as is free shuttle service to all downtown locations. A newer building, the Park East is a fine choice in Yankee Hill. It lacks the charm, perhaps, of some of the neighborhood's older hotels, but it lacks their irregularities as well. ♿ (Downtown)

PFISTER HOTEL
424 E. Wisconsin Ave.
Milwaukee
414/273-8222 or 800/558-8222
$$$$
In some ways, the Pfister is the only hotel in town. That is certainly the case for wealthy entertainers, U.S. presidents, foreign dignitaries, and "luxury" travelers of all stripes. Built in 1893 (with an ungainly 1966 cylindrical high-rise addition on the back), the Pfister is high toned, high Victorian, high service, and high priced. The barrel-vaulted lobby is

plush and elegant, and the rooms and suites are elegant as well, with high ceilings, Queen Anne–style furniture, and tasteful amenities. The staff, needless to say, bends over backward. There are three well-known restaurants in the hotel, and the top floor of that 1960s tower contains a swimming pool with a fantastic view. The Pfister is the first choice of those who can afford it and has hosted a host of well-known names, from Nehru to Truman, Jack London to Robertson Davies, Caruso to Presley. ♿ (Downtown)

PLAZA HOTEL
1007 N. Cass St.
Milwaukee
414/276-2101
$$

The Plaza was never the grandest hotel in town, but it remains a residence hotel in the old style, built in 1925. With its deco friezes and tilework, it's easy to imagine jazz-age traveling salesmen wandering its now somewhat tattered hallways. The Plaza offers a variety of rooms (a few of which still have Murphy beds!) and has always attracted a large number of visiting artists; out-of-town actors performing with the Milwaukee Repertory Theater stay here. On a tree-lined street in Yankee Hill, the Plaza offers rooms for as low as $35 a night, impossibly cheap for lodgings downtown. Don't stay here if you require great comfort or service, but if you want a room with character at an unbeatable price—and don't mind an eccentric neighbor or two—this is the place. ♿ (Downtown)

RAMADA INN DOWNTOWN
633 W. Michigan St.
Milwaukee
414/272-8410 or 800/228-2828
www.execpc.com/~ramadadt
$$$

The Ramada is the workingperson's downtown hotel. The unremarkable 1960s building sits rather desolately on its corner, stuck as an after-

The Pfister Hotel

thought between the bus station and the expressway. Surrounded by parking lots, it presents a gloomy prospect when the weather turns cold and windy. That said, it should be noted that the Ramada, with 155 rooms, is the least expensive and least frivolous of downtown chain hotels, and that alone is a recommendation of a sort. The rooms are adequate, if unattractive, and while the service is haphazard, the staff is congenial. There's an outdoor pool, a just-serviceable restaurant, and a location within walking distance of all downtown attractions—once you get across that parking lot. ♿ (Downtown)

WYNDHAM MILWAUKEE CENTER
139 E. Kilbourn Ave.
Milwaukee
414/276-8686 or 800/WYNDHAM
www.wyndham.com
$$$$
Across Water Street rises City Hall, whose architecture it mimics.

Hyatt Regency, p. 31

Hyatt Regency Milwaukee

Across Kilbourn Avenue stands the Marcus Center, home of the symphony. In the same complex of redbrick buildings is the century-old Pabst Theater, Milwaukee's grandest opera house. The Wyndham Milwaukee Center, in other words, is all about location. Its 221 rooms on 10 floors rise in the very center of downtown Milwaukee and provide all the upscale amenities one could desire, from tasteful polished stone floors and fireplaces in the lobby to quiet piano music in the lounge to all the necessary business accoutrements. The hotel is only 10 years old, the rooms are spacious and offer wonderful views, and the staff, perhaps a little supercilious (but that's what business executives and luxury travelers want for $150 a night, right?), won't let you down. ♿ (Downtown)

EAST SIDE

BAYMONT INN-NORTHEAST
5110 N. Port Washington Rd.
Glendale
414/964-8484 or 800/428-3438
www.baymontinns.com
$$
This is an older Budgetel Inn, but with the new Baymont name, it has undergone the upgrade that the whole chain received. Good prices, nice rooms without extravagance, free breakfast, in-room coffeemakers, voice mail, and irons set Baymont apart from other budget lodgings, as does the competence and friendliness of the staff. Although this hotel is on a very busy street and is visible from the expressway, its placement keeps it

relatively quiet and secluded. Non-smoking rooms and a few suites are available, and it's a quick drive to Bayshore Mall, the Whitefish Bay shopping district, Lake Michigan, and Milwaukee County's Lincoln Park Golf Course. ♿ (East Side)

EXEL INN MILWAUKEE-NORTHEAST
5485 N. Port Washington Rd.
Glendale
414/961-7272 or 800/367-3935
$$
With 125 rooms, this is among the larger of the less-expensive hotels on the east side. Sitting at the Silver Spring Drive exit off I-43, the location is a little noisy and—with traffic whizzing by—definitely not pedestrian friendly. Most of the rooms are plain and bland, but some contain whirlpool baths. Guests receive a continental breakfast (the breakfast nook, frankly, has all the ambience of a turnpike rest stop), free HBO, and discounts for extended stays. Kids stay free and small pets are welcome. This Exel is probably the cheapest lodging in the area, but it could be nicer. Note that it is occasionally the scene of minor, uh, *disturbances,* and the Glendale police regularly cruise the parking lot checking license plates against warrant lists. ♿ (East Side)

MANCHESTER EAST
7065 N. Port Washington Rd.
Glendale
414/351-6960 or 800/723-8280
$$$
Bigge and grander than its cousins in the chain, the Manchester East provides quiet and tasteful lodging for travelers to the North Shore. With 133 rooms and suites, the hotel is organized around an atrium with indoor pool and lounge. Kids love the pool, and adults will find it nicer than the atrium pool in many hotels. There are meeting and banquet facilities, a shuttle to the airport, made-to-order breakfasts, a fairly well-regarded restaurant, sauna and fitness equipment, voice mail, and all the necessary business amenities. In all, the Manchester East deftly treads the line between the needs of business travelers and those of families on the business of pleasure. With rates at the low end of its price range, this hotel is a pretty good bet. ♿ (East Side)

MILWAUKEE RIVER HILTON
4700 N. Port Washington Rd.
Glendale
414/962-6040 or 800/HILTONS
www.hilton.com
$$$
The Milwaukee River Hilton is a very nice hotel, but nicer still is its location. Tucked into a bend of the Milwaukee River, and built horizontally rather than vertically to fit into the landscape, the hotel offers a serene setting—only blocks from a busy expressway, Glendale's industrial parks, and the bustling commercial district of Whitefish Bay. That serenity carries over into the hotel's subdued lobby and 163 upscale rooms, which offer all the amenities a business traveler could desire: dataports, clock radios, and overnight mail services. Travelers demanding a certain level of service will find the Milwaukee River Hilton to their liking as well, with 25-inch televisions, on-command video, and individual thermostats. The Hilton also houses the

GREATER MILWAUKEE

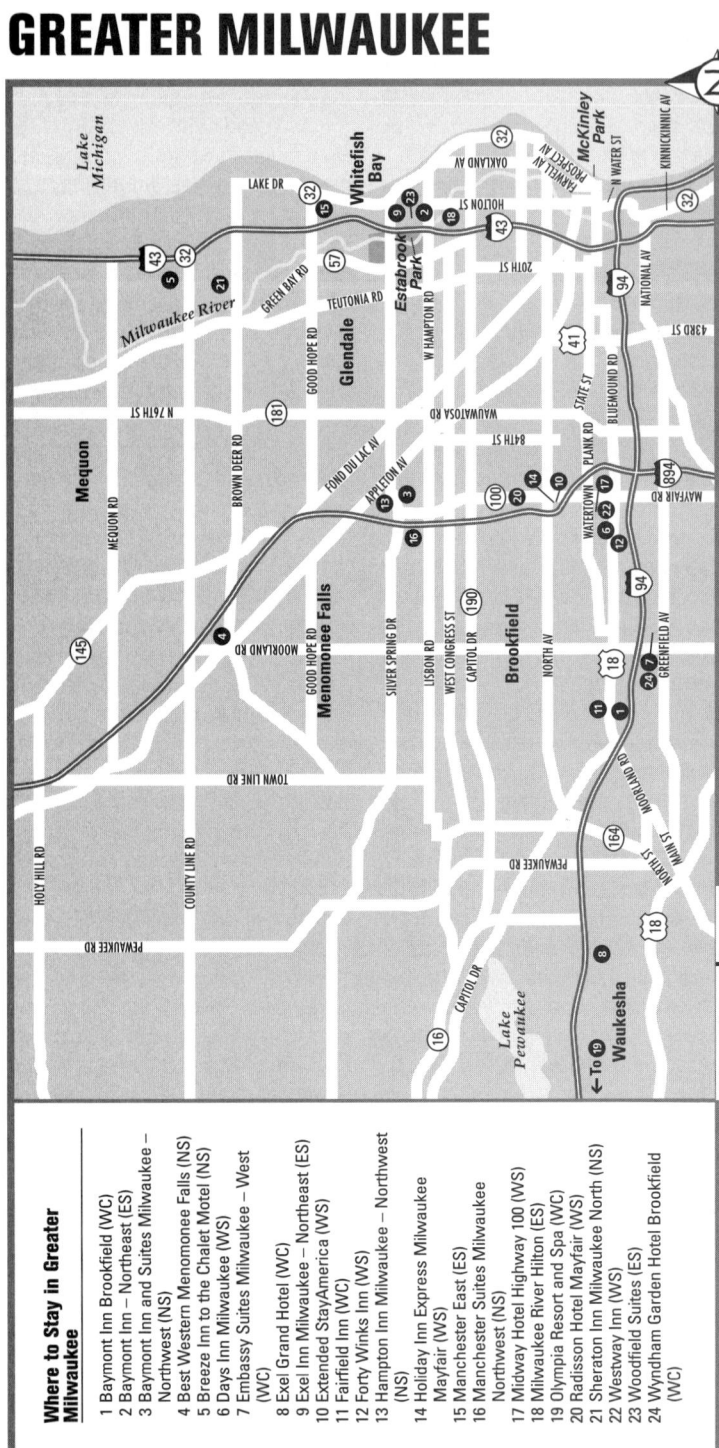

Where to Stay in Greater Milwaukee

1. Baymont Inn Brookfield (WC)
2. Baymont Inn – Northeast (ES)
3. Baymont Inn and Suites Milwaukee – Northwest (NS)
4. Best Western Menomonee Falls (NS)
5. Breeze Inn to the Chalet Motel (NS)
6. Days Inn Milwaukee (WS)
7. Embassy Suites Milwaukee – West (WC)
8. Exel Grand Hotel (WC)
9. Exel Inn Milwaukee – Northeast (ES)
10. Extended StayAmerica (WS)
11. Fairfield Inn (WC)
12. Forty Winks Inn (WS)
13. Hampton Inn Milwaukee – Northwest (NS)
14. Holiday Inn Express Milwaukee Mayfair (WS)
15. Manchester East (ES)
16. Manchester Suites Milwaukee Northwest (NS)
17. Midway Hotel Highway 100 (WS)
18. Milwaukee River Hilton (ES)
19. Olympia Resort and Spa (WC)
20. Radisson Hotel Mayfair (WS)
21. Sheraton Inn Milwaukee North (NS)
22. Westway Inn (WS)
23. Woodfield Suites (ES)
24. Wyndham Garden Hotel Brookfield (WC)

Anchorage, a well-known seafood restaurant (see Chapter 4: "Where to Eat"). ⚒ (East Side)

WOODFIELD SUITES
5423 N. Port Washington Rd.
Glendale
414/962-6767 or 800/338-0008
$$$$
The Marcus Corporation—which also runs the Pfister Hotel, the Milwaukee Hilton, and the Baymont chain of hotels—worked wonders a couple of years ago when they took over this former eyesore of a freewayside hotel for their new Woodfield Suites chain. The lobby is an unexpected delight—spacious and comfortable, unlike many hotels on this busy commercial street—and the desk staff is professional and very pleasant. A variety of rooms is available: whirlpool suites, kitchen suites, and executive suites, with prices ranging from $115 to $165, depending on the number of adults in the room and time of stay. All suites have kitchenettes and an extra sofa bed. Complimentary breakfast is served in a pleasant dining room, and two cocktails are provided each evening. There is a gorgeous indoor swimming pool and a children's play area. ⚒ (East Side)

NORTH SIDE

Hotels

BAYMONT INNS AND SUITES
MILWAUKEE-NORTHWEST
5442 N. Lovers Lane Rd.
Milwaukee
414/535-1300 or 800/428-3438
www.baymontinns.com
$$
When the Budgetel chain—based in Milwaukee—changed its name to Baymont Inns in 1998, it made an attitude upgrade as well. The Baymont Inns are trying hard, and they get most everything right for a low-cost lodging chain. This particular location has just undergone a complete renovation, from carpeting to crown moldings. It offers several types of lodging in its 140 rooms, from the simple single to "Business First" rooms with voice mail, dataports for modems, and ergonomically correct chairs in which to sit while typing on your laptop. In-room coffee, ironing board and iron, hair dryer, and a very basic breakfast are standard, as is pay-per-use Nintendo for the kids. The hotel is within five miles of Harley-Davidson's engine assembly plant, classy shopping at Mayfair Mall, and the County Zoo. ⚒ (North Side)

BEST WESTERN MENOMONEE FALLS
N88 W14776 Main St.
Menomonee Falls
262/255-1700 or 800/528-1234
$$
"Frill-less" is the word for this freewayside hotel. This Best Western Inn has changed hotel chain affiliations a couple of times in the last few years, and the current management is still trying to get things under control. There's a worn-carpet, overworked, smoky atmosphere about the place, but if your travels take you to the far northwest side of Milwaukee and ambience is unimportant, you could conceivably do worse. Fifty of the hotel's 109 rooms have been renovated in the

last 18 months, and more are scheduled for overhaul. There's a restaurant, meeting rooms for up to 50, and an outdoor pool. ♿ (North Side)

HAMPTON INN MILWAUKEE-NORTHWEST
5601 N. Lover's Lane Rd.
Milwaukee
414/466-8881 or 800/426-7866
www.hampton-inn.com
$$$

This Hampton Inn is very much like the others. But a lack of surprises is precisely what makes the chain successful and gives weary travelers peace of mind. The rooms are plain and comfortable enough for a good night's sleep, and they feature 25-inch TVs and micro-fridges on demand. There's an indoor swimming pool and whirlpool, a small conference room, and complimentary breakfast. This Hampton Inn is a little more expensive than the airport location, but it puts guests close to many of Milwaukee's large companies, not to mention good access to points north. ♿ (North Side)

MANCHESTER SUITES MILWAUKEE NORTHWEST
11777 W. Silver Spring Dr.
Milwaukee
414/462-3500 or 800/723-8280
$$

This all-suite hotel is one of the best lodging deals on the northwest side and one that is, surprisingly, underutilized by families traveling to the area. Suite hotels are generally considered appropriate for business travelers, and the Manchester Suites, with their fax machines, voice mail, in-room modem links, and conference space, are certainly that. Guests also enjoy kitchenettes with microwave ovens and refrigerators, sitting rooms with pull-out sleeper couches, made-to-order breakfast, an exercise room, and free basic cable television. Not bad for about $70 night for a double. This particular location features a very courteous staff and is a quick drive from good shopping, outdoor activities, and State Fair Park. ♿ (North Side)

SHERATON INN MILWAUKEE NORTH
8900 N. Kildeer Ct.
Brown Deer
414/355-8585 or 800/325-3535
$$$

Without a supporting cluster of other hotels or direct expressway access, the Sheraton North is a little isolated in the north central part of Milwaukee County. But with its distinctive and enormous circular window facing busy Brown Deer Road, it is a major hotel in every respect. It offers 149 rooms (24 are suites) with distinctly above-average furnishings, a restaurant and nightclub, an indoor swimming pool, and meeting facilities for nearly 400. As the only high-quality hotel in the immediate area, the Sheraton attracts travelers with business in the North Shore suburbs or on the northwest side. ♿ (North Side)

Motels

BREEZE INN TO THE CHALET MOTEL
10401 N. Port Washington Rd.
Mequon
262/241-4510 or 800/343-4510
$$

Newhall House Disaster

Early in the morning of January 10, 1883, a fire broke out at the Newhall House Hotel. Soon, the "finest hotel west of New York" was a blazing inferno, with the screams of trapped guests echoing through the snowy streets of downtown Milwaukee. Firefighters worked valiantly as people leaped from windows—among them the world-famous showman Tom Thumb, who lived to tell the tale. By noon only a smoldering pile of cinders remained on the corner of Michigan Street and Broadway.

The hotel register went up in flames, so there was no way to make an accurate count of the dead, but at least 75 people perished. The disaster made headlines around the country, and a popular ballad was written to commemorate the conflagration: "The fire bells all around were ringing to eternity a hundred souls or more, and the Newhall House was burning to the ground!"

The name is amusing, in the Bide-A-Wee or Fur-E-Nuff vein, and this roadside motel is surprisingly busy and pleasant. Once an outpost between Milwaukee and Cedarburg, suburban Mequon has grown to surround the Chalet, but the building retains a certain minimal 1960s charm, and there are lots of trees around to make you forget that the architecture is nothing special. All rooms have recently been updated, nonsmoking rooms are available, and there is a restaurant and lounge on the premises. Even better, there are a couple of nice restaurants in century-old buildings across the road. You should note that the Breeze Inn enforces a two-night minimum on Saturday, so you've got to stay either Friday or Sunday night as well. (North Side)

SOUTH SIDE

Hotels

BEST WESTERN WOODSVIEW
5501 W. National Ave.
Milwaukee
414/671-6400 or 800/528-1234
$$

The woods to be viewed here is not a forest but rather the enormous Woods Veterans Hospital, now called the Zablocki VA Center, across West National Avenue. Because of that proximity, this hotel is primarily favored by senior citizens with business there. But the Best Western

SOUTH SIDE

Where to Stay on Milwaukee's South Side

1. Best Western Woodsview
2. Clarion Hotel
3. Econolodge Airport
4. Four Points Hotel Milwaukee – Airport
5. Golden Key Motel
6. Hampton Inn Milwaukee – Airport
7. Hospitality Inn
8. Howard Johnson Inn Milwaukee
9. Red Barn Hostel
10. Red Roof Inn
11. Super 8 Milwaukee/Airport

Woodsview is also convenient to County Stadium and the soon-to-be-completed Miller Park, home of the Brewers, as well as major manufacturing companies in West Allis. Everything is fairly standard about this budget hotel—it has an indoor pool, small banquet facilities, a supper club–style restaurant—but you can upgrade to rooms featuring whirlpool spas and kitchenettes. Note that parking is awkward at the Woodsview; be careful in the lot's narrow lanes. ♿ (South Side)

CLARION HOTEL
5311 S. Howell Ave.
Milwaukee
414/481-2400
www.Milwaukee.org/clarion
$$$

Major expansions and renovations in the last decade have made the Clarion one of the favored hotels around Mitchell International Airport. Appealing to business travelers, families, and groups—with meeting space for up to 1,000 people—the Clarion offers a lot in the way of facilities, service, and amenities, without ever losing its relaxed, freewayside-hotel qualities or going overboard on prices. The Clarion features a lovely swimming pool, a restaurant and lounge, fitness center, 24/7 business center, and, in its business-class rooms, large desks with office supplies. One of the best deals here is the "Stay and Park" plan: For around $100, you get a room for a night, plus up to 14 days of free parking in the hotel's fenced-in lot while you're on your flying vacation. ♿ (South Side)

ECONOLODGE AIRPORT
6541 S. 13th St.
Milwaukee
414/764-2510 or 800/553-2666
$

The far south side is a budget-minded part of town, and a dismal one, with weed-strewn vacant industrial lots, heavy equipment storage, and the din of semis on I-94.

Hotel Metro, p. 31

Decquisto Photography

Construction Zone

It's the chicken and egg problem: A city can't attract big conventions without enough hotel rooms, but there's no need to add rooms if the conventions aren't coming. The pressure put on downtown Milwaukee lodging space by the opening of the Midwest Express Convention Center should be somewhat alleviated in the near future. At least three new hotels and one major expansion are in the works, adding more than 500 rooms.

A Courtyard by Marriot is being erected on W. Michigan Street, immediately behind the Grand Avenue Mall. Extended Stay America is building a new hotel in a parking lot north of the Bradley Center, and the Milwaukee Hilton is constructing a gigantic addition. Finally, the upper floors of a former downtown Woolworth's department store will become one- and two-bedroom apartments aimed at long-term business travelers. All of these hotels should be up and running by the turn of the millennium.

Much of the lodging here is a little rundown, but a 1998 exterior renovation turned this budget inn from "must miss" to "not half bad" if you don't expect any more than the minimum for your money. The Econolodge Airport is a frill-free hotel, and priced to reflect that. The desk staff is friendly, a little breakfast is served in a common room, and a shuttle to the airport costs $2 per person. The "Park and Fly" special here is remarkably reasonable: Stay a night and leave your car in the lot for up to two weeks for under $60. ♿ (South Side)

FOUR POINTS HOTEL MILWAUKEE-AIRPORT
4757 S. Howell Ave.
Milwaukee

414/481-8000 or 800/558-3862
$$$
The Sheraton Four Points, formerly the Grand Milwaukee Hotel, is the one airport hotel that goes out of its way in both facilities and service. The sprawling hotel features a whopping 510 rooms of various configurations, a swanky steakhouse and a family restaurant, a pub and a nightclub, an indoor and an outdoor pool, better-than-decent furnishings, meeting space for up to 1,500, and phones in the bathrooms. It is connected to a racquet club at which guests have privileges. There is also a complete business center, the entire building is soundproofed (you're near the airport, after all), and all facilities—including airport transit vehicles—

are accessible to the disabled. ♿ (South Side)

HAMPTON INN MILWAUKEE-AIRPORT
1200 W. College Ave.
Milwaukee
414/762-4240 or 800/426-7866
www.hampton-inn.com
$$

This Hampton Inn makes for perfectly reasonable lodging. The newer, fairly attractive (for a roadside chain) building features clean and unremarkable rooms with ironing boards, an indoor swimming pool, and a fitness area. The fairly inexpensive rates entitle guests to perfunctory service, a breakfast bar, free airport shuttle—Mitchell International is about two miles away—free newspapers, and a family movie channel. This location also offers "Park and Fly" specials for air travelers and significant senior citizen discounts. ♿ (South Side)

HOSPITALITY INN
4400 S. 27th St.
Milwaukee
414/282-8800 or 800/825-8466
www.hospitalityinn.com
$$–$$$$

An odd but not impractical arrangement, two separate facilities comprise the Hospitality Inn. There is a 1960s motor hotel featuring standard rooms and a 10-year-old highrise containing 82 suites. The standard rooms are, well, standard. The suites feature kitchenettes, living rooms, and separate bedrooms. The Hospitality Inn caters largely to travelers with business on the south side and to people visiting family members in nearby hospitals. Of special note are the inn's 11 fantasy suites, themed rooms designed for romantic getaways (in more subdued and slightly better taste than some fantasy hotels). One room has a '57 Caddy for a bed, another offers a waterbed in a space capsule, yet another has a giant wedding-cake bed. Each room features a whirlpool bath as well. Reserve early: The fantasy suites sell out nearly every weekend. ♿ (South Side)

HOWARD JOHNSON INN MILWAUKEE
1716 W. Layton Ave.
Milwaukee
414/282-7000 or 800/446-4656
www.hojo.com
$$

The steeply pitched orange roof still rises above the expressway. The aqua trim still outlines the eaves. Howard Johnson Inns, once synonymous with automobile travel, are largely absent from the landscape now. But this one, built in the early 1960s, remains. All rooms feature door-walls overlooking either the courtyard with outdoor pool (which has, no doubt, seen better days in its landscaping life) or the vast parking area. The rooms have the sort of furniture that is adequate, but needs updating. Still, the place is pretty cheap, and there is a free airport shuttle. This Hojo has seen much smoking in its hallways over the years, and though nonsmoking rooms are available, the telltale scent lingers. So if that bothers you, stay away. ♿ (South Side)

SUPER 8 MILWAUKEE/AIRPORT
5253 S. Howell Ave.
Milwaukee

Hilton Milwaukee City Center, p. 30

414/481-8488 or 800/800-8000
$$
Another budget hotel, but you could do worse around Mitchell International—a lot worse. The building and the rooms are bland, of course, but there is a free, 24-hour airport shuttle, free continental breakfast, a coin-operated laundry facility, free local calls (to check on the status of your flight, say), discounts for senior citizens, and a pleasant and not altogether feckless desk staff. There is a whirlpool, too, but it is unfortunately placed right off the lobby, which makes for a rather public display of relaxation. ♿ (South Side)

Motels

GOLDEN KEY MOTEL
3600 S. 108th St.
Greenfield
414/543-5300
$

When Humbert Humbert made his ill-starred journey across America, this is the sort of motor court in which he spent the night. Nabokov waxes poetic about the subtle glories of these roadside institutions, and it's a pleasure to find one intact. Though it's sited on a busy road, surrounded by car dealerships and expressway ramps, the motel's setback and period landscaping create a fairly quiet haven. The Golden Key's 23 rooms have been recently renovated, and there is an outdoor pool for summertime use. While it's not convenient to anything but I-894, the Golden Key merits a look for budget travelers seeking a bit of the past on the southwest side. (South Side)

RED ROOF INN
6360 S. 13th St.
Oak Creek
414/764-3500 or 800/843-7663
www.redroof.com
$$
The Red Roof Inn looks like a 1970s condo development, with its obliquely placed two-story buildings and steeply pitched (you guessed it) red roof. Recent renovations and landscaping improvements give this motel a tidy and pleasant appearance—the best, really, in the dreary South 13th Street corridor—and a courteous desk staff deepens the impression that, for a budget inn, this Red Roof has a good attitude. Rooms are plain but clean and comfortable enough, kids stay free, and air travelers may leave their cars in the parking lot for nothing while on vacation and take the airport shuttle for $2 per person. ♿ (South Side)

Hostels

RED BARN HOSTEL
6750 W. Loomis Rd.
Greendale
414/529-3299
$

It's a little bit musty, but what do you expect from an 85-year-old barn? The Red Barn Hostel just meets the very minimum requirements to be considered "lodging": bunk beds for a dozen, shared bathrooms, lockers for your gear. But there's a roof over your head, bicycles to cruise nearby Whitnall Park, and a common area in which to get to know other hostelers. A night in the old barn costs $11 for members of Hostelling International and $14 for non-members; reservations are recommended. Please note that it is a little difficult to get to this far-southwest location from downtown without a car, but a long ride on the city bus is possible. The Red Barn is closed in winter. (South Side)

WEST SIDE

Hotels

EXTENDED STAYAMERICA
11121 W. North Ave.
Wauwatosa 53226
414/443-1909 or 800/EXT-STAY ext. 124
www.extstay.com
$

Billed as an "efficiency studio" hotel, Extended StayAmerica offers businesspeople affordable lodgings with at least a hint of the comforts of home. All 122 rooms feature the most complete kitchenettes around:

Bed-and-Breakfasts in Wisconsin

You can stay in a farmhouse, a 19th-century stagecoach stop, or a Victorian painted lady. The Department of Tourism publishes an annual guide to state bed-and-breakfasts, with details on 300 inns, including rates and photographs. The Wisconsin Bed and Breakfast Directory *is available for free by calling 800/432-TRIP.*

Several B&Bs operate in the Milwaukee area. The Crane House in Bayview is sited in a "poor man's" Victorian house. The Little Red House in Wauwatosa is a quiet suburban Cape Cod, and the Brumder Mansion is located in a spectacular 19th-century home in a somewhat thuggish neighborhood on the near west side. Other good bets are found in quaint outlying villages like Cedarburg. Call the Milwaukee Bed and Breakfast Association at 414/277-8066 for up-to-date information and to make reservations.

Under a little-known Wisconsin statute, 31 consecutive days in a hotel makes you a resident. As such, you're not subject to lodging taxes. In Milwaukee, where hotel rooms are taxed at 14 percent, that adds up to a $300 monthly savings on a room that costs $70 per night.

with stoves, microwave ovens, full-sized refrigerators, and cupboards with dishes, utensils, and pots and pans. And while there isn't much in the way of charm here, the building is only two years old and facilities are clean and in great shape. Designed for long-term visits, the prices get cheaper the longer you stay. A single person staying for a week or more will pay under $40 per day, a great deal in the busy Mayfair area. ♿ (West Side)

FORTY WINKS INN
11017 W. Bluemound Rd.
Wauwatosa
414/774-2800
$
With a shallowly sloped roofline and lannonstone masonry, this 1960 motor hotel still gives off a slight whiff of the split-level suburban swank in which it was conceived. The building faces Bluemound Road, and with a long, two-story glass front wall, passing motorists can see into the inn's hallways and all the guest-room doors, one next to another. If your expectations aren't grand, you welcome the slight irregularities offered by non-chain motels, and you need to come in under budget (a room with a king-size bed goes for less than $50), the Forty Winks will do just fine. (West Side)

HOLIDAY INN EXPRESS
MILWAUKEE MAYFAIR
11111 W. North Ave.
Wauwatosa
414/778-0333
$$$
Eight miles from downtown Milwaukee and a hop, skip, and jump from west side attractions like the zoo, the Holiday Inn Express is a great base location for combining business and pleasure. Many of Milwaukee's major manufacturing companies—Harley-Davidson, Briggs and Stratton—are headquartered within a few miles of the hotel, and great shopping is to be found nearby. The hotel's 122 rooms are clean and well appointed, with new carpeting and 25-inch TVs. A complimentary continental breakfast is provided in the Holiday Inn's ground-floor Great Room (which features a fireplace, a nice touch on winter days). The staff is friendly and professional, and adult guests are able to enjoy member privileges at a nearby Bally's health club. ♿ (West Side)

MIDWAY HOTEL HIGHWAY 100
251 N. Mayfair Rd.
Milwaukee
414/774-3600 or 800/528-1234
$$$
It's not much to look at from the outside, located on a busy stretch of

eight-lane Mayfair Road (also called 108th Street and Highway 100, depending on where you are), but this Best Western–affiliated hotel has more to offer on the inside than might be expected. The Midway is built around a large, barrel-vaulted glass atrium, which covers a pool, sauna, whirlpool, deck, and play area for kids, and many of the rooms look out on this not-unpleasant scene. Though there's a distinct early-1980s feel to the rooms and public area, the hotel is undergoing major renovation, adding 15 suites and updating furnishings, carpeting, drapes, and the like, which should make it a decent choice for lodging around the county medical center. ♿ (West Side)

RADISSON HOTEL MAYFAIR
2303 N. Mayfair Rd.
Wauwatosa
414/257-3400
$$$$

The premier hotel on Milwaukee's west side, following a recent top-to-bottom renovation, the Radisson Mayfair is a marvel in understatement. The lobby features plush carpets, subdued lighting, muted artwork, and a quiet and extra-courteous staff. The rooms themselves, with either two double beds or one king-size bed, are very nice (though neither extravagant nor interesting). Creature comforts make this hotel a favorite for corporate travelers who need a certain level of class, but it also provides packages—like bed-and-breakfast weekend specials—designed to attract families. The hotel includes a quiet restaurant, an indoor pool, sauna and fitness center, and complimentary airport shuttle and is sited across a busy street from the region's foremost upscale shopping mall. ♿ (West Side)

WESTWAY INN
201 N. Mayfair Rd.
Wauwatosa
414/771-4400 or 800/531-3965
$$

Perfectly average in almost every respect, this former Ramada hotel cuts a bland figure. It offers average rooms, average meeting space, average rates, averagely dated furnishings, and a decidely average staff—all surrounded by the average suburban parking lot. The only places where the Westway breaks the bonds of mediocrity are at its "Fundome"—a glassed-in atrium with swimming pool and other amusements—and its on-site restaurant, which has recently become the well-regarded Shiva, serving East Indian cuisine. If you're looking for a respectable place serving up few thrills but also few hassles, the Westway is that place. ♿ (West Side)

Motels

DAYS INN MILWAUKEE
11811 W. Bluemound Rd.
Wauwastosa
414/771-4500 or 800/329-7466
www.daysinn.com
$$

A couple of the years ago, this Day's Inn scraped the bottom of the barrel: peeling paint, rundown rooms, terrible parking, and a shuttered coffee shop. Now, under new ownership and undergoing a top-to-bottom remodeling, the hotel offers reasonable facilities to budget-minded travelers (though it's never going to be a four-star establishment, or even two). A 1960s motor hotel, the Days Inn has a two-story L-shaped building wrapping around the hotel offices. There are outdoor walkways, and 135 doors leading to the renovated guest rooms. An indoor pool, huge family restaurant, and new parking structure complete the hotel's leap into respectability. (West Side)

WAUKESHA COUNTY

Hotels

Manchester Suites, p. 38

BAYMONT INN BROOKFIELD
20391 W. Bluemound Rd.
Brookfield
262/782-9100 or 800/428-3438
www.baymontinns.com
$$

Like all the Baymont Inns, this hotel offers a great deal for little money. The building is newish, and the lobby and breakfast area, remodeled in 1998, are lovely. The rooms are tidy, if unremarkable, and many are reserved for nonsmokers. There are irons and ironing boards, coffeemakers and coffee, and pay-per-use Nintendo for the kids. Complimentary breakfast is included, and there are several family restaurants in the same complex as the hotel, along with a multiplex cinema just across the parking lot. The Baymont Inns—and the Brookfield location is no exception—may be Milwaukee's best all-around budget lodging deal. ♿ (Waukesha)

EMBASSY SUITES MILWAUKEE-WEST
1200 S. Moorland Rd.
Brookfield
262/782-2900 or 800/EMBASSY
www.embassy-suites.com
$$$$

All suites, all the time. The Embassy West has more than 200 of them, from doubles to kings to giant two-bedroom, two-bathroom penthouse units that are more luxury apartment than hotel room. Every suite has a queen sofa bed in the living area, dining and work tables, a kitchenette, two telephones, and two TVs. The Embassy is a remarkably swanky and modern hotel. Its five floors are built around a central atrium that rises the entire height of the structure and includes a restaurant, swimming pool and sundeck, car rental office, and gift shop. Combine that with child care, free evening cocktails, and complimentary airport transportation, and there's no reason why a business traveler should ever have to leave the splendor of this far west side hotel. ♿ (Waukesha)

EXEL GRAND HOTEL
2840 N. Grandview Blvd.
Waukesha
262/524-9300 or 800/574-3935
$$

The Exel Grand is the showplace of the otherwise budget Exel Hotel chain, which maintains low rates by cutting back on amenities like pleasant-looking buildings. Located on the far west side of the metropolitan area, about 35 minutes by car from central Milwaukee, this hotel is particularly convenient for travelers who have business in both Milwaukee and Madison. From Waukesha, one can reach the state capital without Beer City traffic hassles. The rooms here are new and relatively spacious, and all units feature coffeemakers, large televisions, and ironing boards. A complimentary breakfast starts the day off right, and a complimentary cocktail and dip in the pool finishes it up. The Exel Grand is a pretty nice hotel, and at these prices, it's a very nice hotel. ⚹ (Waukesha)

OLYMPIA RESORT AND SPA
1350 Royale Mile Rd.
Oconomowoc
262/567-0311 or 800/558-9573
www.olympiaresort.com
$$$

Here's a place for a weekend getaway. Located in the Lake Country, about 45 minutes by car from downtown Milwaukee, the Olympia Resort has everything you need: a restaurant and cocktail lounge, an 18-hole golf course, tennis and racquetball courts, and a complete health club and spa offering the gamut of body wraps, facials, and massage therapy. Most of the resort's rooms have lake or golf-course views, and those that don't are discounted 10 to 15 percent. The Olympia offers some good packages as well. The Weekend Getaway, for example, provides two-night's lodging, Friday fish fry, Saturday prime-rib dinner, and Sunday brunch for about $250 for two people. ⚹ (Waukesha)

WYNDHAM GARDEN HOTEL BROOKFIELD
18155 W. Bluemound Rd.
Brookfield
262/792-1212 or 800/WYNDHAM
www.travelweb.com
$$$

The architecture of this upscale business hotel fails to please. A Greek revival knockoff, the hotel is oversized, and its details look pasted on. But once you're through the doors, the Wyndham Garden is very pleasant indeed. The lobby has plenty of wood, a fireplace, and warm lighting; the restaurant is attractive; and the rooms surround a giant outdoor courtyard with tables, benches, and plantlife. The rooms are attractive without making any statements, and they feature comfortable writing desks. There is a beautiful swimming pool, spa facilities, and an exercise area, plus all the usual business amenities. An airport shuttle is available, but any extended stay in sprawling Brookfield more or less requires a car. ⚹ (Waukesha)

Motels

FAIRFIELD INN
20150 W. Bluemound Rd.
Brookfield

**262/785-0500 or 800/228-2800
$**

Fairfield Inns—the Marriott chain's budget hotels and motels—make for decent, low-frills lodging. This location, at the western end of Brookfield where Blue Mound Road crosses I-94, is no exception. Clean, simple, and affordable are the watchwords, and while there is nothing to make this motel stand out in a crowd, it still has plenty to recommend it: competent staff, small outdoor pool, and 135 rooms, two-thirds of which have outdoor access. The building is about 10 years old and is scheduled for a standard renovation in 1999. ♿ (Waukesha)

4
WHERE TO EAT

It used to be that dining in Milwaukee meant burgers, bratwurst, and beer in a tavern; schnitzel in one of the downtown German food palaces; pizza, or Friday fish fry.

Boy, have things changed. Great German food is still available (probably the best this side of the River Rhein), that Milwaukee-style pizza is still here, with its super-thin crust and checkerboard slices, and fish fries still draw big crowds. But in the last 10 years Milwaukee's restaurant scene has branched out. First came the Thai restaurants, then the sushi bars, then Middle Eastern restaurants, the East Indians, the taquerias. And so on.

Now, whatever you want, you'll find it here. And it will be good. Local specialties include Serbian and Polish food on the south side, Mexican food in Walker's Point, East Indian cuisine on the west side, and frozen custard all over town. Downtown and the lower east side offer a remarkable concentration of out-of-the-ordinary food, from the finest in fine dining to clever experiments with regional cuisine to fantastic international delights.

So, if you're hungry for down-home cooking, Eastern European delicacies, rustic Italian cuisine, tortas al pastor, or just that fantastic burger, Milwaukee's restaurants are saying: "Take your pick."

The following price-rating symbols reflect the average cost of an appetizer, entrée, and dessert.

Price-rating symbols:
- $ Under $10
- $$ $11 to $20
- $$$ $21 and higher

African
African Hut (DT) p. 53

Asian
Ching Hwa (WC) p. 78
Ghengis Khan (WS) p. 76
Ichiban (ES) p. 62
San Dong Express (SS) p. 74
Thai Kitchen (ES) p. 67
Thai Palace (DT) p. 59
West Bank Café (NS) p. 67
Yen Ching (NS) p. 70

Barbeque/Southern
Hal's Ribhouse (NS) p. 68
Mr. Perkins' Restaurant (NS) p. 68
Saz's State House (WS) p. 77
Speed Queen (NS) p. 69

Bistro
Brasserie 143 (DT) p. 54
Café Vecchio Mondo (DT) p. 54

Cajun
Crawdaddy's (SS) p. 70
Jolly's on Harwood (WS) p. 77

California Fusion
Louise's Trattoria (DT) p. 56
Restaurant Hama (ES) p. 68

Classic American
Boder's (NS) p. 67
Café Continental (WC) p. 78
Pleasant Valley Inn (WS) p. 73

Contemporary American
Heaven City (WC) p. 72
Sanford (ES) p. 65

Continental
Boulevard Inn (DT) p. 53
Grenadier's (DT) p. 56
Lake Park Bistro (ES) p. 63
Steven Wade's Café (WC) p. 79

Delicatessen
Benji's Delicatessen (ES) p. 61
Jake's Delicatessen (NS) p. 68

Diners
George Webb (WS) p. 76
Miss Katie's Diner (DT) p. 57
Real Chili (DT) p. 58

East Indian
Dancing Ganesha (ES) p. 62
Taste of India (WS) p. 77

Eastern European
Polonez (SS) p. 74
Three Brothers (SS) p. 75

German
Karl Ratszch's (DT) p. 56
Mader's German Restaurant (DT) p. 57
Kegel's Inn (SS) p. 72

Italian American/Pizza
Albanese's (NS) p. 61
Buca di Beppo (DT) p. 53
Phil and Dom DeMarini's (SS) p. 72

Regional Italian
Di Salvo and Brennan's (ES) p. 62
Mimma's Café (ES) p. 65
Osteria del Mondo (DT) p. 58
Pasta Tree (ES) p. 65
Ristorante Bartolotta (WS) p. 77

Mexican
El Rey (SS) p. 70
La Perla (SS) p. 72
Taqueria Azteca (SS) p. 75
Tres Hermanos (SS) p. 75

Middle Eastern
Sahar (DT) p. 59
Shahrazad (ES) p. 66

Pub Food
Fourth Base (SS) p. 70
M & M Club (DT) p. 57
Milwaukee Ale House (DT) p. 57

Seafood
The Anchorage (ES) p. 61
Eagan's (DT) p. 56
Red Rock Café (ES) p. 65

Soup
Soup Bros. (SS) p. 75

Spanish
Don Quijote (ES) p. 62

Steakhouses
Club Forest (NS) p. 67
Coerper's Five O'Clock Club (DT) p. 54
Eddie Martini's (WS) p. 76
The Porterhouse (SS) p. 73

Tea Rooms
Bits of Britain (WC) p. 78
Watts Tea Shop (DT) p. 59

Vegetarian
Beans and Barley (ES) p. 61

DOWNTOWN

AFRICAN HUT
1107 N. Old World Third St.
Milwaukee
414/765-1110
$$
A popular spot for pre- and post-arts and sports event meals, African Hut specializes in spicy stews from West Africa. The Peanut Stew Banfi, made with chicken breast and fresh peanuts (as opposed to oilier peanut butter) is rich and not too peppery, as are the Cameroon-style collard greens, with a deep vegetable flavor, big chunks of chicken, and a flavorful sauce. The house specialty is *fufu* and *egusi,* a spicy stew with greens, chicken, and beef, served with a firm grain cereal like farina. Just scoop it up with your fingers and dig in. Lunch, dinner, and late night Mon–Sat. ♿ (Downtown)

BOULEVARD INN
925 E. Wells St.
Milwaukee
414/765-1166
$$$
The Boulevard Inn has a reputation for refinement without stuffy pretensions. With a high-ceilinged, hunter-red dining room direct from the continent, the Boulevard is popular among higher-powered businesspeople, ladies who lunch, and diners seeking elegance without stress. The menu is strictly classic: walleyed pike almandine, roast duckling, chicken with pesto, beef goulash. Daily specials and salads—grilled scallops with spinach and roasted tomatoes, say—are highly recommended. The lunch menu is priced remarkably well for food of this quality. Lunch and dinner daily, brunch Sun. Reservations recommended. ♿ (Downtown)

BUCA DI BEPPO
1233 N. Van Buren St.
Milwaukee
414/224-8672
$$$
Buca is the hole-in-the-wall Italian joint of your dreams: Dean Martin records, flowing table wine, meatballs by the ton. A newish restaurant, Buca comes so close to achieving a 1950s authenticity that you simply

won't mind the slight credibility gap. The food is good if not clever, the portions are huge—served family style—and, if fresh, the mussels in white wine are outstanding. Big parties get to sit at a table in the kitchen, the waitstaff will talk your ear off, and everyone gets a doggie bag. Don't miss the spumoni! Dinner daily. ♿ (Downtown)

BRASSERIE 143
143 N. Broadway
Milwaukee
414/273-4411
$$

The emphasis in this chic Eurobistro is lightness. The renovated Third Ward building is delightful and airy, and the food is deftly prepared and delicate. The menu is inventive without straying too far from classic bistro fare, and it focuses on fresh ingredients. One delicious entrée features locally made Italian sausage, a thin red sauce, and perfect polenta. The parkside outdoor seating is particularly pleasant. Lunch and dinner Mon–Sat, brunch Sun. Reservations recommended. ♿ (Downtown)

CAFE VECCHIO MONDO
1137 N. Old World Third St.
Milwaukee
414/273-5700
$$

This restaurant, despite its name, is a quintessentially '90s establishment, bridging cocktail chic (20 kinds of martinis), upscale fusion cooking with a retro twist (the specialty is fondue), and Euro-rehab (the renovated storefront is right out of *Art and Architecture*). The menu is small and *fin-de-siècle*—focaccia-bread sandwiches for lunch, dill-butter swordfish

Grenadier's, p. 56

for dinner, and grilled eggplant cheese soup—and the wine list is huge. Convenient to the Riverwalk and the Bradley Center, the Café Vecchio Mondo is good for a trendy lunch or classy fondue dinner for two. Lunch and dinner Mon–Fri, dinner Sat and Sun. ♿ (Downtown)

COERPER'S FIVE O'CLOCK CLUB
2416 W. State St.
Milwaukee
414/342-3553
$$$

Walk in the door of the Five O'Clock Club and suddenly it's 1946. The war is over, the jazz is jumping, and the manhattans are aflow. Coerper's, the dean of Milwaukee steakhouses and the model to which newcomers aspire, hasn't changed much since that moment, although its Avenues West neighborhood has fallen on hard times. You'll enjoy big steaks cooked to perfection, a relish tray, a potato (a concession to the vegetable kingdom), hard liquor, and a big dessert—definitely not heart

DOWNTOWN MILWAUKEE

Where to Eat in Downtown Milwaukee

1. African Hut
2. Boulevard Inn
3. Buca di Beppo
4. Brasserie 143
5. Cafe Vecchio Mondo
6. Coerper's Five O'Clock Club
7. Eagan's
8. Grenadier's
9. Karl Ratzsch's
10. Louise's Trattoria
11. M&M Club
12. Mader's German Restaurant
13. Milwaukee Ale House
14. Miss Katie's Diner
15. Osteria del Mondo
16. Real Chili
17. Sahar
18. Thai Palace
19. Watts Tea Shop

healthy, but one of the best meals around. A legend. Dinner Tue–Sat. Reservations recommended. Call early. (Downtown)

EAGAN'S
1030 N. Water St.
Milwaukee
414/271-6900
$$$

A swanky and upscale restaurant focusing on seafood, Eagan's has a lovely bar (designed, it seems, for recent converts to the cult of cigars and single malt) and a dining area that is expansive, light, and bubbling with activity. Fresh raw oysters are a hit, as are the large menu's myriad seafood choices. Right across the street from the Marcus Center, and featuring late hours, this restaurant makes a great pre-symphony stop. Dressed up, you'll feel right at home. Finally, if you love bananas Foster or—heaven forbid!—have never eaten that hot caramel, ice cream, and fruit delight, Eagan's has perfected it. Lunch and dinner Mon–Sat, brunch Sun. ♿ (Downtown)

GRENADIER'S
747 N. Broadway
414/276-0747
www.foodspot.com/grenadiers/
$$$

Grenadier's wears its stuffiness like a badge, the last holdout of propriety in a world gone horrendously casual. A hushed, Masterpiece Theater atmosphere creeps between the plush booths on the heels of tuxedo-clad waiters. Serving continental cuisine filtered through an Anglo sensibility, Grenadier's is modeled on the ideal of the Pall Mall men's club: landscape paintings, a wine cellar both deep and broad, and a masterful chef. Expect an opulent menu: turtle soup, sweetbreads, the best cuts of meat and freshest seafood, homemade desserts. The fixed-price dinner, served weeknights, is among the city's better fine-dining offers. Jackets and reservations are required. Lunch Mon–Fri, dinner Mon–Sat. ♿ (Downtown)

KARL RATZSCH'S
320 E. Mason St.
Milwaukee
414/276-2720
$$$

Ratzsch's may be the quintessential Milwaukee restaurant. Operated continuously for nearly a century, it's everything a German restaurant should be, without any concessions to tourist expectations. You'll find murals, staghorn lamps, heavy wooden furniture, a well-used bar, continental glassware, a gracious waitstaff, and a string trio filling in the background on Saturday nights. And don't forget the *sauerbraten*—pork marinated in wine and vinegar—which could be the best in the country. The veal is spectacular, as is the red cabbage and *spätzle* (drop dumplings). You'll leave full, tired, and happy in the knowledge of having experienced a Milwaukee institution. Dinner Mon–Sat. Reservations are required. ♿ (Downtown)

LOUISE'S TRATTORIA
801 N. Jefferson St.
Milwaukee
414/273-4224
$$

The restaurants on Cathedral Square cater to a besuited, cell phone–toting clientelle, which demands interesting interior design, well-mixed drinks, and clever, refined food. Louise's Trattoria has a lot to do with the area's good reputation. Featuring West Coast/urban Italian cuisine, the restaurant's menu is a fine example of the eclectic restaurant movement. The blonde wood interior is clean and contemporary, and the food is the same. No heavy flavors overwhelm the specialty pizzas, fresh salads, and delicate pasta dishes with handmade noodles. Lunch and dinner daily, brunch Sun. ♿ (Downtown)

M&M CLUB
124 N. Water St.
Milwaukee
414/347-1962
$$

By night one of Milwaukee's classier gay bars, the M&M Club is also a great lunch spot, favored by businessmen and women, artists, and people of all stripes. Housed in a narrow glass atrium, the club is bright and relaxed, even on gloomy days. The menu is standard American pub fare—the burgers are huge and delicious, cooked to order—and every day, the M&M's chef concocts a quiche, pasta, and soup and sandwich specials. You won't find a better place for a pleasant and inexpensive lunch. Lunch, dinner, and late night Mon–Sat, brunch Sun. ♿ (Downtown)

MADER'S GERMAN RESTAURANT
1037 N. Old World Third St.
Milwaukee
414/271-3377

Mader's is to German restaurants what Helmut Kohl is to Germans: heavy, serious, and in it for the long haul. Enter the castellated building, walk past suits of armor and what may be the city's most beautiful bar—polished by decades of elbows—and get ready to get full. All the Teutonic specialties are great, but the fact that the menu devotes a separate page to veal *schnitzels*—breaded, with mushroom gravy, and so forth—should tell you something. Leave room for the *schaumtorte*: meringue with ice cream or strawberries. Lunch and dinner daily. Reservations recommended. ♿ (Downtown)

MILWAUKEE ALE HOUSE
233 N. Water St.
Milwaukee
414/226-2337
$$

Brewpubs are ubiquitous nowadays, but this one's better than most. It resides in an 1868 riverside warehouse that at one time housed the makers of the hoola hoop. The architect worked wonders with the renovation, and there's a beautiful two-level patio. The beer is tasty—the Solomon Juneau Ale is particularly good, with a slightly bitter finish like a Czech pilsener. The food is high-end brewpub fare. Salads and enormous burgers are great at lunch, and the dinner menu features ribs, seafood, and grilled steaks. Lunch and dinner Mon–Sat, dinner Sun. (Downtown)

MISS KATIE'S DINER
1900 W. Clybourn Ave.
Milwaukee
414/344-0044
$$

A couple of years ago, German Chancellor Helmut Kohl met President Clinton in Milwaukee for a summit on international relations. Where, people wondered, would the dignitaries eat? That they chose Miss Katie's is no surprise: It's an American classic. As such, it features classic diner fare, though the food is better than that at a normal short-order house. Try omelettes for breakfast, roast beef sandwiches at lunch, and, like the president, a plate of succulent meatloaf for dinner. Near Marquette University on the west end of downtown, Miss Katie's Diner is sure to please. Breakfast, lunch, and dinner daily. & (Downtown)

OSTERIA DEL MONDO
1028 E. Juneau Ave.
Milwaukee
414/291-3770
$$$

Its adroitly stuccoed walls, intimate table groupings, Renaissance-like frescos, and quiet, efficient staff suggest that this is no ordinary Italian restaurant, and a glance at the menu confirms it. With regional Italian specialties such as grilled swordfish steaks with *putanesca* sauce—capers, tomatoes, and a hint of anchovy—the Osteria approaches cuisine with a deft hand. The atmosphere is hushed and classy without being dour, the wine list is extravagant, the desserts heavenly. Dinner daily. & (Downtown)

REAL CHILI
1625 W. Wells St.
Milwaukee
414/342-6955
$

From businesspeople at lunch to students on a study break to those who just can't call it a night at bar time, Real Chili serves everyone the same thing: chili. No frills, no fuss. Start with a red-meat chili base in a deep bowl, then add beans, noodles ("Green Bay-style"), onions, and other extras at your whim. Real Chili offers late hours and a fluorescent-lighted lunch-counter atmosphere that demands nothing but a hearty appetite. There's a second location on Cathedral Square, 20 blocks to the east, at 419 East Wells Street. Lunch,

African Hut, p. 53

dinner, and late night Mon–Sat, lunch and dinner Sun. (Downtown)

SAHAR
307 E. Wisconsin Ave.
Milwaukee
414/270-0970
$$

There are plenty of Middle Eastern restaurants in Milwaukee, but Sahar is the sole purveyor of Persian delights. And some of those delights—like *doogh,* a drink made of yogurt, mint, and lots of salt—are acquired tastes. Sahar utilizes grilled beef and chicken more than lamb (although the lamb shank is outstanding) and basmati rice rather than couscous and also serves many vegetarian dishes. The restaurant is casual and friendly. The lunch buffet is inexpensive, but stick with its Persian specialties, like the delicious *roulette* (hand-ground meatloaf stuffed with carrot, parsley, and egg). Lunch and dinner Mon–Sat. ⚹ (Downtown)

Sanford, p. 65

THAI PALACE
838 N. Old World Third St.
Milwaukee
414/224-7076
$$

Thai Palace is tops for Thai food in Milwaukee. The restaurant is beautifully decorated in red and gold and is comfortable, relaxed, and relatively casual. All the Thai classics are better than good here. The yellow curry with chicken is particularly delicious, and that old standby *pad Thai* is good, too. But the real delights are found on the special board. Example: ocean salmon fillets served on a bed of rice with scallops and holy basil in a light, creamy sauce. Result: an unbelievably delicious meal. Lunch and dinner Mon–Fri, dinner Sat and Sun. ⚹ (Downtown)

WATTS TEA SHOP
761 N. Jefferson St.
Milwaukee
414/291-5120
$$

Found on the second floor of the elegant Watts china, silver, and crystal shop, Watts Tea Shop is the perfect place to take your grandmother for lunch—especially if she is the kind of grandmother who insists on good table manners and polite conversation. This is the classic "ladies-who-lunch" spot, featuring dainty sandwiches—chicken salad, say—dainty pot pies, and dainty croquettes, all served by a slightly stuffy, slightly snooty staff. The room is bright and airy, and no one ever raises his or her voice. One of the great pleasures of Watts, not surprisingly, is tea, served every afternoon. Breakfast and lunch Mon–Sat. ⚹ (Downtown)

EAST SIDE

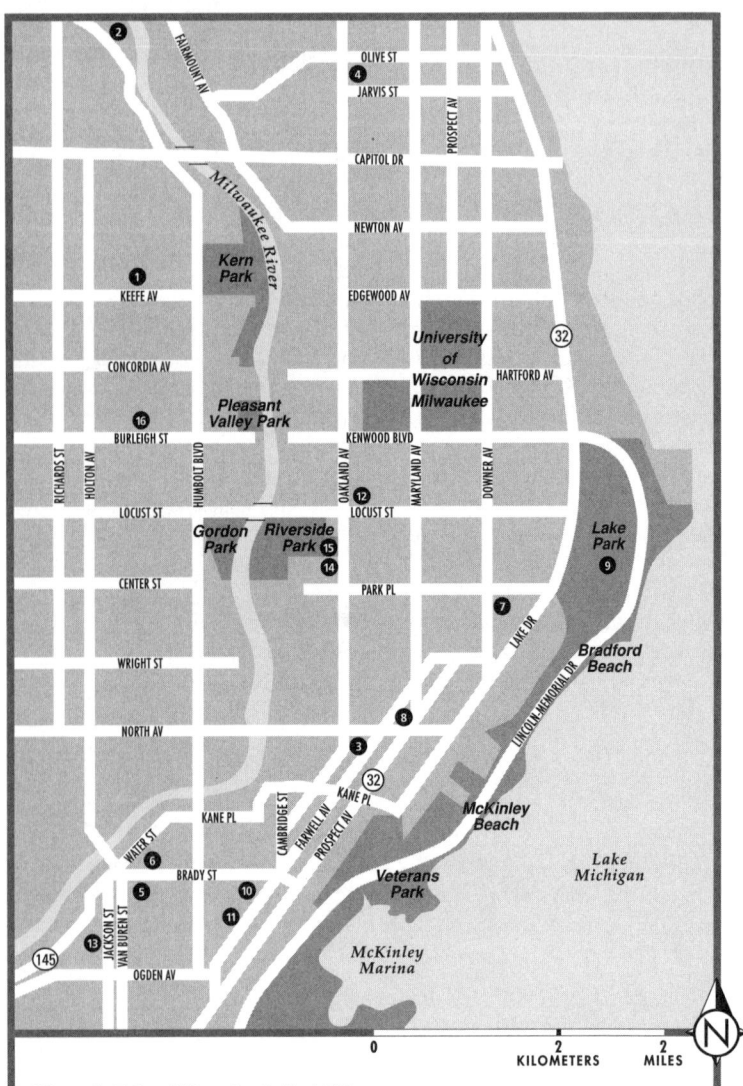

Where to Eat on Milwaukee's East Side

1 Albanese's
2 The Anchorage
3 Beans and Barley
4 Benji's Delicatessen
5 Dancing Ganesha
6 Di Salvo and Brennan's
7 Don Quijote
8 Ichiban
9 Lake Park Bistro
10 Mimma's Cafe
11 The Pasta Tree
12 Red Rock Cafe
13 Sanford
14 Shahrazad
15 Thai Kitchen
16 West Bank Café

EAST SIDE

ALBANESE'S
701 E. Keefe Ave.
Milwaukee
414/964-7270
$$

Pictures of the family on the wall, red-checked tablecloths, bad paneling, boisterous patrons. Other Italian restaurants try for this atmosphere. Albanese's just has it. Albanese's is one of the best Italian American restaurants in town. The menu: homemade egg noodles with red sauce, red sauce and meatballs, red sauce and Italian sausage, mushroom sauce, mushroom sauce with meatballs . . . on and on. Don't miss the house red, sold in half-carafes (actually old beer bottles), carafes, bottles, and cases. It can be loud and smoky on weekends, but kids are welcome here, and everybody leaves happy. Dinner Mon–Sat. (East Side)

THE ANCHORAGE
Milwaukee River Hilton Inn
4700 N. Port Washington Rd.
Glendale
414/962-4710
$$$

The Anchorage has carved out a remarkably serene setting along the upper reaches of the Milwaukee River, with willows weeping and mallards swimming by. Among the city's premiere seafood venues, the restaurant features impeccably prepared versions of the classics—swordfish *au poivre* and walleye pike *amandine*—rather than unexpected pleasures. Steaks and poultry are available, but they take second billing to the fish. The Anchorage is quiet and upscale, a good place for a business dinner with clients who must be impressed but who aren't particularly adventurous. Breakfast and dinner daily, lunch Mon–Sat. ⚹ (East Side)

BEANS AND BARLEY
1901 E. North Ave.
Milwaukee
414/278-7878
$

Beans and Barley was health-conscious before anyone ever heard of vegans or the antioxidant qualities of asparagus. Beans and Barley houses a restaurant—the tables bask in the sunlight coming through a two-story, curved glass wall—deli, and natural foods grocery store. The menu is eclectic, drawing on Middle Eastern and Asian cuisine. Known for light, vegetarian salads (like peanut tofu noodles), delicious soups, and sandwiches (like veggie burgers), Beans is a popular spot for both take-out and eat-in diners. It does a particluraly rousing breakfast business on weekends. Some meat dishes are served. Breakfast, lunch, and dinner daily. ⚹ (East Side)

BENJI'S DELICATESSEN
4156 N. Oakland Ave.
Shorewood
414/332-7777
$$

Everything about Benji's is unassuming. The building is ugly, the atmosphere extremely casual, the decor . . . well, what decor? Nonetheless, Benji's is an east side institution, and the food is great. The bagels and lox, matzoh-ball soup, potato pancakes, and big corned-beef sandwiches stand up to anything in Manhattan. Benji's is crowded—expect to wait for a table at lunchtime and during weekend breakfasts—and noisy with chattering regulars and ebullient waitresses. Wisconsin senator and Milwaukee Bucks owner Herb Kohl is often spotted here, eating a bagel and taking the pulse of his constituency. Breakfast, lunch, and dinner seven days. (East Side)

DANCING GANESHA
1692–94 N. Van Buren St.
Milwaukee
414/220-0202
$$

If there were an award for the city's most exhilarating restaurant, Dancing Ganesha would win hands down. In this quiet and upscale former tavern, the chef starts with East Indian flavors—curry, cardamon, corriander—couples them with a practically boundless creativity, and applies the mix to a startling variety of foods. The result: pure magic. The menu features subtle takes on standard Indian dishes, along with many vegetarian meals. Of particular note are the daily specials, especially if they involve seafood. One dish features tilapia filets marinated in Indian spices, then grilled. If your tastes are slightly adventurous, this is the place. Dinner Tue–Sun. (East Side)

DI SALVO AND BRENNAN'S
728 E. Brady St.
Milwaukee
414/271-9475
$$

A decade ago, Café Di Salvo was at the forefront of a movement in Milwaukee restaurants to return to ethnic cooking's roots. The family-run restaurant went deep into southern Italian cuisine in a small storefront restaurant in Northpoint, with white linen tablecloths and an interesting wine list. Renamed and moved to Brady Street, Di Salvo and Brennan's focuses on pasta with sauces that are familiar—primavera, carbonara—but better than you remember, along with some meat dishes and great pizzas. The *arancini* are particularly good: rice balls stuffed with meat, quickly fried, and served with *salsa di tomate*. Yum. Lunch Mon–Fri. Dinner daily. ⚬ (East Side)

DON QUIJOTE
2624 N. Downer Ave.
Milwaukee
414/967-1322
$$$

Don Quijote is the only Milwaukee restaurant specializing in the cuisine of Spain—land of Goya, flamenco, and blood oranges. Start with tapas—there are several dozen varieties on the menu. Served both hot and cold, these traditional Spanish appetizers—vegetarian empanadas, shrimp sautéed in garlic or mushrooms in parsley sauce—can be a meal in themselves when accompanied by one of the great Spanish wines on the wine list. Or try paella, a seafood platter cooked with fresh herbs in court bouillon and served over saffron rice. The flavors are both delicate and intricate. Lunch Tue–Sun. Dinner daily. ⚬ (East Side)

ICHIBAN
2336 N. Farwell Ave.
Milwaukee
414/278-8056
$$

You might not expect good raw fish in the heart of the heartland, but this ca-

Buns in the Oven

Perhaps because of its strong European heritage, Milwaukee is loaded with incredible bakeries. Many locals wouldn't dream of a Sunday without hot ham and fresh Italian hard rolls. Try these favorites:

- **Hartter's.** Europastries! (2101 N. Prospect Ave., 414/225-0090; additional locations in Shorewood, Hales Corners, Wauwatosa, and Brookfield)
- **Lopez Bakery**. A Mexican bakery with hard rolls for tortas and fascinating cookies. (624 W. National Ave., 414/383-4845)
- **Miller Bakery**. More varieties of rolls than you knew existed. (318 W. Wisconsin Ave., 414/271-3832)
- **Sciortino's**. Hard rolls in three shapes—round, long, and oval. (1101 E. Brady St., 414/272-4623)
- **Simma's Ovens**. The best poppyseed cake in the whole world. (817 N. 68th St., Wauwatosa, 414/257-0998)

---

sual, California-style sushi bar has Milwaukee's best selection of the dainty seafood and vegetable delicacies. The sushi is served à la carte (the *carte* has pictures for the sushi uninitiated, and the staff is more than happy to answer questions and explain the intricacies of the artform). All the usual variations are available, along with specialties like "spicy spider" *maki* stuffed with crab. The tempura, teriyaki, and stir-fried noodles are also good. This is a great lunch spot. Lunch Mon–Fri, dinner daily. (East Side)

LAKE PARK BISTRO
3133 E. Newberry Blvd.
Milwaukee
414/962-6300
$$$

At the top of Lake Park's grand staircase—and the top of restaurant critics' lists—stands the elegant Lake Park Bistro. The Bistro features French cuisine and unparalleled views of Lake Michigan from its majestic bluff site, and the chef's take on classic continental fare is never staid. He works wonders with clever sauces and highlights seasonal foodstuffs from the region, such as morel mushrooms in springtime. With unimpeachable service, the Lake Park Bistro is crowded and pricey, particularly at dinner. A great alternative is the restaurant's scaled-down lunch

GREATER MILWAUKEE

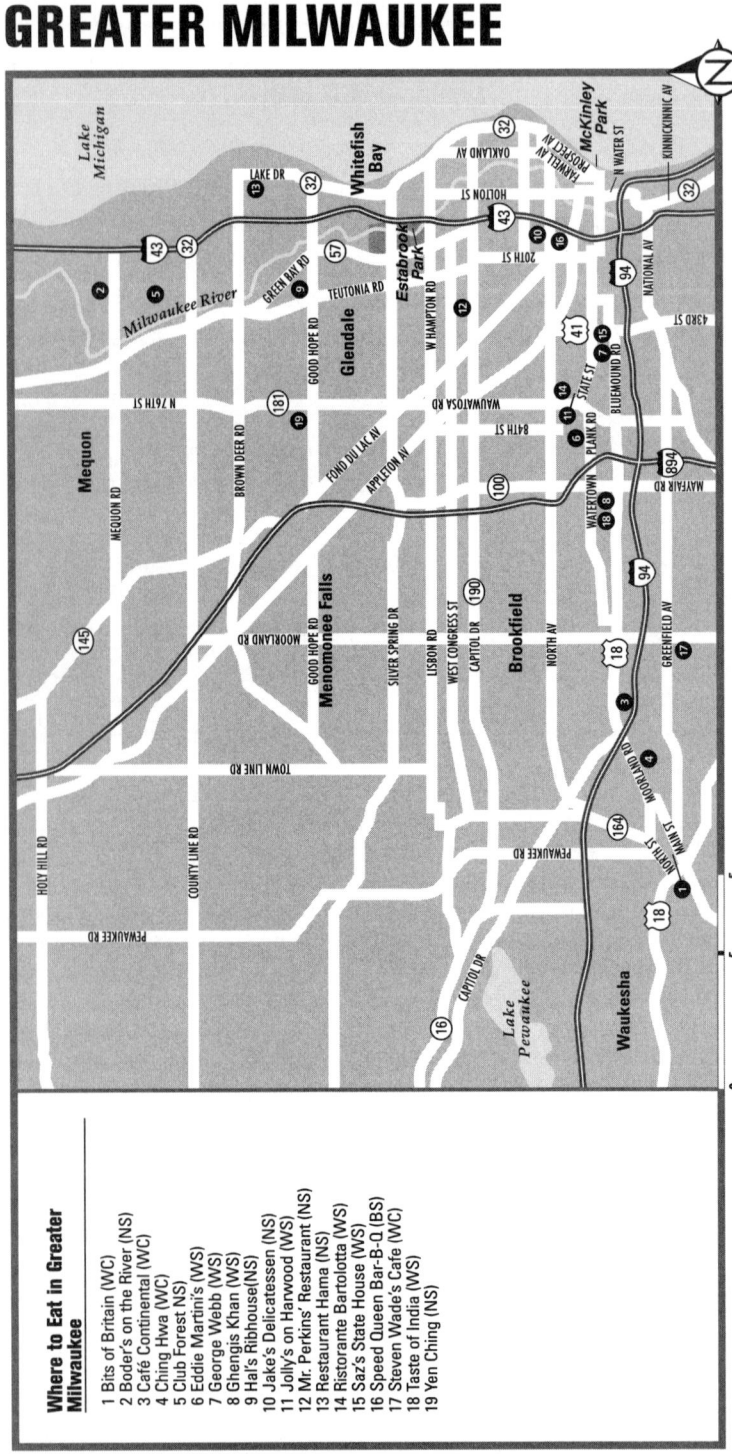

Where to Eat in Greater Milwaukee

1. Bits of Britain (WC)
2. Boder's on the River (NS)
3. Café Continental (WC)
4. Ching Hwa (WC)
5. Club Forest NS
6. Eddie Martini's (WS)
7. George Webb (WS)
8. Ghengis Khan (WS)
9. Hal's Ribhouse (NS)
10. Jake's Delicatessen (NS)
11. Jolly's on Harwood (WS)
12. Mr. Perkins' Restaurant (NS)
13. Restaurant Hama (NS)
14. Ristorante Bartolotta (WS)
15. Saz's State House (WS)
16. Speed Queen Bar-B-Q (BS)
17. Steven Wade's Cafe (WC)
18. Taste of India (WS)
19. Yen Ching (NS)

menu, featuring less-formal delights like *escargots en croute* and *croque monsieur*. Lunch Mon–Fri, dinner daily, brunch Sun. Reservations required. ♿ (East Side)

MIMMA'S CAFE
1307 E. Brady St.
Milwaukee
414/271-7337
$$$

A decade ago, Mimma's was the talk of the town, heralding as it did the eminent revival of Brady Street, which had fallen on hard times. Since then, the area has indeed revived into the city's most happening nine blocks, and Mimma's, though with less hype than before, continues to delight with its upscale regional Italian menu. The restaurant's connected 19th-century storefronts are beautifully renovated, with a decor remarkable mostly for its lack of ostentation. All the pasta dishes are great, but special attention should be paid to the weekly specials board, which features meat, fish, vegetarian, and polenta concoctions guaranteed to please. Dinner daily. ♿ (East Side)

THE PASTA TREE
1503 N. Farwell Ave.
Milwaukee
414/276-8867
$$

The Pasta Tree is probably the most romantic restaurant in Milwaukee. Located in a narrow storefront, the tiny restaurant holds only two dozen diners in the cozy glow of dim lighting, antique fixtures comfortably worn with use, and walls tastefully painted in rich earth tones. Serving, of course, homemade pasta, the Pasta Tree has a changing menu of perhaps 15 different dishes that reflect the availability of fresh ingredients and the chef's whim. From an almost sinfully rich *Bolognese* sauce (meat, tomatoes, and cream) on semolina penne to salmon with basil on fettucini, the flavors are classically grounded but creative enough to thrill the discerning palate. Lunch Tue–Sat, dinner Tue–Sun. ♿ (East Side)

RED ROCK CAFE
4022 N. Oakland Ave.
Shorewood
414/962-4545
$$

In a city where seafood means fish fries, the Red Rock Café breaks the mold. Relying on the day's fresh catch and the chef's imagination, the Red Rock serves a startling variety of fish and shellfish from the ocean and the Great Lakes. Because availability of ingredients ebbs and flows, the menu changes almost daily—you'll find trout in the spring, for example, and seven or eight crab dishes in crab season—and depends on clever but simple combinations of food and sauces rather than pomp. No need for a suit and tie at the Red Rock, but they certainly aren't out of place, either. Lunch and dinner daily. Reservations recommended. (East Side)

SANFORD
1547 N. Jackson St.
Milwaukee
414/276-9608
$$$

When Frank Lloyd Wright was called the greatest living American architect, he replied: "What do you mean 'American?' What do mean, 'living?'" Well, Sanford has the reputation as

WHERE TO EAT

Milwaukee's very best restaurant. Not the best "fine dining" restaurant, not the best "contemporary American" restaurant—simply, the best. Sanford is incapable of disappointing, because the former corner grocery store is intimate and tasteful, because the staff is polite without being obsequious, and because the kitchen is more magician's workshop than standard cooking place. Examples: seared sea scallop tournedos, rack of lamb with Mediterranean eggplant. Eat here. Dinner Mon–Sat. Reservations required. (East Side)

SHAHRAZAD
2847 N. Oakland Ave.
Milwaukee
414/964–5475

$$
The Shahrazad is among the east side's more venerable Middle Eastern restaurants. The owners hail from Palestine, and the menu focuses on lamb, couscous, and subtle sauces. Great choices include *schawirma*—similar to a Greek gyro, but delicate—and spinach pie, which features pine nuts instead of feta cheese. Or you can make a meal of appetizers like *baba ganousz* (eggplant spread), hummus (chickpea dip), and tabbouleh (bulgar wheat, tomato, and parsley salad). The Shahrazad's atmosphere is casual but quiet and tidy: students mingle with businesspeople, and neither feels out of place. Lunch and dinner daily. (East Side)

Don't Call It Ice Cream

One bite from a cone, one sip from a malt, one spoon from a sundae, and you'll see why Milwaukeeans would never eat mere ice cream when frozen custard is available. It's richer, creamier, and at least 100 times more delicious than any ice cream ever created. It's only eaten fresh, just as it emerges from the custard machine, and local custard stands have only three flavors: vanilla, chocolate, and a changing flavor of the day. Standouts include:

- **Gille's**. *A Wauwatosa fixture since 1938. (7515 W. Bluemound Rd., Wauwatosa, 414/453-4875)*
- **Kopp's**. *If you can eat in only one Milwaukee restaurant, this should be it. (7631 W. Layton Ave., 414/282-4080)*
- **Leon's Drive-In**. *"Neon Leon's" is said to be the model for Al's in the* Happy Days *sitcom. (3131 S. 27th St., 414/383-1784)*
- **Robert's**. *Old-school burgers, onion rings, and sundaes. (6005 W. Appleton Ave., 414/444-4199)*

THAI KITCHEN
2851 N. Oakland Ave.
Milwaukee
414/962-8851
$$

Most of the food at this storefront restaurant is about average. Standard Thai dishes like pad Thai (spicy rice noodles with shrimp and ground peanuts) are good, certainly, but nothing to write home about. Where Thai Kitchen shines, however, is in its fantastic selection of salads. Dishes like *som tum* (papaya and tomato salad in lemon juice with peanuts), *pla goong* (grilled shrimp, red onion, mint leaves, and ginger), and a fabulous *nam sod* (ground pork, ginger, lime juice, and hot pepper) make for indescribable taste combinations: tangy, deep, and with a delightful bite. Lunch and dinner Mon–Fri, Dinner Sat. (East Side)

WEST BANK CAFE
732 E. Burleigh St.
Milwaukee
414/562-5555
$$

The West Bank Café, an intimate and charming Riverwest institution, is the city's number one Vietnamese restaurant. The menu, though decidedly Asian, emphasizes light flavor rather than the gummy sauces associated with Chinese cooking in America or the fiery exclamation points of Thai cuisine. Fresh spring rolls are outstanding appetizers, and the house specialty, catfish cooked in a clay pot, greets your tongue with a series of subtle flavors, one after another. The West Bank features a number of vegetarian selections, too, like tofu and vegetable stir fry. Dinner daily. (East Side)

NORTH SIDE

BODER'S ON THE RIVER
11919 N. River Rd.
Mequon
262/242-0335
$$$

In 1929, when Boder's opened, Mequon was a quiet rural suburb far removed from the bustle of the big city. Now Mequon is one of Milwaukee's most affluent and fastest-growing North Shore suburbs. But Boder's remains committed to simple elegance—both its atmosphere and food pull no punches. There are no outrageous flavors, just classic American cuisine. Entrées like medaillons of veal with apple compote and baked rainbow trout stuffed with white-wine dressing make Boder's one of Milwaukee's favorite places to celebrate memorable events. Lunch and dinner Tue–Sun, brunch Sun. Reservations required. (North Side)

CLUB FOREST
4200 W. County Line Rd.
Mequon
262/238-0876
$$$

Forget eclecticism. Forget California fusion. Forget nouvelle this and nouvelle that. When you walk in the door of Club Forest, you've entered the meat and potatoes zone. Milwaukee's first exponent of the early 1990s bull-market trend toward old-style steakhouses, Club Forest remains the best of the breed. The historic building—a former speakeasy—is understated, and you can hear the cocktail shakers being shaken and the sizzle of USDA prime filets being grilled. Though the menu branches out into seafood and poultry, don't be fooled. Beef is the specialty. Enough said. Lunch Tue–Fri, dinner Tue–Sun. & (North Side)

HAL'S RIBHOUSE
7600 N. Teutonia Ave.
Milwaukee
414/228-8108
$$

Hal's is among the city's very best spots for down-home southern cooking: black-eyed peas, smoked ham hocks, beef tips, corn bread, ribs (of course), catfish, yams, okra, and what may be the best stewed greens—collard, mustard, beet, and the like—this side of the Ohio River. Hal's features a Friday fish fry, Sunday buffet (a steal at under $10), and an easygoing, family atmosphere. The desserts, all homemade, are incredible: peach cobbler, caramel cake, and bread pudding. Lunch Tue–Fri, dinner Tue–Sun. (North Side)

JAKE'S DELICATESSEN
1634 W. North Ave.
Milwaukee
414/562-1272
$$

Up through the 1950s, the North Division neighborhood was the center of Jewish-German Milwaukee. Now, except for a few Stars of David on temples converted to Baptist churches, Jake's is the last trace of that legacy. Jake's hasn't changed in 40 years: a lunch counter, a handful of booths, and a long line of people waiting for take-out sandwiches. Those sandwiches—roast beef, tongue, salami—are huge, and the matzoh ball soup is the best in town. The neighborhood struggles with poverty and crime, but people who know wouldn't get their corned beef elsewhere, because Jake's is the mother of all kosher delis. Breakfast and lunch Mon–Sat. (North Side)

MR. PERKINS' RESTAURANT
2001 W. Atkinson Ave.
Milwaukee
414/447-6660
$$

Just because Mr. Perkins' has the best breakfast in town, that's no reason to shy away from the soul-food insitution for lunch and dinner. For three decades, the Perkins family has been satisfying Milwaukee families with their recipes—perfected recipes—that bring down-home southern cooking to the frozen North. Breakfast features ham (cut thick) and eggs with grits or home fries, biscuits, pancakes, hash, and other heart-stopping delights. Other meals continue the theme: chicken and dressing, catfish, smothered steak, turnip greens. Desserts—sweet-potato pie—are a must. Breakfast, lunch, dinner Mon–Sat. (North Side)

RESTAURANT HAMA
333 W. Brown Deer Rd.
Fox Point
414/352-5051
$$$

This upscale North Shore restaurant specializes in Japanese fare by way of a California filter; the chef takes traditional food and makes it distinctly his own. The results: generally outstanding. Standard sushi is available, and it's some of the best in town, but the real deal is found on the special board: grilled squid served with saki and field greens, seared black-bean chicken in a noodle basket, roasted salmon with Chinese hot mustard. Hama is light, West-Coasty, and quite fashionable. Dinner Mon–Sat. (North Side)

SPEED QUEEN BAR-B-Q
1130 W. Walnut St.
Milwaukee
414/265-2900
$
No relation to the appliances, Speed Queen is the place to fix your hankering for ribs—or chicken, or beef—in a hurry. Owned by the Partee family since 1952, this busy restaurant (in a neighborhood that has, admittedly, seen better times) has no windows and no table service—take-out is the order of the day. Walk in, check the menu board, place your order through the safety glass, and you'll be handed a bag full of succulent barbeque, spicy sauce, and coleslaw. Try any of the half-and-half combos: beef ribs and pork shoulder, pork ribs and beef tips, you name it. Lunch, dinner, and late night Mon–Sat. No credit cards accepted. (North Side)

YEN CHING
7630 W. Good Hope Rd.
Milwaukee
414/353-6677

The Daily Grind

Sure, you could get your coffee from a machine at the gas station, but Milwaukee is loaded with great coffeehouses and chic cafés including:

- *Alterra Coffee Roasters. Coffee roasters to Milwaukee and a funky café. (2211 N. Prospect Ave., 414/273-3753)*
- *Bear Brew. It's stylish and full of businesspeople trying to get an edge. (708 N. Milwaukee St., 414/224-8877)*
- *Brewed Awakenings. Relaxed Brady Street hipness and good vegetarian food. (1208 E. Brady St., 414/276-2739)*
- *Capoochino's. Espresso hut and self-service dog wash. Very amusing. (3640 S. Moorland Rd., New Berlin, 414/789-5210)*
- *Fuel Café. Cool music, 'zines, coffee, tattoos, cigarette smoke. (818 E. Center St., 414/374-3835)*
- *Hi-Fi Café. Sunny, friendly, with a wonderful jukebox. (2640 S. Kinnickinnic Ave., 414/486-0504)*
- *Milwaukee Coffee Company. Great architecture, great coffee. (5010 W. Vliet St., 414/257-1001)*

$$

The far northwest side is a slightly desolate region for restaurant seekers, but there are gems to be found among the downtrodden strip malls and less-than-elegant apartment complexes. In this environment, you wouldn't expect to come across a gorgeous Chinese restaurant with carved dragons, pagoda roof, and gold leaf. Even better, in a world where tastebuds are tempted by a startling variety of Asian food, Yen Ching more than holds its own with Mandarin classics of the highest quality. Chicken with snow peas and pork in garlic sauce are just a few of the dishes to be found on the huge menu. Lunch and dinner daily. ♿ (North Side)

SOUTH SIDE

CRAWDADDY'S
6414 W. Greenfield Ave.
West Allis
414/778-2228
$$

Try to find a place at the bar, order a Sazerac, and wait (and wait) to be seated. Crawdaddy's is tremendously popular. Of all the Cajun joints in Milwaukee, this is the swingingest. It's big, bold, and busy, with traditional New Orleans favorites like gumbo, po' boys, and blackened snapper and a changing menu of creative specials featuring seafood and previously unimagined uses of alligator. There are no disappointments at Crawdaddy's; a taste of the red beans and rice with andouille sausage should prove that. It's casual, loud, and smoky. Lunch Tue–Fri, dinner Tue–Sat. (South Side)

EL REY
1023 S. Cesar Chavez St.
Milwaukee
414/643-1640
$

If you want Mexican food without the Anglo filter, this diner inside the bustling El Rey grocery store on South 16th Street is the place to find it. The service can be slow and the fluorescent lights make for low ambience, but the food is incredible. There are burritos and tacos, but don't miss the *tortas al pastor*, Mexican sandwiches of cubed beef and pork in a savory red sauce on grilled bread with tomato, avocado, lettuce, and *pico de gallo* salsa. There is another diner in the even larger El Rey grocery store at 3524 West Burnham Street. Breakfast, lunch, and dinner daily. ♿ (South Side)

THE FOURTH BASE
5117 W. National Ave.
West Allis
414/647-8509
$$

In the shadows cast by the I-beam infrastructure of the nascent Miller Park, the Fourth Base is a restaurant of contradictory motives. The best description: a pub on steroids. At least, the Fourth Base's incredible menu is on steroids. Don't be put off by the pub's noisy, tipsy tavern atmosphere: The food is remarkable. The changing menu features elegantly simple fare—from lobster tails to prime rib, all of which is a far cry from the burgers and fries typical of a place like this. The Fourth Base is widely known for an outstanding Sunday brunch. Not bad for a sports bar. Lunch and dinner daily. ♿ (South Side)

SOUTH SIDE

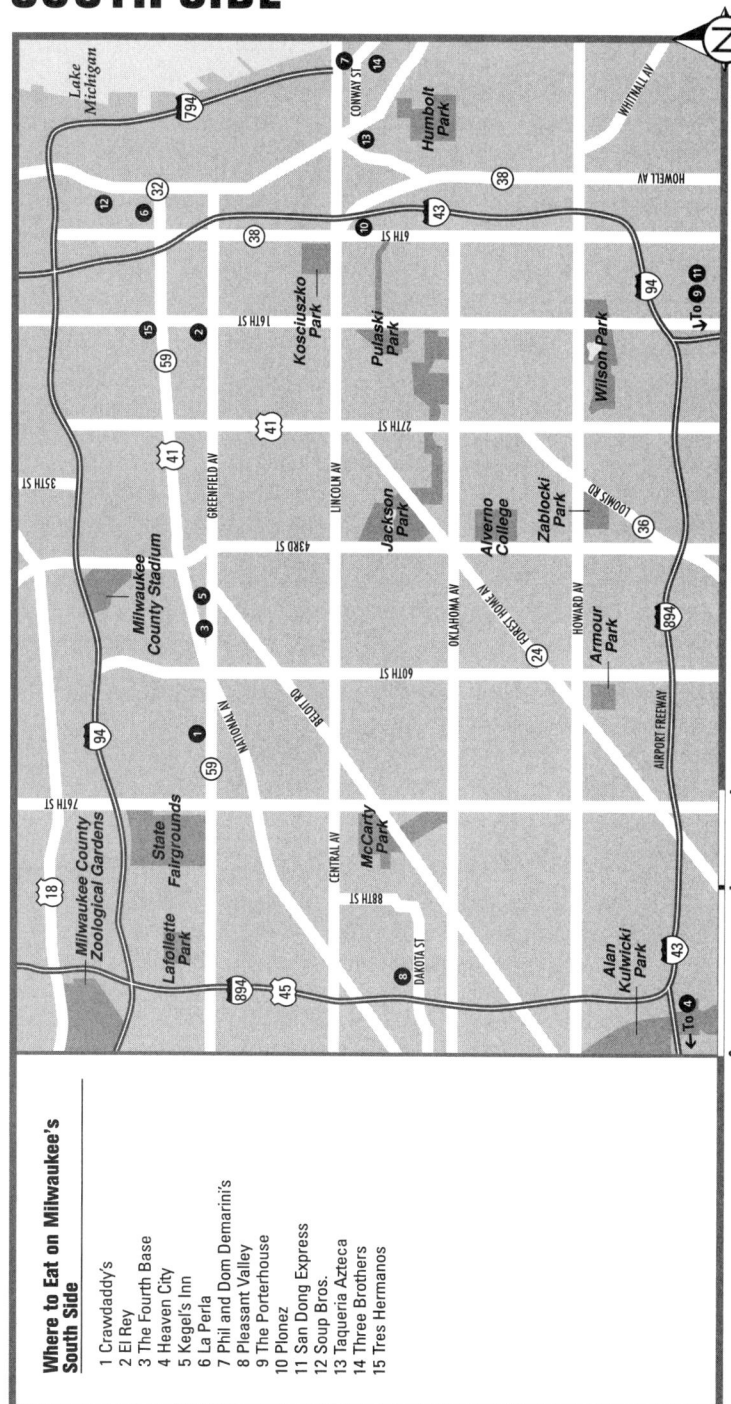

Where to Eat on Milwaukee's South Side

1 Crawdaddy's
2 El Rey
3 The Fourth Base
4 Heaven City
5 Kegel's Inn
6 La Perla
7 Phil and Dom Demarini's
8 Pleasant Valley
9 The Porterhouse
10 Plonez
11 San Dong Express
12 Soup Bros.
13 Taqueria Azteca
14 Three Brothers
15 Tres Hermanos

HEAVEN CITY
S91 W27850 Highway ES
(National Ave.)
Mukwonago
262/363-5191
$$$

Heaven City is found in an old art deco resort, built in the 1920s to satisfy the weekend whims of Chicago gangsters and the Gatsby set. Curving walls, rich wood trim, an indoor palm garden, and a warren of small dining areas make Heaven City a treat for the eyes. And chef Scott McGlinchey's concoctions are a treat for the palette. Using local ingredients and with a flair for eclectic flavors, he makes delicious surprises like sautéed fiddlehead ferns, sturgeon filets in saffron butter, and grilled lamb. Lunch Mon–Fri, dinner Mon–Sat. Reservations required. & (South Side)

KEGEL'S INN
5901 W. National Ave.
West Allis
414/257-9999
$$

There are many justly famous German restaurants in Milwaukee. Kegel's is, unjustly, not one of them. Less formal and less pricey than its downtown cousins, Kegel's features the old German tavern atmosphere, plenty of imported beer on tap, a decent wine list, and a number of house specialties to delight those seeking authentic fare. While all of the German entrées are good, the don't-miss meal at Kegel's is the roasted duck. Succulent and juicy with a crispy skin, served with dressing and mild red cabbage, this meal is nearly perfect. Lunch Mon–Fri, dinner Mon–Sat. (South Side)

LA PERLA
734 S. Fifth St.
Milwaukee
414/645-9888
$$

Walker's Point is home to dozens of Mexican restaurants, sliding along an authenticity scale from Suburban to Sonoran. La Perla falls right in the middle. Good food (leaning toward the unadventurous) and a funky atmosphere combine to make a popular eating place that is easy on the eyes and stomach. The nice bar is busy at Happy Hour, refilling margarita glasses as fast as the blender will blend, and the fare is standard, well-prepared Mexican. There is a beautiful outdoor patio for summer evenings, and kids can ride the wiggling jalapeño ride for a quarter, with proceeds going to charity. Lunch and dinner daily. & (South Side)

PHIL AND DOM DEMARINI'S
1211 E. Conway St.
Milwaukee
414/481-2348
$$

This Italian American restaurant is informed by a tale of family intrigue and betrayal worthy of Shakespeare. The original DeMarini family restaurant—famous for Milwaukee-style thin-crust pizza—is around the corner at 2754 South Wentworth Street. After an acrimonious family battle, it's now known as Mama DeMarini's, and the new restaurant is owned by Mama's sons. What makes sons betray their mother? The real question is: Who has the pizza recipe? They both do. Mama's is a little more downscale (but only a little), but both restaurants are casual. Lunch and dinner daily. & (South Side)

Friday Fare

Friday night means one thing in Milwaukee: fish fry. Stemming from the Catholic Church's prohibition on eating meat at the end of the work week, this weekly culinary orgy of perch, french fries, cole slaw, and beer is is served by hundreds of restaurants and taverns in Milwaukee. If you ask a dozen Milwaukeeans which one is best, you'll get a dozen different answers. But here are a few favorites:

- **Benjamin Brigg's Pub**. *A former Schlitz beer garden, this is old Milwaukee all the way. (2501 W. Greenfield Ave., 414/383-2337)*
- **Five & Ten Tap**. *This smoky tavern is beloved by cops, and they ought to know. (1850 N. Water St., 414/272-1599)*
- **Historic Turner Restaurant**. *A German gymnastic club with 19th-century murals and great fish. (1034 N. Fourth St., 414/276-4844)*
- **Serb Hall**. *The fish fry of the gods! Serving thousands every Friday. (5101 W. Oklahoma Ave., 414/545-6030)*

PLEASANT VALLEY INN
9801 W. Dakota St.
West Allis
414/321-4321
$$$
This family-owned restaurant, tucked into a residential neighborhood, generates a lot of good buzz. And it's reputation as "casually elegant" is well earned. It's the atmosphere that's casual (but not downscale—you don't need a tie, but blue jeans aren't welcome either). It's the food that's elegant: fresh seafood specials, delicate meat dishes, and steaks cooked as you like them. The wine list is not huge, but it's broadly conceived, and desserts are a wonder. If you seek an upscale but unpretentious dinner in a quiet and out-of-the-way locale, this is the place. Make weekend dinner reservations early. Dinner Tue–Sun. ♿ (South Side)

THE PORTERHOUSE
800 W. Layton Ave.
Milwaukee
414/744-1750
$$$
The Porterhouse, a stone's throw from Mitchell International, is more like a rural Wisconsin supper club than swanky urban steakhouse. It's not fancy or formal, but the Porterhouse is a place for the kind of meal your grandparents would enjoy. Its low-key, slow, and steady approach

Ichiban, p. 62

to meat and potatoes make it a great place to eat if you're looking not for adventure but for quality. Steaks and chops are cooked to your order perfectly every time and are served with starch and the more normal sorts of vegetables. You'll find poultry, ribs, and some seafood, too. Lunch Tue–Sat, dinner Tue–Sun. (South Side)

POLONEZ
2316 S. Sixth St.
Milwaukee
414/384-8766
$$

In the shadow cast by the towering copper dome of St. Josaphat Basilica stands the humble Polonez. Humble, that is, of atmosphere, because from the first spoonful of borscht to the last pierogi, the food is positively transporting. This family-run restaurant is one of Milwaukee's best purveyors of Polish cuisine—kielbasa, duck's blood soup—in the heart of the old Polish south side. Best bets: meatloaf with mushroom gravy, which is better than your mother's, and the sampler platter featuring Polish sausage, stuffed cabbage, and several other delights. Lunch and dinner Tue–Sun. (South Side)

SAN DONG EXPRESS
220 W. Layton Ave.
Milwaukee
414/744-3399
$

Milwaukee's best Hong Kong noodle restaurant is found in a former fast-food joint near the airport. Though the exterior of the building is done up red pagoda–style, the interior offers plastic chairs, little tables, and no creature comforts. You can see the chefs working their wok magic, though, and the noodles are homemade. The best bet is the seafood stew—a slurpy delight with all kinds of shellfish. Note that chicken is chopped in little cubes, bone in, in the traditional Chinese style, which can be disconcerting. Lunch and dinner daily. (South Side)

SOUP BROS.
209 W. Florida St.
Milwaukee
414/860-7687
$

You've seen the *Seinfeld* episode, now dip a spoon into the soup. The chef at Soup Bros. it's rumored, worked for the infamous "Soup Nazi" in Manhattan, and his Walker's Point storefront dishes out some of the finest and cleverest soups you've ever tasted—and nothing else. With half a dozen varieties changing daily, you'll find gumbos and chowders, cream soups and clear, hot soup, cold soup, and a vegetarian choice. Of particular note are the honey-roasted carrot soup with fresh herbs and the chicken chowder, all served with fresh bread. Soup Bros. is take-out only, serves a few sandwiches, and makes a great quick stop before a lunch in the park. Breakfast, lunch, and early dinner Mon–Fri, lunch Sat. (South Side)

TAQUERIA AZTECA
2301 S. Howell Ave.
Milwaukee
414/486-9447
$$

Milwaukee has been fortunate in the last several years to see an explosion in the number of taquerias. Of these unpretentious Mexican diners, Bay View's Taqueria Azteca operates on a somewhat higher plane than many. The menu is simple—tacos, tortas, burritos—but the daily specials surpass the everyday. Fish tacos, for example, feature small pieces of fried perch, shredded red cabbage, lime juice, and chipotle sauce. More extravagant is an Oaxacan specialty like *enogada:* a *poblano* pepper stuffed with meat, nuts, and fruit, served cold with a walnut cream sauce. The Taqueria Azteca is casual and comfortable. Lunch and dinner Mon–Sat. (South Side)

THREE BROTHERS
2414 S. St. Clair Ave.
Milwaukee
414/481-7530
$$

At the end of the last century, Schlitz Brewery dotted Milwaukee with beer gardens, taverns with distinctive globes adorning their rooflines. Three Brothers, a remarkable restaurant serving Serbian cuisine, is housed in one of those beer gardens and maintains the atmosphere perfectly. Dark wood, dim lights, a slightly imperious staff: it adds up to a great place for dinner. No one is in a hurry here, and you can expect your meal to last a couple of delicious hours. Veal, lamb, and *burek*—a flaky filo-dough pie filled with savory meat or spinach—are all great choices, especially when accompanied by the delicious house red. Reservations recommended. Dinner Tue–Sun. (South Side)

TRES HERMANOS
1100 W. National Ave.
Milwaukee
414/384-8850
$$

Tres Hermanos may be the best all-around Mexican restaurant in town, drawing more and more diners from the well-known restaurants a few blocks to the east with its growing reputation for great food at great prices in an unpretentious atmosphere. All the Mexican standards are good here, and the daily lunch special is exceptionally cheap. But for a real treat try the *ceviche* (chopped shrimp marinated in lime juice with serrano peppers and tomatoes) and the *caldo de camarones* (cold shrimp and tomato soup). Breakfast, lunch, dinner and late-night daily. (South Side)

WEST SIDE

EDDIE MARTINI'S
8612 W. Watertown Plank Rd.
Wauwatosa
414/771-6680
$$$

The 1950s meant cars with fins, cocktails, and, above all, red meat. At Eddie Martini's, a gracious reminder of life during the Eisenhower era, two out of three ain't bad. Without any cruddy affectation, the restaurant captures the glory of a time when the future was bright and cholesterol wasn't bad for you. Quite simply, the place is a class act. Drink a cocktail, indulge in the perfect porterhouse *au poivre* or *à point*, and finish off an elegant evening with a sumptuous and non-heart-healthy dessert. Lunch Mon–Fri, dinner daily. Reservations required. ♿ (West Side)

GEORGE WEBB
6108 W. Bluemound Rd.
Milwaukee
414/453-2392
$

Ah, George Webb, Milwaukee's homegrown greasy spoon, as inseparable from the city's sense of identity as Miller High Life or Harley hogs. Found throughout the metropolitan area, in strip malls and on street corners, George Webb restaurants provide what other burger joints can't:

atmosphere. Granted, it's not a great atmosphere, but it is reassuring: fluorescent lights, vinyl booths, chatty waitresses. Cheap breakfasts, great french fries, and passable burgers are the chain's hallmarks. George Webb is where Milwaukee eats, especially after the taverns close. Hours: 24/7. No credit cards accepted. ♿ (West Side)

GHENGIS KHAN
725 N. Mayfair Rd.
Wauwatosa
414/774-5540
$$

Serving Mongolian barbecue, Ghengis Khan is a novelty restaurant. But the novelty doesn't wear thin. Ghengis Khan's focus is the huge griddles on which the chefs work their Mongolian magic. Choose from a variety of meat, fresh vegetables, and sauces laid out on a buffet table. Hand the concoction to the chefs, who then grill the whole mess with a spectacular display of manual dexter-

Boulevard Inn, p. 53

© Grace Natoli Sheldon/Eric Oxendorf

JOLLY'S ON HARWOOD
7754 Harwood Ave.
Wauwatosa
414/476-7393
$$$

Once upon a time, there was a legendary restaurant called Jolly Vnuk's, Milwaukee's first and foremost Cajun restaurant. It burned to the ground, but lo! From the ashes a new restaurant, called simply Jolly's, has risen. Located in a tastefully renovated industrial building, the restaurant now starts at New Orleans and works its way west. You can still get alligator, but look for items like chicken in chipotle sauce, broiled steaks, and marinated seafood dishes. Soups are very good here, as are desserts. A great lunch choice is the catfish po' boy sandwich; the filet is dredged in spices and baked—to juicy perfection—rather than deep fried. Lunch and dinner Wed–Mon. & (West Side)

RISTORANTE BARTOLOTTA
7616 W. State St.
Wauwatosa
414/771-7910
$$$

Found in a lovely Cream City brick storefront in quaint Wauwatosa, Bartolotta specializes in rustic Italian cuisine—which is about as far from overcooked pasta with cloying red sauce as St. Mark's is from Mulberry Street. Among the dinner choices: Riviera-style seafood stew, veal chops in Marsala cream sauce with potato-chard puree, and homemade artichoke-filled ravioli with rock shrimp, tarragon, and white truffles. If that's too much, Bartolotta has a scaled-down lunch menu that is equally elegant, but a trifle less unapproachable in its perfection. Lunch Mon–Fri, dinner daily. (West Side)

SAZ'S STATE HOUSE
5539 W. State St.
Milwaukee
414/453–2410
www.sazsbbq.com
$$

In Milwaukee, "Saz's" is another word for "ribs." Though Saz's offers a full menu of American fare, seafood, and steaks, you'd be a fool to order anything without barbecue sauce. Try pork sandwiches at lunchtime and half a rack for dinner. Saz's is just up the railroad tracks from Miller Brewing and a favorite among Milwaukee Brewers fans. You can catch a bus to the game from here or just hang around the beautiful wooden bar with the regulars to talk about the team's chances. There's an outdoor patio, too, where conversation competes with passing freight trains. Lunch Mon–Sat, dinner daily. (West Side)

TASTE OF INDIA
10900 W. Bluemound Rd.
Wauwatosa
414/259–9200
$$

There was a grim period in the early 1990s when Milwaukee was without a single East Indian restaurant. That *annus horribilis* ended, thankfully, with the establishment of Taste of India. And while many Indian restaurants have opened since, this one

TIP: Want to avoid the hotel restaurant but don't want to leave the hotel? Try the Takeout Taxi, a delivery service that will bring food to you for a $4 surcharge. Restaurants involved in the project include Maharaja for good Indian food, Red Rock Cafe for outstanding seafood, and Benji's kosher deli. Call 414/427-0088.

remains the standard. Don't let the rundown-motel setting fool you: The food is outstanding. Delicious vegetable-filled flat breads complement classic subcontinental fare—curries, vindaloos (hot!), and many vegetarian choices. Finish off with a mango dessert and a cup of chai, sweet hot tea with milk, cinnamon, and cardamon. Lunch and dinner daily. (West Side)

WAUKESHA COUNTY

BITS OF BRITAIN
294 W. Main St.
Waukesha
262/896-7772
$

Jolly good, old chap! Bits of Britain, an expatriate from Bay View to suburban Waukesha, does its best to imitate a tearoom in merry old England. English newspapers and magazines, groceries, and baked goods abound, and the tea is excellent, of course. This is the perfect spot for lunch on a rainy day. Mulligatawny soup, Cornish pasties, kidney pie, and mushy peas are the most pleasant ticket to London you can find. Lunch Tue–Sat. ♿ (Waukesha County)

CAFÉ CONTINENTAL
19035 W. Bluemound Rd.
Brookfield
262/786-9139
$$

Housed in a strip mall on daunting Blue Mound Road, this restaurant is an island in a sea of fast-food and second-rate chains. Café Continental is casual and easygoing, but the menu is delightfully broad and the food is high quality. Homemade soups and sandwiches, light dinners—chicken Florentine, for example—and creative pasta dishes are sure to please. Most importantly, Café Continental's homemade baked goods, eggs of all stripes, and griddlecakes make a wonderful alternative to greasy-spoon breakfasts. Breakfast and lunch daily, dinner Mon–Sat. Brunch Sun. ♿ (Waukesha County)

CHING HWA
1947 E. Main St.
Waukesha
262/544-1983
$$

Milwaukee is home to a huge number of merely adequate Chinese restaurants, but Ching Hwa rises above the fray. Ching Hwa won't surprise you: The comfortable, gracious atmosphere is old-school Chinese restaurant, and the food is traditional Mandarin and Szechuan. But everything on the extensive menu is made with a light touch and fresh ingredients, a hundred miles from the gooey,

MSG-laden junk that used to pass for Chinese food in the Midwest. Lunch Sun–Fri, dinner daily. ♿ (Waukesha County)

STEVEN WADE'S CAFE
17001 W. Greenfield Ave.
New Berlin
262/784-0774
$$$

The last word in elegant dining on Milwaukee's far west side, Steven Wade's is known for creativity and attention to detail. The menu changes daily to reflect seasonally available ingredients and specializes in quality food with a continental flair. Fresh seafood specials, roast loin of lamb, and duck are among the treats that pop up. This restaurant is a perfect choice for visitors with business in Brookfield who want to lavish themselves with good taste. Desserts are out of this world. Lunch Tue–Fri, dinner Mon–Sat. Reservations recommended. ♿ (Waukesha County)

5

SIGHTS AND ATTRACTIONS

Whatever Milwaukee's identity may be in the national consciousness, it does not revolve around a single, unique landmark. While there are lovely bridges, monuments, and architecture, there's no Golden Gate, no Statue of Liberty, no Sears Tower.

In many ways, that's befitting of a city of Milwaukee's history—a city of immigrants, of working people, of unself-conscious achievement. Milwaukeeans have long eschewed expressions of self-aggrandizement, and the city's greatest monument to that modesty is an open space. The Milwaukee lakefront is entirely public parkland, a legacy of socialist government. Milwaukee keeps its greatest resource accessible and open to everyone, to the people. So instead of lakefront highrises and monuments to capitalism, Milwaukee's sights and attractions include trees, grass, and beach.

Still, the city's history of hard work and its sense of community spirit— for it is nothing less—have paid off. The results are a wealth of achievements in architecture, monuments, and attractions for visitors. And there is something to appeal to every taste.

Love historic architecture but only have a few hours to sightsee? Head to the Third Ward, a neighborhood of 19th-century warehouses on the southern edge of downtown. Want to learn about Great Lakes maritime history? Visit the Lake Schooner project. One of the few medieval buildings in the United States is on the Marquette University campus. You can watch motorcycles—Milwaukee Iron—being made on the Harley-Davidson factory tour. Or sip beer at the end of a Miller Brewery excursion. The world's greatest collection of historic maps is housed at the Univeristy of Wisconsin-Milwaukee. And there's more, of course, much more.

DOWNTOWN

BRADLEY CENTER
1001 N. Fourth St.
Milwaukee
414/227-0400

The Bradley Center arena, home to many of Milwaukee's professional sports teams as well as concerts and other events, was a gift to the city from philanthropists Jane and Lloyd Pettit. Built in 1988, the Bradley Center rises 14 stories and seats 20,000 fans with no obstructed views. The Bradley Center's architecture pays subtle homage to the Allen-Bradley Company, source of Jane Pettit's family wealth: The huge octagonal air vents that punctuate the building's exterior mimic the faces of the giant Allen-Bradley factory clock tower in Walker's Point. (Downtown)

THE CALLING
O'Donnell Park
E. Wisconsin and
N. Prospect Aves.
Milwaukee

One of the greatest pleasures in Milwaukee is seeing the sun rise over Lake Michigan. But if sunrise is too early for you, seeing Mark di Suvero's monumental sculpture is a close second. *The Calling* was commissioned by the Milwaukee Art Museum in 1981, with funds from an anonymous donor.

Installed in the city's most prominent public art site, the work has caused no end of controversy. It was accused to being too big, too abstract, too weird. Two decades later, the sculpture seems perfectly natural atop the bluff, its bright orange I-beams and subtly assymetrical proportions lending an almost kinetic energy to the monument. (Downtown)

CAPTAIN FREDERICK PABST MANSION
2000 W. Wisconsin Ave.
Milwaukee
414/931-0808

Ship captain-turned-brewer Frederick Pabst was among Milwaukee's richest citizens. To prove it, he erected an opulent, 37-room home, built in the Flemish Renaissance Revival style, in 1893. Pabst spared no expense on his stunning house—there are tons of stone putti, an enormous staircase, carved wooden panels imported from a 17th-century Bavarian castle, and 14 fireplaces. A tour of the mansion is a great way to see how the other half lived in Edwardian-era America. Tue–Sat 10–3:30, Sun 12–3:30. Adults $7, seniors $6, ages 6 to 17 $3. (Downtown)

CLOWN HALL OF FAME
161 W. Wisconsin Ave.
Milwaukee
414/319-0848

Wisconsin is Circus-Central, with the Circus World Museum in Baraboo and Milwaukee's Great Circus Parade, an extravaganza of century-old circus wagons, acrobats, and wild animals, held every August. Add to that the Clown Hall of Fame, recently relocated into the museum space in the center of the Grand Avenue Mall, and you've got three rings of fun. The Clown Hall of Fame is dedicated to celebrating the grand masters of the art of laughter, with exhibits, an archive, and, of course, the hall of fame itself, featuring relics from famous bygone clowns.

Mon–Sat 10–4. Admission: $2. (Downtown)

DOWNTOWN SKYWALKS

Milwaukee is cold in the wintertime. The wind blows down Wisconsin Avenue, and flurries of snow whirl through the arcs of the streetlights. Instead of fighting the chill, take to the skywalks! A series of enclosed second-story walkways in Kilbourntown, the skywalks connect hotels, shopping areas, theaters, office towers, parking structures, and even the Midwest Express Convention Center. Beyond convenience, among the best uses of the skywalk system are Sky-Waukee architecture and history tours, held every Saturday in climate-controlled comfort (See City Tours, page 102). ♿ (Downtown)

GERMANIA BUILDING
134 W. Wells St.
Milwaukee

In the 1890s, Milwaukee's *Die Germania* was the largest German-language newspaper in the world. This "Wagnerian skyscraper" was built in 1896 as the paper's headquarters. At the time, it was the tallest building in Kilbourntown, not to mention the most splendid, with its marble floors, Ionic and Doric columns, carved cherubs, and copper domes. Stone lions guard the entrance, and the building has carved ceilings, arched windows, and a neoclassical pediment. A 10-foot bronze statue once stood above the entrance, allegorically representing Germany. It was removed during the First World War. (Downtown)

GRAIN EXCHANGE BUILDING
225 E. Michigan St.
Milwaukee
414/272-6230

In the years after the Civil War, Milwaukee was the leading grain exporting city in the nation, and fortunes hinged on the price of a bushel of wheat. Built in 1879, the Grain Exchange Building is a landmark of Victorian excess: The 175-foot bell and clock tower is guarded by gargoyles, the trading room rises three stories, surrounded by frescoes, stained glass, arches, and columns. This was once the busiest commodities exchange in the country, the pits bustling with speculators and dealers. Now it's used for elegant weddings, antiques shows, and other social functions. Open during business hours, but call ahead. Admission: free. (Downtown)

HISTORIC THIRD WARD
Bounded by the Milwaukee River, E. St. Paul Ave., and Lake Michigan
Milwaukee
www.milwaukee-htw.org

In the 1970s and '80s, artists were attracted to the rundown Old Third Ward, the city's warehouse district, for its large spaces and cheap rents. Slowly, the neighborhood was transformed, from wholesale grocers to chic specialty stores, trendy cafés, theaters, antiques shops, loft condos, and art galleries. It's a quick walk from any of the downtown hotels, and the Third Ward, with its beautiful historic buildings, is a great place to see a play, drink a latte, or find that perfect Mission library table. Stop in at the Historic Third Ward Association office at 219 North Milwaukee Street for a walking-tour map. (Downtown)

DOWNTOWN MILWAUKEE

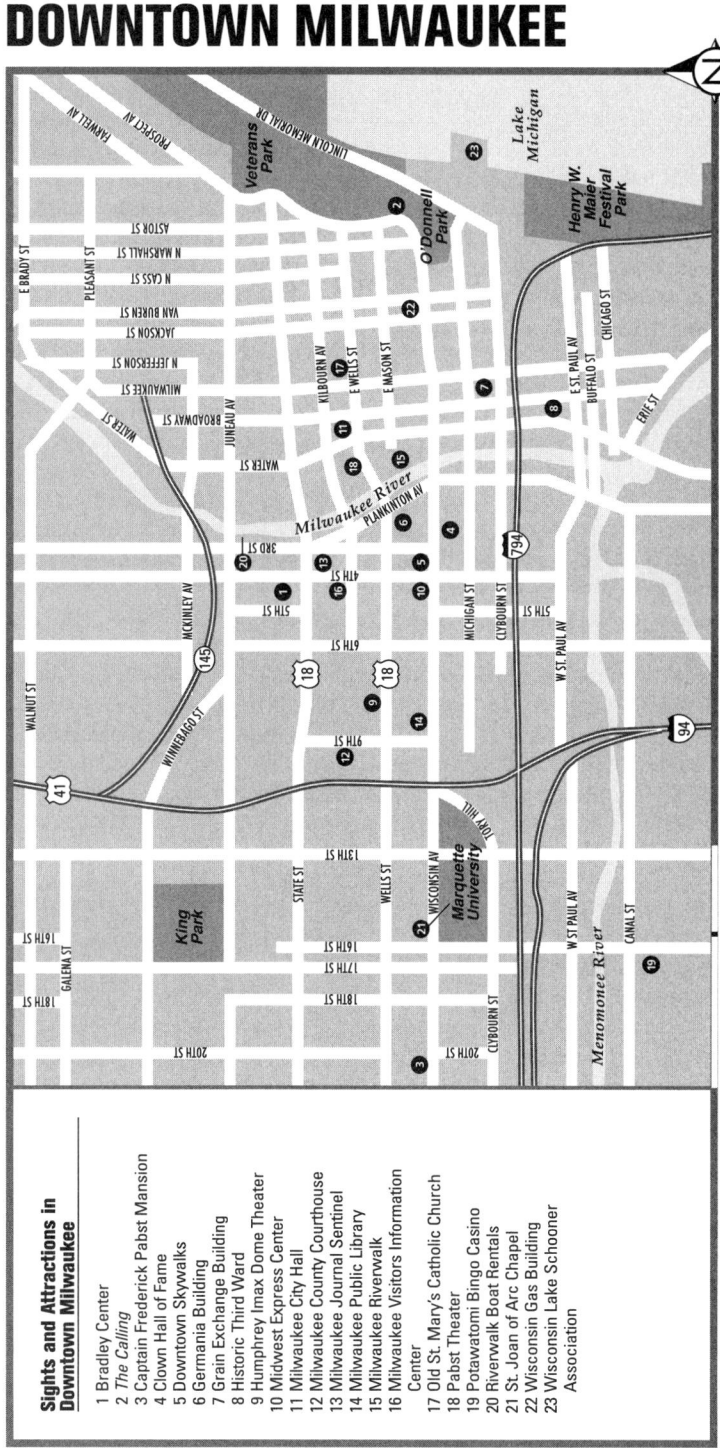

Sights and Attractions in Downtown Milwaukee

1. Bradley Center
2. *The Calling*
3. Captain Frederick Pabst Mansion
4. Clown Hall of Fame
5. Downtown Skywalks
6. Germania Building
7. Grain Exchange Building
8. Historic Third Ward
9. Humphrey Imax Dome Theater
10. Midwest Express Center
11. Milwaukee City Hall
12. Milwaukee County Courthouse
13. Milwaukee Journal Sentinel
14. Milwaukee Public Library
15. Milwaukee Riverwalk
16. Milwaukee Visitors Information Center
17. Old St. Mary's Catholic Church
18. Pabst Theater
19. Potawatomi Bingo Casino
20. Riverwalk Boat Rentals
21. St. Joan of Arc Chapel
22. Wisconsin Gas Building
23. Wisconsin Lake Schooner Association

HUMPHREY IMAX DOME THEATER
**Museum Center
710 W. Wells St.
Milwaukee
414/319-4629**
The Humphrey IMAX Theater, the only cinema of its kind in Wisconsin, lies beneath the Museum Center's copper dome. Lie back—way back—in the tall seats and watch the world unfold in virtual 3D on the wrap-around screen. Scale Everest, dive into the deep-blue sea, or ride out into space. The movies change regularly, but there are always two or three heart-pounders from which to choose. One of the best parts of the show is the helicopter ride through downtown Milwaukee that starts each program. Sun–Wed 11:30–4:30, Thur–Fri 11:30 –8:30, Sat 10:30–8:30. Adults $6.50, seniors $5.50, children $4.50. (Downtown)

MIDWEST EXPRESS CENTER
**400 W. Wisconsin Ave.
Milwaukee
414/908-6000**
Milwaukee's old convention center, built in the 1970s, was likened by Mayor Norquist to a giant VCR. All that changed in July 1998, when the first phase of the Midwest Express Center opened. Covering two square blocks (and eventually four) in the heart of the city, the convention center is state of the art, with airy reception rooms, bright hallways, glass towers reminiscent of City Hall, and more than $1 million worth of integrated artwork. The exhibition space is enormous and flexible, featuring 30-foot ceilings. In short, the Midwest Express Center puts Milwaukee on the convention map like never before. (Downtown)

MILWAUKEE CITY HALL
**200 E. Wells St.
Milwaukee
414/286-3200**
Called by architect and critic Witold Rybczinski "the most beautiful city hall in America," it is, without a doubt,

Historic Third Ward, p. 82

the most resplendent building in town. Based on guildhall architecture of the Flemish renaissance, City Hall was the third tallest building in the United States when it was completed in 1896. The Roman arches and brick and granite exterior bespeak solidity, while the decorative wolf heads, dragons, eagles, and more than 100 infants and cherubs embody a sort of sensuousness not often found in civic architecture. The interior is impressive, too: The central atrium—ringed by hallways—rises nine stories to a skylight that runs the length of the building. Mon–Fri 8–5. (Downtown)

MILWAUKEE COUNTY COURTHOUSE
901 N. Ninth St.
Milwaukee
414/278-4987

Built in 1931, the courthouse is the anchor of a grand civic center that includes the Central Library and the Public Museum. Rising at the foot of Kilbourn Avenue, the County Courthouse is a serious and imposing structure. Modeled after Roman public buildings, the courthouse is surrounded by 68 gigantic Corinthian columns, is watched over by 5,000-pound stone owls (the symbols of wisdom), and is inscribed with the words *Vox Populi Vox Dei:* "The voice of the people is the voice of the gods." (Downtown)

MILWAUKEE JOURNAL SENTINEL
333 W. State St.
Milwaukee
414/224-2419

Now the sole daily newspaper in Milwaukee, the *Journal Sentinel* reaches into hundreds of thousands of homes each day. The bustling offices and production facility are open to the public, who may tour the building. The most fascinating part is the printing area—all those newspapers whizzing past! Tours must be scheduled in advance. Wed–Fri. Admission: free. (Downtown)

MILWAUKEE PUBLIC LIBRARY
814 W. Wisconsin Ave.
Milwaukee
414/286-3000
www.mpl.org

The Milwaukee Public Library was founded in 1878, and the Central Library building, one of the most imposing and beautiful structures in the city, celebrated its centennial in 1998. The building, with Corinthian columns, stone eagle pediments, a spectacular mosaic floor, and a neo-Renaissance dome, received additions in 1909, 1930, and in the 1950s. A complete interior renovation in the last decade has brought the library into compliance with the 21st century, with loads of computers, new book stacks, and a stunning children's area (see also Chapter 7: "Kids' Stuff"). (Downtown)

MILWAUKEE RIVERWALK
Milwaukee

The river is the heart of Milwaukee. A commercial throughway and recreational haven, the river has over the years provided transportation, ice for the city's breweries, and swimming spots. The Riverwalk—a series of water-level walkways, docks, artwork, and bridges—opens up the Milwaukee's banks to strollers, café-sitters, and sightseers. The walkways, now about 75 percent complete, will eventually run from Brewer's Hill to the Summerfest grounds at the harbor mouth. Restaurants, parks, concert venues, and taverns sit along Riverwalk's length. It's a great place to stroll or to sit and eat your lunch. (Downtown)

MILWAUKEE VISITORS INFORMATION CENTER
510 W. Kilbourn Ave.
Milwaukee
414/273-7222 or 800/554-1448
www.milwaukee.org
Get the facts. Check the schedule. Reserve a place. Visit the Milwaukee Visitors Information Center to do all this and more. Located in the offices of the Greater Milwaukee Visitors and Convention Bureau, the Info Center stocks literature on just about every major attraction in the metropolitan area. You'll find information on lodging and restaurants, festivals and events, tours and transit, as well as "Milwaukee: Genuine American" gear. The Visitors Information Center makes a good first stop for anyone visiting the city. Mon–Fri 9–5. (Downtown)

OLD ST. MARY'S CATHOLIC CHURCH
844 N. Broadway
Milwaukee
414/271-6180
Old St. Mary's is remarkable for two reasons: first, because it is the oldest standing ecclesiastical building in the city, and, second, for its delightful interior decoration. Built in 1847, only a few months after the Milwaukee city charter was ratified, St. Mary's was the area's first German Catholic church. Built in the German *Zopstil*, the building is distinguished by clean lines, regular rectangular proportions, and a solid, sober character. Inside the church you'll find a delightful set of German Romantic paintings, given to this outpost of the faith by King Ludwig II of Bavaria. Mon–Fri 11–1. (Downtown)

PABST THEATER
144 E. Wells St.
Milwaukee
414/286-3665
Built in 1895 by Captain Frederick Pabst, the Pabst Theater is Milwaukee's most lavish opera house. The German Baroque–style edifice, with its elegant staircase, plush seats, and gently curving balustrades, has hosted many of the world's greatest orchestras and performers. The Pabst seats 1,400, although its vertical orientation creates an impression of intimacy. Of special note is the huge chandelier in the theater's dome: The fixture includes nearly 3,000 feet of strung crystal. Free tours of the Pabst are available on Saturday at 11:30. Please call ahead, as rehearsals may interrupt tours. (Downtown)

POTAWATOMI BINGO CASINO
1721 W. Canal St.
Milwaukee
414/645-8888 or 800/PAYS BIG
www.paysbig.com
Hundreds of slot machines humming around the clock. Five million dollars paid out in high-stakes bingo every day. Potawatomi Bingo is as close as Milwaukee gets to Vegas, baby. Indian gaming is big in Wisconsin, and, despite general opposition from Mayor Norquist, Potawatomi is a major destination. This casino is better than many: The atmosphere is Nevada with a touch of Milwaukee frumpery. It's safe and secure enough

Ten Underrated Architectural Jewels
by Dan Taylor, (non-practicing) architect and proprietor of Taylor's Bar

1. **St. Francis Seminary** (S. Lake Dr. at Bay View Park)
2. **VA Building** (W. National Ave. at Hwy. 41, Wood, Wisconsin)
3. **Annason Apartments** (2121 E. Capitol Dr.)
4. **Fatima Shrine** (N. 68th and W. Mt.Vernon Sts.)
5. **Sheridan Park Neighborhood** (S. Lake Dr. at E. Layton Ave.)
6. **"Flamingo House"** (529 E. Oklahoma Ave.)
7. **Cherry Street Bridge House** (E. Cherry St. at Milwaukee River)
8. **Grant Park Bridge** (E. Oak Creek Pkwy. at S. Lake Dr.)
9. **Enclosed Water Tower** (S. Sixth St. at E. Morgan Ave.)
10. **Schlitz Audubon Center Tower** (1111 E. Brown Deer Rd.)

for senior citizens to feel comfortable, but happening enough for would-be high rollers to feel like they're in on some action. Hours: 24/7. Admission: free. (Downtown)

RIVERWALK BOAT RENTALS
Pere Marquette Park
1137 N. Old World Third St.
Milwaukee
414/283-9999
Do it yourself on the Milwaukee River—rent a pontoon boat and see the sights. Docked along the Riverwalk, RBR provides two-person "mini-toons" by the half-hour, hour, or half-day. Boats can be operated by leg power or an environmentally friendly (and blissfully silent) electric motor. A pontoon boat accommodating up to 12 people is also available. There are public docks, restaurants, taverns, and entertainment venues along the length of the river, or you can cruise out into the harbor or shipping canals that line the Menomonee Valley, where the freighters dock. Daily 11–dusk, weather permitting. Prices start at $15 per half hour. (Downtown)

ST. JOAN OF ARC CHAPEL
Marquette University
N. 14th St. and W. Wisconsin Ave.
Milwaukee
414/288-6873
Half a millenium old, the St. Joan of Arc Chapel is the only truly Gothic church in Milwaukee. Built in the 15th century in France, it was in this edifice that Joan had a vision from God. Transported to Milwaukee 35 years ago, as an architectural monument the chapel is remarkable for its austere beauty. As a monument to religious history it is something far grander. St. Joan is said to have kissed a stone in the chapel after her vision, and to this day it feels colder to the touch than any of the others!

Mon–Sat 10–4, Sun 12–4. Admission: free. (Downtown)

WISCONSIN GAS BUILDING
626 E. Wisconsin Ave.
Milwaukee
Gorgeous by day and stunning at night, the 20-story Wisconsin Gas building, built in 1930, is among the country's best examples of the art deco skyscraper. The building's faces step back toward the top, and the orange brick becomes progressively lighter. The effect is that the building seems taller than it actually is. And speaking of architectural devices, the Wisconsin Gas building is replete with metal relief sunbursts, leaf patterns, and even images of the building itself. Most notable of all is the "Weather Flame" that adorns the roof. Milwaukeeans trust the flame's color each night to accurately predict the following day's weather! (see Trivia on page 102). (Downtown)

WISCONSIN LAKE SCHOONER ASSOCIATION
500 N. Harbor Dr.
Milwaukee
414/276-7700
www.wis-schooner.org
Milwaukee's heritage is largely a maritime one, its location and harbor ideal for shipborne trade. That exciting past comes alive at the Wisconsin Lake Schooner Association. Volunteers, students, and skilled craftspeople have spent more than five years building a 103-foot "tall ship," just like the ones that plied the lakes a century ago. The gorgeous vessel, to be completed by the turn of the century, is open for tours, and there is a little museum documenting its construction and the history of shipping in Milwaukee. Tue–Sat 10:30–3. Admission: $3. (Downtown)

EAST SIDE

AMERICAN GEOGRAPHICAL SOCIETY COLLECTION
Golda Meir Library
University of Wisconsin-Milwaukee
2311 E. Hartford Ave.
Milwaukee
414/229-6282
What did the world look like in the year 1500? Visit the American Geographical Society Collection to find out. Museum, research center, focal point for the world's geographers, the AGS collection was moved to Milwaukee from New York City in 1978, when the one-time rival to the National Geographic Society went bankrupt. The enormous collection of maps, globes, and geographic commentary includes rare works, very old

---

TRIVIA

In 1893 the Milwaukee Public Library held a competition to choose the architect for its new central facility. Among the 78 entrants was a young, unknown Wisconsin artist named Frank Lloyd Wright. Though he didn't get the commission, Wright would build a number of churches and houses in Milwaukee in the 20th century.

Giraffes at the Milwaukee County Zoo, p. 99

maps, famous maps, and fascinating peripheral materials. The AGS organizes regular exhibitions. Mon–Fri 8–5. Admission: free. (East Side)

THE BOAT HOUSE
3138 N. Cambridge Ave.
Milwaukee

There are a number of architectural oddities in Milwaukee, but none, perhaps, is odder than the boat house. It's not a house for boats, you see, but a boat-shaped house. Everything about the one-bedroom home, perched on the bluff over the Milwaukee River, is nautically accurate—from gunwales to pilothouse. The local legend runs thus: In the 1930s, after years of saving, a Milwaukee man who had long dreamed of a seafaring life was ready to buy the boat of his dreams. His spouse said: "Over my dead body." "Well," he told her, "how would you like a new house?" The boat house is not open to the public. (East Side)

FREDERICK BOGK HOUSE
2420 N. Terrace Ave.
Milwaukee

Frank Lloyd Wright was called an architectural genius, arrogant iconoclast, moribund philanderer. While he may have been all of these, he is without a doubt Wisconsin's most famous native son. The Bogk House, designed for politician Frederick C. Bogk in 1916, is perhaps the only Milwaukee structure to fully manifest Wright's mature Urban Prairie School phase. The low-pitched roof and wide eaves are standard-issue, but Wright varies the theme with "Mayan" elements in the house's cast-concrete decoration, while the distinctly Japanese slit windows prefigure the artist's work in that country. The Bogk House is privately owned and not open to tours. (East Side)

HISTORIC BRADY STREET
E. Brady St. between N. Van Buren St. and Lake Michigan
Milwaukee

Brady Street. For Milwaukeeans, the name conjures a mishmash of conflicting images: Italian grocery stores, drug-addled hippie madness, stylish coffee bars. Historically the main artery of the Lower East Side, Brady Street's densely built nine-block shopping and residential district represents the essence of the urban experience in Milwaukee. Like its diverse architecture, Brady Street's current incarnation fuses the past—Sicilian *ristoranti,* flower-power alterna-culture—into a forward-facing, eclectic shopping, dining, and nightlife district. Interesting stores (see Chapter 9: "Shopping"), international restaurants (see Chapter 4: "Where to Eat"), Old World taverns,

GREATER MILWAUKEE

Sights and Attractions in Greater Milwaukee

1. American Geographical Society Collection (ES)
2. Annunciaton Greek Orthodox Church (WS)
3. The Boat House (ES)
4. Frederick Bogk House (ES)
5. Harley-Davidson Factory Tours (NS)
6. Heirloom Doll Museum (WC)
7. Historic Brady Street (ES)
8. Holy Hill (NS)
9. Kilbourntown House (ES)
10. Lowell Damon House (WS)
11. Manfred Olsen Planetarium (ES)
12. Milwaukee County Stadium (WS)
13. Milwaukee County Zoo (WS)
14. North Harbor Breakwall (ES)
15. Northpoint Lighthouse (ES)
16. Northpoint Watertower (ES)
17. Notre Dame Convent (WC)
18. Old Falls Village (NS)
19. Old World Wisconsin (WC)
20. Pettit National Ice Center (WS)
21. Tripoli Shrine Temple (WS)
22. Wisconsin State Fair Park (WS)

trendy cocktail lounges, a coffeehouse on every block, and a good dose of street culture await you on Brady Street. (East Side)

KILBOURNTOWN HOUSE
Estabrook Park
4400 N. Estabrook Pkwy.
Shorewood
414/273-8288

Kilbourntown, the area of downtown Milwaukee immediately to the west of the Milwaukee River, was one of the city's three original settlements. This building was slated for demolition until newspapers, dated 1844, were found in the walls, proving that the house was in fact among the very oldest extant buildings in the city. Clean lines and Doric columns make the house, now located in Estabrook Park, a fine example of classical revival architecture and remarkably gracious for a frontier settlement. July 1–Labor Day Tue, Thur, Sat 9–5, Sun 1–5. Admission: free. (East Side)

MANFRED OLSEN PLANETARIUM
1900 E. Kenwood Ave.
Milwaukee
414/229-4961

Where's Orion? Can you see the northern lights from here? The star shows at the Olsen Planetarium bring the night sky to life every weekend. The planetarium, in the physics building at the University of Wisconsin-Milwaukee, presents seasonal shows exploring the wonders of the firmament throughout the academic year. Because the presentations are timely—"The Autumn Sky" is shown throughout the fall, for example—you can use your newfound knowledge of the stars immediately by, say, taking a walk on Government Pier (see next entry). Fri 7 and 8:15; call to confirm showtimes. Admission: $1, no children under 6 admitted. (East Side)

NORTH HARBOR BREAKWALL
McKinley Park
1750 N. Lincoln Memorial Dr.
Milwaukee

Everyone calls it Government Pier (it was built by the Army Corps of Engineers), and a stroll along its sturdy length may be the closest you'll ever come to walking on water. Jutting half a mile out into Lake Michigan, the breakwall provides unmatched views of downtown, Yankee Hill, the Gold Coast highrise apartments, and Northpoint. Government Pier is favored by pedestrians, anglers, in-line skaters, and cyclists, and there is no better place in town for an after-dinner walk. If you drive down here, free parking is available in the huge lot north of McKinley Marina. Hours: 24/7, except during high seas. Admission: free. (East Side)

NORTHPOINT LIGHTHOUSE
N. Terrace at N. Wahl Aves.
Milwaukee

Tucked into the woods at the south end of Lake Park, the Northpoint Lighthouse rises 160 feet above Lake Michigan. Built just after the Civil War as a navigation aid for the city's busy harbor, the lighthouse is made entirely of cast-iron sections bolted together, a common construction technique at the time. (The Iron Block Building, 205 East Wisconsin Avenue, was built in a similar fashion.) The lighthouse's first lantern burned mineral oil, and though the light is now electric, the original lens is still in

> **TRIVIA**
>
> On the Wisconsin Avenue bridge downtown, you'll find a bronze statue commemorating Gertie the Duck, the patriotic waterfowl that raised Milwaukee's spirits during the darkest days of World War II. Gertie built her nest on a piling in the Milwaukee River adjacent to the bridge. Through thick and thin, high water and terrible storms, she laid eggs, they hatched, and the story of the urban duck was picked up by the newspapers. Gertie become a national symbol of hope and new beginnings in a time aching for hopefulness.

place. The light is visible 25 miles out into the lake. (East Side)

NORTHPOINT WATERTOWER
E. North at N. Terrace Ave.
Milwaukee

Visible for miles from the lake, the Northpoint Watertower is Milwaukee's answer to Cinderella's castle. Standing at the top of an 80-foot bluff, this high-Victorian creampuff of a structure is a delight to all passersby. Fully frilly, the 175-foot tower with copper-clad Gothic spires houses an iron standpipe designed to relieve pressure on Milwaukee's water mains. The watertower was built in 1874 and to this day remains the singular landmark of the Northpoint neighborhood. (East Side)

NORTH SIDE

ANNUNCIATION GREEK ORTHODOX CHURCH
9400 W. Congress St.
Wauwatosa
414/461-9400

Toward the end of his life, Frank Lloyd Wright increasingly used circles in his designs. It seems almost natural that one of his final commissions should be this oddly stunning Greek Orthodox church (historically based on a plan of a cross intersecting a circle). Holding 1,000 worshipers, this church is a shallow concrete dish covered by a mirror-image dome, with arched stained-glass windows. Most interesting of all, to allow for expansion, the dome is not actually attached to the body of the church but rides in a steel track on hundreds of thousands of ball bearings. Theoretically, it could be set spinning! Tours by appointment only. (North Side)

HARLEY-DAVIDSON FACTORY TOURS
11700 W. Capitol Dr.
Wauwatosa
414/535-3666

Along with Miller Beer, perhaps no consumer product is so allied with Milwaukee's image as the Harley-Davidson motorcycle. From the macho rumble of the exhaust system to the attendant leather jackets and fringed saddlebags, Harley culture is famous throughout world. So when in Milwaukee, don't miss your opportunity to tour the Harley-Davidson engine plant, the original home of Milwaukee Iron. Watch the assembly of engines and transmissions and get an eyeful of the Hog mystique. No cameras or open shoes are allowed on the tour. Hours vary; call in advance for tour times. Admission: free, children under 12 not admitted. (North Side)

**HOLY HILL
1525 Carmel Rd.
Hubertus
262/628-1838**
The spires of the neo-Gothic cathedral, situated on an impressive glacial moraine, rise high above the rolling countryside. The site was first consecrated in the 1850s as the home of a Flemish hermit and currently includes a monastery, shrine, and the monumental cathedral itself. Visitors will find 400 beautiful acres, a picnic area, wooded trails to the stations of the cross and Lourdes grotto, unparalleled hilltop views, and, in summer, a bell tower to climb for even better vistas. Holy Hill is located 30 miles northwest of downtown Milwaukee via Highway 41 north to Highway 167 west. Open daily. Admission: free. (North Side)

**OLD FALLS VILLAGE
N96 W15791 County Line Rd.
Menomonee Falls
414/255-8436**
Before expressways and suburban sprawl, Menomonee Falls was a charming town on the fringe of Milwaukee. Before that, it was a frontier village on the fringe of the wilderness. This outdoor museum preserves a glimpse of the life of its pioneers. Eight buildings containing artifacts used by 19th-century farmers and townspeople provide insights into both the joys and hardships of frontier America. Special tours may be arranged by calling ahead. May–Sept Sun 1–4. Adults $3, children $1. (North Side)

SOUTH SIDE

**ALLEN BRADLEY CLOCK TOWER
1201 S. Second St.
Milwaukee**
The largest four-faced clock in the world (twice the size of London's Big Ben), the Allen-Bradley tower rises nearly 300 feet above Walker's Point. Brightly lit at night, the clocktower is among the principal landmarks of the south side. Now called Rockwell Automation, the Allen-Bradley Company makes electronic equipment and industrial controls for robotics systems, and the tower serves as the company's headquarters and main research facility. Each of the clock's minute hands is 20 feet long and weighs more than 500 pounds. The tower is not open for tours. (South Side)

Mark di Suvero's The Calling, *p. 81*

Milwaukee Art Museum

SIGHTS AND ATTRACTIONS

SOUTH SIDE

Sights and Attractions on Milwaukee's South Side

1. Allen Bradley Clocktower
2. American System Built Homes
3. Froemming Park Observatory
4. Jeremiah Curtin House
5. Mitchell Park Horticultural Conservatory
6. Pryor Street Well
7. St. Josaphat Basilica
8. St. Sava Serbian Orthodox Cathedral
9. Timber Wolf Farm
10. Trimborn Farm Park

AMERICAN SYSTEM BUILT HOMES
2714–2732 W. Burnham St.
Milwaukee

The 2700 block of West Burnham Street is one of the most architecturally interesting in the whole city. In 1911, committed to the idea that working people should be able to live in decent homes, Frank Lloyd Wright designed these mass-producible American System Built Homes, four Prairie-style duplexes and two single-family houses. The flat-roofed buildings are dignified, airy, and well-lit. Some unfortunate renovations—siding, in one case—have altered their character, but the buildings are undeniably charming and intriguing. They are not open for tours. (South Side)

FROEMMING PARK OBSERVATORY
9000 block of S. 51st St.
Franklin
414/425-8550
www.execpc.com/~tgrunwa/astro/was.html

Operated by a group of star enthusiasts based at the Wehr Nature Center (see Chapter 8: "Parks and Gardens"), the Froemming Park Observatory offers free public sky viewings once a week throughout the year. The observatory, with a permanent telescope, is located far enough from downtown Milwaukee to allow decent views of the moon, constellations, and distant galaxies. Each program includes a general overview of the week's sky and telescope observations of timely space phenomena. Open Friday, call for times. Admission: free. (South Side)

JEREMIAH CURTIN HOUSE
8400 block of W. Grange Ave.
Greendale
414/273-8288

Jeremiah Curtin was a diplomat, linguist, anthropologist, and translator (the great Polish novel *Quo Vadis* is among his accomplishments). Built in 1846, this charming house—the first stone dwelling in Greenfield—was occupied by the Curtin family for twenty years and eventually passed into the hands of the Milwaukee County Historical Society. Important not only for its architectural value, the building is also a physical monument to the lives of early Irish settlers in Wisconsin and is furnished with items typical of frontier life in the mid-19th century.

TRIVIA

No neighborhood feels the holiday spirit quite like the southwest district known as Candycane Lane: seven or eight blocks of the most spectacularly lit and decorated houses imaginable. You'll see flying sleighs, glowing crèches, moving Santas, and much more. Around the holiday, lines of cars travel South 92nd through 96th Streets between West Oklahoma Avenue and West Montana Street from sundown until late in the evening. Neighbors collect a small donation, which is given to charity, from each car.

Riverwalk Boat Rentals, p. 87

Open summers, call for hours. Admission: free. (South Side)

MITCHELL PARK HORTICULTURAL CONSERVATORY
524 S. 27th St.
Milwaukee
414/649-9800
Known simply as the Domes, the Mitchell Park Conservatory's three seven-story glass domes tower above its south side neighborhood. Inside, that neighborhood is left behind. The tropical dome contains a jungle, and the arid dome a desert environment. The third dome houses six changing exhibitions yearly, including an annual poinsettia blowout during the holidays. There is no better place to feel as though you've left the hemisphere for a few hours. Of special note are the tropical birds inhabiting the jungle dome, moved here during construction of a new aviary at the zoo. Daily 9–5. Adults $3.25, children and seniors $1.25. (South Side)

PRYOR STREET WELL
1700 block of E. Pryor St.
Milwaukee
A working fragment of history resides unobtrusively on Pryor Street. A natural artesian spring bubbles up out of the ground at this spot, and, in the health-conscious 19th century, the mineral properties of the water were considered particularly invigorating. Protected by a little hut between the sidewalk and street, the water runs out constantly. Though the minerals have long since been dissolved, people still line up to fill jugs from this spring, and during Milwaukee's 1993 cryptosporidium crisis, when the city's water supply was contaminated, the lines went around the block. (South Side)

ST. JOSAPHAT BASILICA
2333 S. Sixth St.
Milwaukee
414/645-5623
Built "with the pennies of Polish immigrants," St. Josaphat Basilica is

the grandest cathedral in Milwaukee. Its enormous copper dome—larger than the Taj Mahal's—towers over the neighborhoods called Lincoln Village and Polonia. Made of materials salvaged from a Chicago post office, the building was dedicated in 1901. The interior features Austrian stained glass, a hand-carved marble pulpit, tons of gold leaf, and wonderful ceiling murals, all of which have been recently restored to their original glory. Tours Sunday following 10 a.m. mass or for groups by appointment. Admission: free. (South Side)

ST. SAVA SERBIAN ORTHODOX CATHEDRAL
3201 S. 51st St.
Milwaukee
414/545-4080

In the 1950s, when churches were turning to Modern designs for new buildings, the Serbian Orthodox congregation of St. Sava bucked the trend. Its cathedral, completed in 1958, is based on traditional Byzantine designs. The result is spectacular, with five copper domes topped by gold crosses, narrow arched windows lending an eastern air to the limestone building, and the interior a blazing display of cobalt-blue tile, barrel-vaulted chambers, and golden icons. As is traditional in Serbian Orthodox churches, the congregation faces east, toward the rising sun. Tours are not available; call for a schedule of services. (South Side)

TIMBER WOLF FARM
6669 S. 76th St., Greendale
414/425-8264

The Timberwolf Preservation Society operates a farm housing more than a dozen of the misunderstood and endangered animals at the edge of Whitnall Park. Timberwolves in Wisconsin were hunted nearly to extinction in the early part of this century, and they retreated to the north. Since becoming protected, the noble beasts have made a comeback. Most of the animals at Timber Wolf Farm were rescued from people who (very) mistakenly thought that wolves would make good pets. The farm is a great place to learn about the progress of this endangered species. Sat and Sun 10–3. Admission: $1. (South Side)

TRIMBORN FARM PARK
8881 W. Grange Ave.
Hales Corners
414/529-7744

Trimborn Farm is a restored, mid-19th-century farm and lime business. An essential ingredient in mortar, lime was once manufactured in huge brick kilns that burned limestone at very high temperatures. Trimborn Farm has a farmhouse, barn, smoke-

The City of Milwaukee publishes a series of brochures outlining informal walking tours of historic neighborhoods. Focusing on Juneautown, Kilbourntown, Northpoint, Walker's Point, and elsewhere, the brochures provide fascinating information on significant buildings and architectural history. They're available free at the city's Tourist Information Center, 510 West Kilbourn Avenue, downtown.

Beer City

The beer that made Milwaukee famous is long gone. And so are Pabst and Blatz. It's been decades since the city was the nation's leading brewer. But, still, Milwaukeeans love their beer, and there's plenty of it to go around in corner taverns—Milwaukee has more bars per capita than anyplace else—and in the breweries that remain. If you want to soak up some suds (and learn a little about the glory of malted hops), check out these brewery tours:

Miller Brewing Company. *The maker of High Life, MGD, Lite, and Red Dog packages half a million cases of beer daily at it flagship Milwaukee brewery. Free tours—and free samples— are available nearly every day. Call 414/931-2337 for tour times. (4251 W. State St., Milwaukee)*

Sprecher Brewing. *When Randy Sprecher opened his microbrewery 15 years ago, it was the first new brewery licensed in Milwaukee since the end of Prohibition. Well known in Wisconsin for its Special Amber and Black Bavarian beers, Sprecher offers tours on Saturday by reservation. Admission: $2. Call 414/964-2739 for information. (701 W. Glendale Ave., Glendale)*

Lakefront Brewing. *Lakefront beers are, without a doubt, consistently the best microbrews in Milwaukee. Started in a Riverwest storefront a decade ago by the Klisch Brothers, the company now brews several thousand barrels every year in its new quarters near downtown. Lakefront Stein Beer, Pale Ale, Organic Extra Special Bitter, and seasonal brews are available before, during, and after tours on Friday at 5:30 and Saturday at 1:30, 2:30, and 3:30. Admission: $3. Call 414/372-8800 for information. (1872 N. Commerce St., Milwaukee)*

house, and the old kilns, big enough to walk through, along with other outbuildings. Now surrounded by housing developments and busy streets, all of the buildings are open for tours, and special events recall the days when the dairy farm and lime operations were in full swing. Call for program details. Admission: free. (South Side)

International Clown Hall of Fame, p. 81

WEST SIDE

LOWELL DAMON HOUSE
2107 N. Wauwatosa Ave. (76th St.)
Wauwatosa
414/273-8288
In 1844, New Hampshire native Oliver Damon built one of the first houses in the village of Wauwatosa, and over the next three years his son, Lowell, completed a four-room addition. That makes the Damon house the oldest extant dwelling in the village and among the very oldest in the whole metropolitan area. The humble colonial-revival architecture is unusual in Milwaukee, and a small museum is maintained in the house, with antique objects from the early period of settlement. Sun 1–5, Wed 3–5. Admission: free. (West Side)

MILWAUKEE COUNTY STADIUM
201 S. 46th St.
Milwaukee
414/933-6100
When the Braves moved to town in 1952, Milwaukeeans thronged the new stadium in record numbers, screaming with such abandon that one sportswriter called the stadium "an insane asylum with bases." Now, as state-of-the-art Miller Park rises in the stadium's center field parking lot, an era of baseball history will soon close. But it's not too late to get in on some of that history. Ballpark tours are available April through September when the team is out of town. You can see the locker rooms, sit in the dugout, and imagine the glory days of Hammerin' Hank Aaron and Robin Yount. Tours by appointment. (West Side)

MILWAUKEE COUNTY ZOO
10001 W. Bluemound Rd.
Wauwatosa
414/771-3040
The zoo is, hands down, Milwaukee's top attraction. A pioneer in naturalistic environments, the park groups animals in displays that function like gigantic, living dioramas, with preda-

tors and prey in close proximity but separated by invisible moats. It makes for exciting zoo-going: African watering holes feature gazelles, zebras, elephants, giraffes, and big cats, each eyeing the other suspiciously. The zoo explores the wildlife of five continents, with special emphasis on primates, felines, penguins, and some very entertaining bears. Of special note is the new aviary, with birds of the world in free flight. (See Chapter 7: "Kids' Stuff" for more information.) Summer daily 9–5, winter daily 9–4:30. Adults $6.50–$8, ages 3 to 12 $4.50–$6, seniors $5–$7. Parking: $5. (West Side)

PETTIT NATIONAL ICE CENTER
500 S. 84th St.
West Allis
414/266-0100
www.thepettit.com
A U.S. Olympic training facility, the Pettit Center holds the only indoor 400-meter speed-skating track in the country—and one of very few in the world. Because it can be used all year round, the Pettit is home to the U.S. Speed-skating Team, along with many national and international competitions, and casual skaters often find themselves in the presence of Dan Jansen, Bonnie Blair, and other winter sports heroes. The enormous oval—big enough to hold three 747s—surrounds several full-sized hockey and figure-skating rinks. Open skating daily; call for times. (See Chapter 10: "Sports and Recreation" for more information.) (West Side)

TRIPOLI SHRINE TEMPLE
3000 W. Wisconsin Ave.
Milwaukee
The Tripoli Shrine Temple is hard to miss. Driving west out of downtown toward, say, County Stadium, there suddenly arises an enormous Islamic-style temple, complete with onion dome and missile-shaped minarets. Built in 1928 on the city's main street in what was then the high-rent district, the Tripoli temple may be the grandest Masonic lodge in Wisconsin. It is certainly among

Humphrey IMAX Dome Theater, p. 84

Greater Milwaukee Conv. and Visitors Bureau

> **TRIVIA**
>
> The Allen-Bradley clock tower, brightly lit at night and hovering above its heavily Eastern European south side neighborhood, is often called the Polish Moon. The largest four-faced clock in the world, it's visible for more than 40 miles out in Lake Michigan and is definitely the brightest satellite in the Milwaukee firmament.

the oddest buildings in town. Besides the tiled dome, the temple is adorned with orange and brown brick, colorful tiles, and windows with graceful, pointed arches. Giant reclining camels guard the entrance staircase. The building is not open to the public. (West Side)

WISCONSIN STATE FAIR PARK
8100 W. Greenfield Ave.
West Allis
800/884-3247
The beloved Wisconsin State Fair—an orgy of cheese, livestock, beer, and food, food, food—has been held on these grounds for more than a century. The sprawling complex, which houses cattle barns, a draft-horse colliseum, restaurants, a midway, a pig race course, beer tents galore, and a cream-puff factory, also includes the Milwaukee Mile speedway (see Chapter 10: "Sports and Recreation") and the Pettit National Ice Center (see page 100). The park is used all year for antique shows, sporting events, and home remodeling expos. About those cream puffs: tens of thousands of them are consumed each day during the fair. Piled high with real whipped cream, they are, perhaps, the perfect expression of America's dairyland. Hours and admission fees vary. (West Side)

WAUKESHA COUNTY

HEIRLOOM DOLL MUSEUM
416 E. Broadway
Waukesha
262/544-4739
Come to the Heirloom Doll Museum to have an old toy repaired and stay to explore the incredible collection of dolls. More than 2,000 dolls of all flavors line the shelves of this remarkable museum, from 1960s Barbies in their little coupes to Raggedy Annes and Andys from a bygone era. China dollies from the 19th century sit down to tea, baby dolls ride in baby carriages, glamour dolls find themselves all dressed up for a night on the town. Doll parts and a repair service round out the attractions at this unusual spot. Tue–Fri 10–6, Sat 10–5. (Waukesha County)

NOTRE DAME CONVENT
13125 W. Watertown Plank Rd.
Elm Grove
262/782-1450
Among the more imposing works of ecclesiastical architecture in Milwaukee, this grand structure is the provincial headquarters and motherhouse of the School Sisters of Notre Dame, an order of Catholic nuns devoted to the education of women.

TRIVIA

Check out the 21-foot-tall "Weather Flame" atop the Wisconsin Gas building. It's color and motion predict tomorrow's weather. Just remember this little rhyme:
> If the flame is red, warmer weather's ahead
> If gold, watch out for cold
> If the flame is blue, no change is due
> When the flame's in agitation, watch out for precipitation

Founded in Milwaukee nearly a century and a half ago, this complex of buildings is modeled on a Bavarian castle in homage to the order's German origins. The convent includes a spectacular chapel, bell tower, offices, and communal living space for 170 sisters. A cemetery on the grounds houses the grave of Sr. Caroline Freiss, the order's North American founder. Closed to the public, a gift shop is open daily 1–4. (Waukesha County)

OLD WORLD WISCONSIN
S103 W37890 Hwy. 67
Eagle
262/594-6300
The Wisconsin State Historical Society's answer to Williamsburg, Old World Wisconsin is a living history museum. More than 50 historic farmhouses, barns, houses from village settlements, and commercial buildings have been moved to this site in the Kettle-Moraine State Forest and are arranged across the park's 600 acres in ethnic groupings. The houses, shops, and inns of Poles, Germans, Scandinavians, and Yankees demonstrate firsthand how Old World traditions were transported to—and transformed the landscape of—the frontier. Craftspeople in authentic costumes reenact events from daily life throughout the grounds. Old World Wisconsin is a fascinating place to get a taste of history. May, June, Sept, Oct Mon–Fri 10–4, Sat and Sun 10–5, July and Aug daily 10–5. (Waukesha County)

CITY TOURS

AMERICAN SIGHTSEEING INTERNATIONAL
1122 W. Boden Ct.
Milwaukee
414/282-6465 or 800/236-8687
Boarding at major downtown hotels, American Sightseeing International bus tours showcase "the genuine Milwaukee experience." That, you may rightly assume, means historic neighborhoods, historic buildings, and historic monuments. Choose from a pair of tours, lasting two or three and a half hours, sit back in a climate-controlled motorcoach, and see the sights. One tour focuses on downtown, the mansions of Northpoint, and the Mitchell Park horticultural conservatory. The other highlights St. Josaphat's Basilica, the Hoan Bridge, and Miller Brewing.

Wed–Fri 9:30 and 12:30. Adults $12–$14, children $7–$9. (Downtown)

GRAY LINE OF MILWAUKEE
744 N. Fourth St.
Milwaukee
414/271-0996 or 800/998-2325
www.grayline.com
Old churches or new breweries, historic theaters, day spas, or outlet malls: Gray Line caters to a variety of whims. While most Gray Line tours require a minimum of 10 participants and advanced reservations, the "Milwaukee in a Nutshell" tour runs regularly, winding for an hour and a half through interesting ethnic neighborhoods, past museums and the Domes, and highlighting shopping, dining, and nightlife options. While Gray Line is relatively new, and the information given isn't always exactly accurate, "Milwaukee in a Nutshell" is a great introduction to the city. Thu, Fri, Sun, Mon 1–2:30, Sat 9:30–11. Adults $19. (Downtown)

HISTORIC MILWAUKEE WALKING TOURS
414/277-7795
Historic Milwaukee is dedicated to increasing awareness of the city's historical roots and their expression in architecture and city planning. The group leads an ambitious series of walking tours year-round, from the SkyWaukee series—held every Saturday in the enclosed downtown

---

Down by the Riverside

The Riverwalk—a series of walkways that line the Milwaukee River—is already a pleasant place to while away an afternoon, but it is about to get a lot better. Renowned artist Mary Miss has designed the next segment of the project, running through the Historic Third Ward, to focus on the river's historical and environmental significance to the city.

Miss's vision blends aesthetics with science and engineering to create a transporting experience for strollers, joggers, anglers, lunch eaters, and other lollygaggers. It features a series of wetlands—the Third Ward was once an enormous marsh—transected by multilevel walkways, boating channels, and natural systems to purify water running off from surrounding streets. Among the segment's highlights are a giant observation tower and a lighted excavation shaft for viewing the Deep Tunnel, the city's huge storm drainage system, which lies more than 300 feet beneath the riverbed.

skywalk system—to in-depth neighborhood tours. The 90-minute tours, led by exceptionally knowledgeable guides, are the very best way to get a handle on Milwaukee history and architecture. From June to October, HM offers specialty tours each weekend. Call for complete information on upcoming programs. Sat 10 and 1, Sun 1. Adults $5, children $2. (Downtown)

IROQUOIS HARBOR CRUISES
**Milwaukee River at
E. Clybourn St.
Milwaukee
414/332-4194**

There was a time when hundreds of boats, loaded with goods and bound for points east, crowded the Milwaukee River downtown. The *Iroquois* recalls that era, belching smoke and delighting tourists with cruises of Milwaukee's waterways. Holding 150 people, the *Iroquois* tours the river and inner and outer harbors and takes in sights like the Summerfest Grounds, art museum, and—from below—a great view of the Hoan Bridge suspended in a graceful arc over the harbor entrance. An hour and a half on the *Iroquois* is a fun way to see the city. June–Sept sailings at 1 and 3. Adults $8.50, children $4.50–$5.50. (Downtown)

MILWAUKEE IRON MOTORCYCLE TOURS
414/628-9421

Fatboys, hogs, or soft tails. To a motorcycle aficionado, it all adds up to one thing: Harley-Davidson, synonymous the world over with freedom, the code of the road, and a slightly bad attitude. Hop on the back of a chauffered hog and head out on the highway. Up to 50 riders can go out at once for group tours, and Milwaukee Iron will customize routes to your whim, 24 hours a day. There's no better way to be an Easy Rider. Advance registration of three days is required, and weekend rides may require a week's notice. Tour prices start at $45 per hour.

Milwaukee County Historical Society

6

MUSEUMS AND GALLERIES

Milwaukee loves its museums. And there is a lot to love. The city's history, science, and art museums are its cultural backbone, delighting hundreds of thousands of visitors annually.

Recently, Milwaukeeans have translated that love into financial support, allowing several of the city's bigger institutions to add galleries, theaters, and exhibits and, in a couple of cases, build whole new museums. The new Museum Center—housing the Milwaukee Public Museum, an institution of natural and cultural history, Discovery World science museum, and the Humphrey IMAX dome theater—has focused a lot of the city's museum-going attention onto the corner of Seventh and Wells Streets. The Milwaukee Art Museum's spectacular addition, set to open in summer 2000, will add another dimension to that renowned museum's facilities and a grand sculptural building to the lakefront. The Betty Brinn Children's Museum, an addition to the Charles Allis Art Museum, big changes at the University of Wisconsin-Milwaukee's art museums, and a planned museum of advertising art are adding further excitement to the city's museum scene.

Similarly, there is a remarkable abundance of galleries in Milwaukee—largely concentrated in the Third Ward—showing everything from the least commercial conceptual installations imaginable to prints, paintings, jewelry, and furniture that you would gladly display in your own living room. So set a day aside and spend it in Milwaukee's museums and galleries. You'll go home richer for the experience.

ART MUSEUMS

BRADLEY SCULPTURE GARDEN
2115 W. Brown Deer Rd.
Milwaukee
414/276-6840
The Bradley Sculpture Garden may be Milwaukee's most perfect green space: 40 acres of rolling lawns, shade trees, ponds, and waterfalls. And then there are the 60 world-class outdoor sculptures—from huge geometric abstractions of gracefully rusting cor-ten steel to subtler works by modern masters Gerhard Marcks, Henry Moore, and Barbara Hepworth. Open daily by appointment only, with hour-and-a-half docent-guided tours. $2.50 adults, plus $1-per-person docent fee (with $10 minimum). (North Side)

CHARLES ALLIS ART MUSEUM
1801 N. Prospect Ave.
Milwaukee
414/278-8295
Reflecting a peculiarly midwestern blend of pragmatism and opulence, the 1910 Tudor-style mansion of industrialist Charles Allis is made of reinforced concrete (practical) faced with Lake Superior sandstone (extravagant). As art collectors, the Allises' taste was Victorian: landscape paintings, Asian art, the occasional antique sculpture. And they bought a lot of art. The stairway alone, besides showcasing a marvelous prayer rug (owned, they say, by a Sultan of Turkey), holds paintings by Homer, Gainsborough, and Rosa Bonheur. This house museum is a great place to while away an afternoon and is particularly cozy on snowy days. Wed–Sun 1–5, Wed 7–9. $2 adults. & (East Side)

FREDERICK LAYTON GALLERIES
Milwaukee Institute of Art and Design
273 E. Erie St.
Milwaukee
414/276-7889
As the Milwaukee Institute of Art and Design has grown into one of the nation's better-regarded art colleges, its gallery program has grown in stature. Housed in a fantastically renovated riverfront warehouse, the Layton Galleries get better all the time, featuring well-conceived changing exhibitions for the edification of the students and the enjoyment of the public. Recent shows have focused on emerging Asian American artists, the visual culture of raves, and public art. MIAD is the only art institution in town to regularly feature exhibitions on graphic and industrial design. Tue–Sat 10–5. Admission: free. & (Downtown)

HAGGERTY MUSEUM OF ART
Marquette University
W. Clybourn at N. 13th St.
Milwaukee

Thanks to admission packages, it's good fiscal sense to make a day of a visit to the Museum Center—the Milwaukee Public Museum, Discovery World, and IMAX cinema. For example, adult admission to the MPM and IMAX theater on the same day costs $9.75, as opposed to $12 if purchased separately.

414/288-1669

Although Marquette University doesn't grant a visual-arts degree, the Haggerty is one of Wisconsin's finest art museums. Housed in a beautiful contemporary building, with plenty of natural light, the Haggerty's collection of old masters is outstanding, containing no end of surprises. Displayed "salon-style," as they would have been in the past, the paintings cover every inch of available wall space from floor to ceiling. The modern and contemporary galleries, on the other hand, are clean and spare, with a collection of significant breadth, including a well-known painting by Salvador Dali. Mon–Sat 10–4:30, Sun 12–5. Admission: free. ♿ (Downtown)

INOVA
University of Wisconsin-Milwaukee
3253 N. Downer Ave.
Milwaukee
414/229-5070
inova@csd.uwm.edu

This place is hot. With consulting curators on the West Coast, in Europe, and in Latin America, Inova shows the work of emerging artists from around the globe. It's the best place in town to get a preview of the art world's next big (potential) thing, and a curatorial predilection for video, installation, and other non-traditional media makes Inova ultra-happening indeed. The art is sometimes a little obtuse, but it's often great, and the institute's comfortable old campus building goes a long way to mitigate what might otherwise be a stifling hipper-than-thou atmosphere. Wed–Sun 12-5. Admission: free. ♿ (East Side)

MILWAUKEE ART MUSEUM
750 N. Lincoln Memorial Dr.
Milwaukee
414/224–3200
www.mam.org

Wisconsin's largest fine-arts institution, the Milwaukee Art Museum houses nearly 20,000 artworks dating from the Middle Ages to last year. The MAM is recognized internationally for its collections of modern and contemporary art, School of the Eight and German Expressionist paintings, American folk art, the Frank Lloyd Wright/Prairie School archives, Georgia O'Keeffe paintings, and the biggest assembly of Haitian art in the country. Combine that with 20 or so changing exhibitions annually, and you've got an impressive art museum. More impressive than anything inside the building right now, however, is the spectacular addition scheduled to open in June 2000. Designed by Spanish architect Santiago Calatrava, the building features two enormous sail-like wings that open and close to control the temperature and sunlight inside the glass structure. Tue, Wed, Fri, Sat 10–5, Thur noon–9, Sun noon–5. Adults $5, students and senior citizens $3, children free. ♿ (Downtown)

VILLA TERRACE DECORATIVE ARTS MUSEUM
2220 N. Terrace Ave.
Milwaukee
414/271-3656

Built as a bluff-top home in 1923, Villa Terrace is an architectural oddity in these northern climes: an Italian villa complete with courtyard fountain. The collection is a monument to eclecticism—the library is Queen Anne, the great hall is Renaissance palazzo, the bedrooms American Federal. Seventeenth-century porcelain sits beside a 1970s paperweight sits next to a Renaissance terra-cotta. Still, Villa Terrace is a charming house museum; one highlight is a fine collection of American art pottery—including a very funky teepee incense burner. The building's fabulous renaissance gardens are being restored. Wed–Sun 12–5. Adults $2. (East Side)

HISTORY AND SCIENCE MUSEUMS

AMERICA'S BLACK HOLOCAUST MUSEUM
2233 N. Fourth St.
Milwaukee
414/264-2500
In 1930, James Cameron—falsely accused of murder—was dragged from his southern Ohio jail cell by a mob of angry vigilantes. A noose was thrown around his neck, and the end was near. More than 50 years later, Cameron opened this museum to tell the story of his escape and struggle to forgive his would-be murderers. The combination of personal history and an impressive collection of photographs, documents, and exhibits chillingly traces the grim history of violence perpetrated against black people in America. This is an unusual and moving museum. Mon–Sat 9–5. $5 adults, $2.50 children. (North Side)

DISCOVERY WORLD MUSEUM
Museum Center
712 W. Wells St.
Milwaukee
414/765-0777
Discovery World drives kids wild. It features 140 hands-on exhibits to open minds to the wonders of mechanics, the weather, laser beams, and Tesla coils, all in a futuristic new building. Daily 9–5. Admission: $3–$5. (See also Chapter 7: "Kids' Stuff.") ♿ (Downtown)

GREENE GEOLOGICAL GALLERY
University of Wisconsin-Milwaukee
Lapham Hall
3210 N. Maryland Ave.
Milwaukee
414/229-5067 or 414/229-4561
This little-known "gem" of a museum contains the collection of a 19th-century amateur geologist. Working in the best Victorian collecting tradition, Greene amassed hundreds of rocks, minerals, fossils, and crystals, with a special focus on the geology of southeastern Wisconsin. Some of the samples are very rare, thanks to

---

TRIVIA

Milwaukee has long been a hotbed for visionary art. Matthias Wernerus, who made the famous *Dickeyville Grotto* in southwestern Wisconsin, built his first sculpture in suburban St. Francis at the turn of the century. Masters like Eugene von Bruenchenhein and Prophet Blackmon are from Milwaukee, and the Milwaukee Art Museum's Hall Collection is recognized as one of the top folk-art collections anywhere.

quarrying and development. Regular viewing hours change each semester (the gallery is staffed by students), so call first. Viewings may also be arranged by appointment. Admission: free. (East Side)

MILWAUKEE COUNTY HISTORICAL CENTER
910 N. Old World Third St.
Milwaukee
414/273-8288
The majestic former First Wisconsin Bank building, in Père Marquette Park along the Milwaukee River downtown, is an apt repository for the documents that narrate the city's history. This museum houses exhibits on Milwaukee's recent and distant past, including the Newhall House disaster, children's life in the early days of settlement, and the industries that built Beer City. A particularly engaging gallery is devoted to the use of the Milwaukee River, from the shipyards and docks on its lower stretches to the swimming schools, steamboat landings, and skating rinks upstream. Mon–Fri 9:30–5, Sat 10–5, Sun 1–5. Admission: free, $1 per day for research. (Downtown)

MILWAUKEE PUBLIC MUSEUM
Museum Center
800 W. Wells St.
Milwaukee
414/278-2702
www.mpm.edu
In 1890, Carl Akeley, a taxidermist at the Milwaukee Public Museum, made the first diorama—showing a muskrat swimming into its swampy den. With that diorama, the modern natural history museum was born. Today, a visit to the MPM is a whirlwind world tour through time and space, thanks to a collection of 6 million artifacts and specimens. See the animals of every continent, huge geodes, and the world's largest dinosaur skull. Distant cultures are brought to life with displays of art objects and artifacts from Samoa to the Arctic Circle. Among noteworthy exhibits are an exquisite Rain Forest and "The Streets of Old Milwaukee," a 19th-century city built with architectural objects from the period. The Milwaukee Public Museum is tremendously popular, always crowded, and always exciting. Daily 9–5. Admission: $3.50–$5.50. ♿ (Downtown)

OTHER MUSEUMS

BETTY BRINN CHILDREN'S MUSEUM
929 E. Wisconsin Ave.
Milwaukee
414/291-0888
Where else can kids crawl through a giant human heart, anchor a TV news program, or learn to act like a sound

Milwaukee Art Museum, p.107

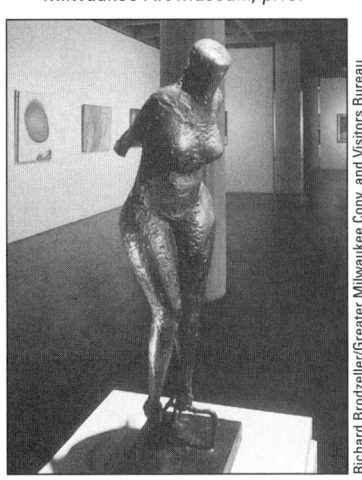

wave? Designed for children ages 1 to 10, the Brinn employs a philosophy that hands-on, imaginative role-playing is the best way to learn about our bodies, physics, and the world at large. Tue–Sat 9–5, Sun 12–5. Admission: $4. See also Chapter 7: "Kids' Stuff". ♿ (Downtown)

BROOKS STEVENS AUTOMOTIVE MUSEUM
10325 N. Port Washington Rd.
Mequon
262/241-4185
Brooks Stevens may have been the most important industrial designer of the 20th century, and his handiwork is visible in a staggering array of consumer and industrial products. He's the man who put windows in commercial clothes dryers. He designed streamlined passenger trains in the 1930s. He also had a lot to do with automobiles, and this museum presents a portion of Stevens's private collection. You'll find sports cars, racing cars, and vintage autos here, along with a few surprises. Mon–Fri 8–5. $4–$5 adults, $2 children. (North Side)

GALLERIES

DEAN JENSEN GALLERY
759 N. Water St.
Milwaukee
414/278-7100

Recently moved from the Third Ward to an historic building in the shadow of City Hall, the Dean Jensen Gallery showcases some of the finest new artwork in town. The gallery director is a former art critic, and he organizes outstanding solo exhibitions, focusing for the most part on edgy figurative work of very high quality. The gallery represents some of Wisconsin's most acclaimed painters—such as Fred Stonehouse, Norbert Kox, and Laura Dronzek—and shows outsider and untrained artists from around the country several times a year. ♿ (Downtown)

DELIND FINE ART
811 N. Jefferson St.
Milwaukee
414/271-8225
Specializing in 19th-century posters, contemporary landscapes, and floral still lifes, this Cathedral Square space is stuffed with paintings, prints, and sculpture. Though the artwork is a little prosaic, DeLind is a fun place to browse and is loved by informal art collectors. Of special note are large, fantastic animal sculptures painted in bright primary colors that often creep out onto the sidewalk. (Downtown)

GALERIE ART TODAY!
218 N. Water St.
Milwaukee
414/278-1211

Four times a year, Milwaukee's downtown art museums and galleries throw a party called Gallery Night, with late hours, openings, and tours. Thousands of people hobnob and check out the latest from local and national artists. Call the East Town Association at 414/271-1416 for dates.

Artist's rendition of the Milwaukee Public Museum, p. 109

In a lovely Soho-style space, Galerie Art Today focuses on contemporary European art, particularly French minimalism. While that might seem like an awfully narrow niche, it works well in this instance. First, there is no one else in town showing it, and, second, the high-ceilinged gallery is well-suited to large abstract paintings. ♿ (Downtown)

HERMETIC GALLERY
**226 S. First St.
Milwaukee
414/226-2098**

A few years ago, just when Milwaukee's gallery scene was getting stale, along came Hermetic. A home for conceptual and installation art, as well as more broadly considered exercises in painting, photography, and drawing, Hermetic consistently mounts some of the city's best exhibitions. Shows are often laced with humor and loaded with humanity, although the artwork is sometimes not particularly commercial—or even approachable. Gallery director Nicholas Frank never pretends he's cooler than you are, and in his hands even the most obtuse installation isn't off-putting. Hermetic is hip and shouldn't be missed. (South Side)

INSTINCT
**733 N. Milwaukee St.
Milwaukee
414/276-6363**

With the Milwaukee Art Museum's acquisition of the huge Hall Collection of American Folk Art a decade ago and with a number of nationally known artists calling the region home, the city is something of a mecca for collectors of outsider art. Located on a quickly gentrifying block of Queen Anne–style buildings, Instinct capitalizes on the raw power contained in the sculptures, drawings, and paintings of visionary, untrained artists. Even a peek through this gallery's windows is rewarding. (Downtown)

KATIE GINGRASS GALLERY
241 N. Broadway

Milwaukee
414/289-0855
Katie Gingrass Gallery specializes in American realist landscapes, glass, and decorative objects, but the gallery's more interesting focus, especially to the casual collector, is wearable art. The space is bright, airy, and well lit, better to show off the artist-made clothing, scarves, and other textiles. This, along with a conscientious staff and a huge selection of beautiful jewelry, makes Gingrass Gallery worth a stop on any Third Ward gallery hop. ♿ (Downtown)

KM ART
226 S. First St.
Milwaukee
414/226-2272
A decade ago, the opening of Kent Mueller's Metropolitan Gallery was among the first indications that Milwaukee might have a future as an art town. Mueller's new gallery, KM Art (pun intended), shows funk, outsider, and otherwise interesting regional art that wouldn't have a chance to show at any of Milwaukee's stodgier galleries. Recent shows have featured the work of merchant marine/memory painter Clare Mente and the photographs of environmental artist Roy Staab. The space, in an old industrial building, is a little rough, but what KM Art lacks in polish is more than made up for by Mueller's impeccable eye. (South Side)

MICHAEL LORD GALLERY
420 E. Wisconsin Ave.
Milwaukee
414/272-1007
One of the city's top-end art dealers, the Michael Lord Gallery carries the work of artists of international repute—such as Sam Gilliam and Nicholas Africano—as well as established local artists and those who seem to have a future. Managerial disorganization had caused a falling-off in the quality of exhibitions recently, but new staff has turned that situation around, and the Michael Lord Gallery is once again one of the best places in town for a good art experience. Of special note is the photography gallery down the hall from the main space. ♿ (Downtown)

TORY FOLLIARD GALLERY
233 N. Milwaukee St.
Milwaukee
414/273-7311
The Third Ward, a neighborhood of 19th-century warehouses and commercial buildings, has a high concentration of high-end galleries. Tory Folliard is one of the best in the area, showing primarily contemporary

---

TRIVIA

Don't be surprised if, walking down the street, you come across a slightly disconcerting window display. Art Street Window, a project of Milwaukee sculptor Paul Druecke, organizes installations by local artists, usually conceptual, in vacant commercial space downtown. One recent ASW installation featured a delicately balanced pile of rocks, beautiful to contemplate as trucks rumbled by on the busy street.

"Exhibits Come Alive" at the Milwaukee County Historical Center, p. 109

landscape and still-life paintings. The gallery shies away from art that is oppressive and portentous, and much of the work is lyrical, light-filled, and pleasant. Tory Folliard is also the Milwaukee representative of internationally acclaimed painter John Wilde, Wisconsin's most famous surrealist. ϟ (Downtown)

WALKER'S POINT CENTER FOR THE ARTS
911 W. National Ave.
Milwaukee
414/672-2787
Walker's Point, with its warehouses and factories, harbors a lot of artists looking for cheap rent and a vibrant neighborhood. Walker's Point Center for the Arts, a nonprofit gallery, features art exhibitions, performances, and after-school art classes for neighborhood kids. Consulting curators organize fascinating theme exhibitions of little-seen local and national artwork (recent shows have focused on handguns and art that uses plant life), most of which can reasonably be described as "cutting edge." (South Side)

PUBLIC ART

RICHARD HAAS MURAL
Centre Building
212 W. Wisconsin Ave.
Milwaukee
You probably won't even notice this gigantic mural, so seamlessly does noted photorealist Richard Haas integrate his painting with the architecture of the Centre Building. Painted on the blank east wall of the high rise, the mural creates a facade of an imaginary glass and steel skyscraper. Its "windows" even reflect the erstwhile Pabst Building, which once stood on the corner of Water Street and Wisconsin Avenue. (Downtown)

VALIANT IMMIGRANT MOTHERS
Cathedral Square Park
Wells and Jefferson Sts.
Milwaukee
The public sculptures that typically attract the most attention are the grandest: Solomon Juneau, the city's founder, stands in Juneau Park; DiSuvero's controversial sunburst anchors the foot of Wisconsin Avenue. This little statue, out of the way and forgotten in some shrubs near the fountain in Cathedral Square, commemorates the sacrifices of female immigrants in a city of immigrants. Depicting a woman carrying a baby, the expressionist sculpture is an apt testament to the fortitude of the anonymous millions who really built this city. (Downtown)

Discovery World

7
KIDS' STUFF

Milwaukee is a pretty good place to be a kid—from both a kid's point of view and a parent's. Parents, of course, love to see their children involved in educational, creative, and healthy activities. Kids just want to play, and they know that fun comes in many shapes and sizes.

The trick is for parents to learn what attractions and activities fit both bills. It's fun to make art, for example, and if your kids are learning how their own art projects fit into big exhibitions at the art museum, well, that's even better. If going to see a play is fun, isn't it doubly fun if that play provides you with some lasting message? Sure it is.

That's what kids' stuff is all about in Milwaukee. There are museums just for kids, nature centers that specialize in fun programs for children, and a brand new library for people under 14—with computers galore, CDs, and even a lighthouse.

And, lest your kids despair that every activity in Milwaukee has an educational component, there are plenty that are just plain fun. Go to the beach, play at the Milwaukee County water park, tour a candy factory, make your own ceramic dishes, shop for toys, and play video games. Just don't sit around complaining that there's nothing to do.

ANIMALS AND NATURE

APPLE WORKS
W179 N12536 Fond du Lac Ave.
Germantown
800/306-8888

In autumn, the Apple Works orchard and farm becomes a kid's paradise. Ride the hay wagon out to the pumpkin patch or the apple trees to find that perfect jack-o-lantern or to pick the basis for an outstanding apple pie. The organically grown fruit at Apple Works tastes great. When you're done picking fruit, visit the petting zoo, which has the world's fattest goats, then bug your parents for a carmel apple from the farm market. You pay for what you pick. (North Side)

RIVERSIDE URBAN ENVIRONMENTAL CENTER
Riverside Park
N. Oakland Ave. and E. Newberry Blvd.
Milwaukee
414/964-8505

In the heart of the densely populated east side, nature comes alive along a wild stretch of the Milwaukee River in a hands-on environmental laboratory for children. The Riverside Urban Environmental Center has a full-time naturalist and educator and offers a dozen programs each month—most of them free—for kids of all ages. Kids can count butterflies, learn to identify animal tracks in the snow, or explore the geology of the river bluff in short classes that combine fun, learning, and a walk in the woods. (See also Chapter 8: "Parks and Gardens.") (East Side)

SCHLITZ AUDUBON CENTER
1111 E. Brown Deer Rd.
Bayside
414/352-2880

Besides the observation tower with great views of Lake Michigan, the Schlitz Audubon Center presents children's environmental education programs each weekend. The programs make extensive use of the center's 250 acres of wilderness, combining outdoor exploration with in-depth research indoors. Learn about the winter constellations, maple-syrup making, songbird migration, and other subjects. (See also Chapter 8: "Parks and Gardens.") Call for current program information. Tue–Sun 9–5. Adults $4, ages 2 to 12 $2. & (East Side)

STACKNER HERITAGE FARM
Milwaukee County Zoo
10001 W. Bluemound Rd.
Wauwatosa
414/771-5500

Life on the farm is anything but laid back at the Milwaukee County Zoo's working dairy farm. Complete with octagonal barn, the Heritage Farm features milking presentations and a petting area where kids may handle Wisconsin animals—don't worry: Badgers are not on the list. One of the best displays at the children's area is the fascinating Birds of Prey show, presented at 11, 1, and 3 daily, and featuring real hawks, eagles, and falcons. As though children need another reason to visit the zoo. Daily 9–5 in summer, 9–4:30 in winter. Free with zoo admission (See also Chapter 5: "Sights and Attractions.") & (West Side)

URBAN FISHING PROGRAM
Milwaukee County Parks

Many of Milwaukee's parks feature lagoons—large ponds, really—and in summer they're stocked with game fish. The county's Urban Fishing Program is designed to introduce youngsters to the joy of dipping a line and the even greater joy of the wily bluegill's strike. Children under 16 may fish where posted without a Wisconsin fishing license—limits must be obeyed—and anything they catch may go home to the dinner table. Try

Humboldt (South Side), Washington (North Side), Veterans' (Downtown), or Kozsciousko (South Side) Parks. &

MUSEUMS AND LIBRARIES

BETTY BRINN CHILDREN'S MUSEUM
929 E. Wisconsin Ave.
Milwaukee
414/291-0888 or 414/390-5437 (info)
Kids love to head downtown to Milwaukee's newest museum; it's usually crammed with children having so much fun they don't realize they're learning. Named after child welfare advocate Betty Brinn, the children's museum features interactive exhibits exploring anatomy, economics, communications, mechanics, and the physics of sound. Kids can crawl through the digestion tunnel, build toys, and get into a working video studio to produce a TV show. There's a space especially for toddlers to explore a lake freighter, and more—all overlooking Lake Michigan. Tue–Sat 9–5, Sun 12–5. $4 ages 2 and up. & (Downtown)

BETTY BRINN CHILDREN'S ROOM
Milwaukee Public Library
814 W. Wisconsin Ave.
Milwaukee
414/286-3091
www.mpl.org
In 1998 the Central Library opened this new children's library. A huge area housing more than 70,000 books and other materials, the Brinn Children's Room is so sensitively designed that kids never feel lost in space. Readers are greeted by a giant book, showing quotes from children's classics. There is a lighthouse

Botswain Chair at Discovery World Museum

for young children to climb, a toddlers' area, comfortable chairs, window carrels for curling up with a good book as the sunshine pours in, dozens of computers, a theater, and a mosaic floor created by acclaimed children's author Lois Ehlert. & (Downtown)

DISCOVERY WORLD MUSEUM
Museum Center
712 W. Wells St.
Milwaukee
414/765-0777
From laser beams to boatswain's chairs, from Tesla coils to lightning tracks, at Discovery World older kids can really get into science. In the futuristic museum, "futurenauts," as visitors are called, play with 140 hands-on exhibits. They can learn about mechanics in the Milwaukee Muscle area, use teamwork to solve problems on the space shuttle, enter a real weather station complete with radar, and let the sparks fly on the

Van de Graff generator. Discovery World is a real blast. Daily 9–5. Adults $5, seniors $4, ages 4 to 17 $3. ♿ (Downtown)

EXPLORATION STATION
Milwaukee Public Museum
Museum Center
800 W. Wells St.
Milwaukee
414/278-2702
www.mpm.edu

With the dinosaurs, mummies, and shrunken heads, every nook and cranny of the Milwaukee Public Museum is fun for kids (see also Chapter 6: "Museums and Galleries"). But the MPM's Exploration Station is designed especially with them in mind. Children can use scientists' tools to explore the natural world: compare animal skulls, look at fossils, examine plant cells under a microscope. In each project, kids are given a series of problems to solve and the tools to do it. The Exploration Station has, without a doubt, spawned a new generation of naturalists-to-be. Daily 9–5. Admission: $3.50–$5.50. ♿ (Downtown)

FAMILY SUNDAYS
Milwaukee Art Museum
750 N. Lincoln Memorial Dr.
Milwaukee
414/224-3200
www.mam.org

Kids love to work on art projects, and the Milwaukee Art Museum's Family Sundays make creativity doubly fun by tying it to current exhibitions. Led by working artists, Family Sundays feature art projects for kids of all ages, tours tailored to the interests of young people, and gallery games that make learning seem more like playing. Family Sundays are a great way for children and their parents to explore the museum and their creative urges. Call for a current schedule. Sun 12:30–4. Adults $5, students $3, under 12 free. ♿ (Downtown)

CHILDREN'S THEATER

FIRST STAGE MILWAUKEE
Todd Wehr Theater
Marcus Center for the Performing Arts
929 N. Water St.
Milwaukee
414/273-7121

The most visible of Milwaukee children's theater companies, First Stage presents plays for young audiences based, most often, on classic literature like *Caddie Woodlawn* and *Charlotte's Web*. Generally written for grade-school audiences, First Stage plays are performed by professional actors and children who have graduated from the company's acting workshops. Known for thoughtful writing,

Milwaukee has a number of children's theaters and puppet groups, presenting shows in various theaters around town. In addition to First Stage Milwaukee and M&W Productions, check out the African American Children's Theater (414/283-9588), Mask & Puppet Co. (414/372-8058), and the Milwaukee Children's Theater (414/277-9357).

beautiful costumes, and great sets, First Stage has a well-earned reputation for staging high-quality children's theater throughout the arts season. ♿ (Downtown)

M & W PRODUCTIONS
Cooley Auditorium
1015 N. Sixth St.
Milwaukee
414/272-7701

"And they lived happily ever after" is the motto of M&W Productions. On the big proscenium in the Milwaukee Area Technical College's Cooley Auditorium, M&W presents children's mythology like *Rapunzel, Cinderella,* and the holiday chestnut *The Story of the Nutcracker*—geared for children from preschool through elementary grades. These are full-scale musical productions, with professional adult actors, full-stage sets, and great special effects—and kids go wild for them. Musicals are presented in October, December, and May. Admission: $8. ♿ (Downtown)

Betty Brinn Children's Museum, p. 116

STORES KIDS LOVE

AMERICAN SCIENCE AND SURPLUS
6901 W. Oklahoma Ave.
Milwaukee
414/541-7777

American Science and Surplus is, in a word, unbelievable. Need a beaker or test tube? ASAS has several thousand from which to choose. How about a glass eye? Or a bag of 500 model rocket engines? You get the picture. Wandering the overstuffed aisles at American Science and Surplus is an adventure—you never know what you might find. The overstocked science equipment includes glass slides, electrical clips, cameras, telescopes, even stoplight lenses, fancy kites, and Canadian mailbags. This is one wonderful store. (South Side)

ART SMART'S DART MART
1695 N. Humboldt Ave.
Milwaukee
414/273-3278

Like Peter Pan, the man known as Art Smart is a kid who never grew up: he supplies the city with darts and dartboards, obviously, but he also stocks an unbelievable selection of frisbees, boomerangs, yo-yos, and other marvelous time killers. So, if your pleasure is disc golf, juggling—bean bags for beginners, bowling pins for experts—hackey sack, or flying a kite, Art Smart's will fill all your needs. Best of all, not only is this store a load of fun for kids, it's also a great place for adults to find gifts for children. (East Side)

BUDDY SQUIRREL/QUALITY CANDY OUTLET

1801 E. Bolivar Ave.
Milwaukee
414/483-4500

Willie Wonka's wonderland comes to life at the Quality Candy factory outlet. Owing to Wisconsin's status as dairy heaven, the Milwaukee area has a number of chocolate factories—that's *milk* chocolate, after all. Quality Candy is a big-time chocolate and candy factory: dipped caramels, fairy food, turtles—the whole mother lode. Free tours of the factory are available by appointment (tours include a number of samples), and the outlet store is open to everyone. If you've ever wondered how they make nonpareils, this is your chance to find out. (South Side)

THE LEARNING SHOP
17435 W. Bluemound Rd.
Brookfield
262/789-6994
www.learningshop.com

The Learning Shop is a class act. (Get it?) This local chain specializes in "toys that teach," but the real emphasis is on quality: wooden toys, imported toys, and names like Brio and Lego. Kids will have a field day browsing the aisles stocked with trucks, dolls, games, puzzles, and books. Parents will appreciate the educational toys, so everyone leaves happy. The Learning Shop has additional locations in Shorewood, on the south side, and on the North Shore. (Waukesha County)

SPUTNIK
Discovery World
Museum Center
712 W. Wells St.
Milwaukee
414/765-0777

Located in the Discovery World science museum, Sputnik is a mighty cool gift store. How cool? you ask. Well, the main counter is built from an actual airplane wing. Featuring science games, techno-toys, and oddly futuristic Japanese amusements, Sputnik is a store for budding Einsteins and Oppenheimers, Galileos and Galens. Visitors can pick up

Schlitz Audubon Center, p. 115

David Stokes/Schlitz Audubon Center

Forget the stroller? Don't worry. Your trip to Milwaukee can be hassle-free even if you have small children. Call Kids on the Go—888/738-1600—to rent cribs, strollers, high chairs, rocking chairs, car seats, and other equipment. They even deliver—and include a box of toys with each rental.

spaceship and monster models and official Discovery World apparel here too. & (Downtown)

TIME TO KILN
2565 N. Downer Ave.
Milwaukee
414/967-4959
Time to Kiln is a you-decorate-it ceramic boutique. Kids and parents choose from a large assortment of unfired greenware—dishes, cups and mugs, vases, flowerpots, bowls—then (with some instruction, of course) paint glazes onto the pottery. You can be as simple or complicated as you want, and, after the pros fire up the kiln and bake your creation, you'll have a personal and unique gift or memento—or a new set of dishes. (East Side)

WIZ KIDS COMPUTERS
4479 N. Oakland Ave.
Shorewood
414/967-9265
Geeks of the world, unite! You have nothing to lose but your boredom! Specializing in educational and entertainment software for the under-15 set, Wiz Kids helps children tune in and turn on to the digital future. Boot up the machine, plug in the CD-ROM, and watch reading comprehension, math skills, and geography knowledge bloom. There are games, too, of course. Wiz Kids offers computer classes for kids and is also a fabulous party place, particularly for children whose birthdays, falling in the chilly months, require indoor celebrations. (East Side)

PLACES TO PLAY

COOL WATERS
Greenfield Park
2028 S. 124th St.
Greenfield
414/321-7530
Cool Waters, a public water park, is among the reasons Milwaukee County Parks are considered to be among the nation's best. Cool Waters provides serious summer fun: two huge water slides twist and turn into the heated pool, causing kids to twist and shout. The park has interactive water toys—arch jets, sprayers, and the like—a sand volleyball court, and, when the kids need a break, a restaurant and picnic area. Cool Waters is open in summer only. Call for hours and admission prices. (South Side)

DISCOVERY ZONE
5008 S. 74th St.
Greenfield
414/281-3220
To an adult, Discovery Zone seems like a kiddie insane asylum—boys and girls bounce from one attraction to another like pinballs. But kids know

that it's just a great place to go crazy for a while. An indoor amusement center, DZ focuses on activities that use a lot of energy: laser tag, tube mazes, kiddie karaoke (now, that's a hoot), and games of skill like skee-ball. Bland-ish food is available, too. Entrance fees are computed by the child's height. (South Side)

FUN WORLD
620 N. Elizabeth Ct.
Brookfield
262/789-5370
It's raining, it's snowing, the north wind is blowing, the kids are complaining that there's nothing to do. Where, oh where, are you going to take them? Well, Fun World lives up to its name: it's the biggest indoor amusement park around—big enough to hold mechanical rides like a Ferris wheel and a motion simulator, laser tag, games of skill, and a full 18 holes of miniature golf. That ought to keep 'em busy for a while. (Waukesha County)

GIFT OF WINGS
1300 N. Lincoln Memorial Dr.
Milwaukee
414/273-5483
Veteran's Park, projecting into Lake Michigan, with steady winds and few tall trees, is thought to be one of the finest places in the country for kite flying. At Gift of Wings, you can put the theory to the test by renting kites—from simple airfoils to geohedric stunt wonders. Many people

Window on the Past

A century-old stained-glass window hangs on the south wall of the Betty Brinn Children's Room at the Central Library. It shows author Hans Christian Andersen surrounded by three children who look up at him with rapt attention as he weaves a tale.

The window was made in 1896 by German-born Milwaukee artist Marie Herndl, the only successful female stained-glass artist of her time. Well known, she was also commissioned by Congress to create skylights showing the seals of the original 13 colonies for the U.S. Senate.

The window, which had been stored in pieces in a library closet, was carefully restored for the new children's room. An inscription across the bottom reads "Exegi monumentum aere. Perennium." *It means,* "I have erected a monument more lasting than bronze," *an apt sentiment for a library, whose books live on forever in the imaginations of readers.*

fly kites here on breezy days all year long, and kids have a great time feeling the tug of the lake wind on the line. (Downtown)

JOHNSON'S PARK
7350 N. 76th St.
Milwaukee
414/353-9548
When the kids ask what you did for fun when you were their age, you can point them in the direction of Johnson's Park, an amusement center from an era when fun was real, not virtual. The park features three mini-golf courses (the huge fiberglass dinosaurs under which you must putt are visible for blocks), a giant slide, a go-cart racetrack where older kids can drive at breakneck speeds, baseball and softball batting cages, an arcade, and, of course, the ubiquitous snack bar, selling the same bad-for-you stuff on which you gorged yourself as a kid. (North Side)

PETTIT NATIONAL ICE CENTER
500 S. 84th St.
West Allis
414/266-0100
www.thepettit.com
The Pettit Center is one of the biggest ice rinks in the world, and, since it's home base for the U.S. Olympic Speed-skating Team, you and your kids can skate with the big boys and girls. Open skating is held daily, but schedules change as the team's training schedule does. (See also Chapter 5: "Sights and Attractions" and Chapter 10: "Sports and Recreation.") Admission: $4–$5, skate rental $2. (West Side)

VIRTUAL MAGIC
11112 N. Port Washington Rd.
Mequon
262/241-8739
It's not playing in the physical sense, but surely a couple of hours hooked up the machines at Virtual Magic will stimulate some primitive and reptilian part of your child's brain. Virtual Magic is a more or less barren room in a North Shore strip mall, stuffed with high-powered computer terminals. Those terminals run very high-res, very high-intensity computer role-playing games in which people combat the evil whatzit, blowing holes in opponents, walls, and their own digital personae. (North Side)

8
PARKS AND GARDENS

With the sort of long cold winters that besiege Milwaukee, it's no wonder that its citizens take particular pride in their parks. This city needs all the green it can get for the nine months of the year that aren't marked by snow cover.

The roots of the outstanding county park system go back to 1889, when a newly formed parks commission began acquiring land along the lake and river. It also hired Frederick Law Olmsted, creator of Central Park in Manhattan, to design three parks in Milwaukee: Lake Park, Riverside Park, and Washington Park. Over the years, the parks were expanded and facilities were added: swimming beaches and pools, two botanical gardens, an arboretum, a marina, even Milwaukee County Stadium, home of Brewers baseball.

Currently, Milwaukee County parks cover 15,000 acres and serve millions of picnickers, boaters, swimmers, stargazers, nature lovers, dog walkers, and more every year. Couple the county system with nearby state-park facilities and municipal green spaces in suburban Milwaukee, and you've got a lot of opportunities to get outside.

Oh yeah, speaking of those snowy months, Milwaukeeans use their parks then, too. Sleds come out, skis are waxed, the pad on the toboggan is tightened, and ice skates are sharpened. A little snow and sub-zero temperatures aren't going to stop the Cream City from having fun. Plus, you can always go inside for hot chocolate afterward.

So what are you waiting for? Put on your bathing suit (hiking boots, bicycle shorts, cross-country skis, bug spray, sunglasses) and head for the great outdoors.

BOERNER BOTANICAL GARDENS
Whitnall Park
5879 S. 92nd St.
Hales Corners
414/425-1132

Thousands of years ago, glaciers carved the rolling landscape of Whitnall Park. During the Great Depression, the CCC built the foundation of the Boerner Botanical Gardens on 120 acres of that parkland. Today one of the nation's premier public gardens, Boerner features formal landscaping, trellised walkways, perennial beds, and rock gardens that attract thousands of visitors every year. Of particular interest are the bog walk, shrub mall, and trial gardens, at which new hybrids are developed. May–Oct daily 8–sunset. Free admission, $3 parking fee. (South Side)

Havenwoods State Forest

BRADFORD BEACH
2400 N. Lincoln Memorial Dr.
Milwaukee

Bradford Beach is the home of Milwaukee's bikini set. On summer weekends the beach and the area around it are packed with frisbee players, in-line skaters, strapping lifeguards, and people of all flavors hanging out in the sunshine. They picnic in the green spaces adjacent to the sand, throw sticks into the lake for their dogs, listen to radios, and practice tae kwon do. In other words, you name it. If you want to be seen on the beach, this is the beach to visit. (East Side)

CATHEDRAL SQUARE
N. Jefferson and E. Wells Sts.
Milwaukee

Cathedral Square is downtown's premier urban park, surrounded by tony restaurants, galleries, coffee bars, and nightspots—as well as the glorious Cathedral of St. John from which the park takes its name. The park is home to a summer farmer's market, a well-regarded series of weekly jazz concerts, a small tot playground, and a popcorn wagon and picnic tables. Rumor has it that a movement is afoot to restore the park's original beaux arts fountain—a grand wedding cake spouting water. (Downtown)

THE DOG PARK
W. Good Hope Rd. at U.S. 45
Milwaukee

Dogs, you have a friend in the Milwaukee County Park System. This off-leash dog park, with trails winding through woods and meadows and along the Menomonee River, is a lovely spot for pooches and their people to romp, safely fenced off from roads. All dogs under voice command (or on leash) are welcome for sniffing, gleeful playing, and the chasing of sticks. From the south on Highway 45, use the left exit for Highway 175, turn left at the first frontage road, and double back to the south to the parking lot. (North Side)

GRANT PARK
100 Hawthorne Ave.
South Milwaukee
Grant Park should perhaps be named Grand Park. One of the county's largest parks, it is located at the point where Oak Creek empties into Lake Michigan. The park contains a public golf course, walking and skiing trails through lakeside ravines, picnic areas, and playgrounds. Grant Park's best feature, though, is its glorious beach, which is wide, long, and well used in summer. (South Side)

HAVENWOODS STATE FOREST
6141 N. Hopkins St.
Milwaukee
414/527-0232
Once the site of the Milwaukee House of Corrections, a camp for German prisoners during the Second World War, and a Nike missile installation, Havenwoods State Forest was reclaimed as wild land at the end of the 1970s. The 237-acre forest provides much-needed green relief in the middle of the city, with six miles of hiking, off-road biking, and ski trails, an environmental education area, and a children's resource center. Havenwoods is unique in that it is the only state forest accessible by city bus. Daily 6–8. Admission: free (North Side)

JACOBUS PARK
6501 W. Hillside Ln.
Wauwatosa
A delightful ribbon park nestled in an older neighborhood along the Menomonee River, Jacobus Park is notable for its outstanding playground. A wading pool for toddlers is complemented by two play complexes, one for kids under six and one for those a little older. There are slides in all shapes and sizes, ladders of various configurations, and suspended walkways. Swings for big kids and little kids, and one that will hold a parent and child, round out the equipment at this popular and busy play spot. (West Side)

KLODE PARK
5900 N. Shore Dr.
Whitefish Bay
Terraced down the precipitous drop to Lake Michigan, Klode Park is perhaps the most pleasant of several North Shore beaches. This small park includes picnic areas, a pair of tennis courts, some lovely elm trees, and one of the area's best playgrounds. But the park's real glory is invisible from street level: A wheelchair-accessible pathway winds down the steep bluff to a pair of crescent-shaped beaches, a great and

---

Perhaps the very best view of downtown Milwaukee is found in the South Shore and Bay View Parks along South Superior Street. Looking across the bay, with the majestic Hoan Harbor Bridge in the foreground, you can see all of the downtown, Gold Coast, and east-side skyscrapers.

Boerner Botanical Gardens, p. 124

sheltered spot for sunbathing and swimming. ♿ (East Side)

KOSCIUSZKO PARK
W. Lincoln Ave. at S. Seventh St.
Milwaukee
This bustling urban park is named for Thaddeus Kosciuszko, Polish hero of the American Revolution, and is located across the street from St. Josaphat's Basilica (see Chapter 5: "Sights and Attractions"). The greenspace features rolling terrain, a senior center, a playground and picnic area, and a lovely lagoon for the Urban Fishing program in summer and ice-skating in winter. The park is one of the city's multicultural crossroads, with Latinos playing soccer, Poles strolling the paths, and Hmong kids playing a game like volleyball, except using their feet. (South Side)

LAKE PARK
E. Kenwood Blvd. at N. Lake Dr.
Milwaukee
In 1889, Milwaukee County hired landscape architect Frederick Law Olmsted—exponent of the city-beautiful movement and designer of Central Park—to plan a series of parks for the city. Lake Park, a triumph of 19th-century design on a bluff over Lake Michigan, remains the jewel of the entire park system. Olmsted's paths through the gullies of the rolling landscape, delicate bridges spanning wooded ravines, curving staircases, and statuary are joined by a par-three golf course, lighted tennis courts, lovely picnic areas, and one of the best playgrounds in the city. (East Side)

LAPHAM PEAK
Kettle Moraine State Forest
N846 W329 County Highway C
Delafield
262/646-3025
The highest point in Waukesha County, Lapham Peak has historical as well as recreational significance. It was from the top of this hill that Increase Lapham established the U.S. Signal Corps, a series of signal towers used to relay weather information

to sailors on Lake Michigan. The Signal Corps eventually became the National Weather Service. This state-forest unit features 12 miles of hiking trails over rolling terrain and some off-road bike trails. It is also the area's major site for cross-country ski and dogsled races in winter. Lapham Peak is the state-forest area closest to downtown Milwaukee. (Waukesha County)

LOWELL PARK
Madison and Grandview Sts.
Waukesha

Lowell Park beckons when the Wisconsin winter lies heavily across the landscape. Grab your sled and climb the big ridge that runs across the south edge of the park. Besides great sledding trails—from gentle to terrifying—Lowell Park has two permanent toboggan runs. The wooden troughs are flooded in winter and become an icy racetrack for the big wooden sleds. The thrill, as you tear down the hillside in the chilly air, is, well, thrilling. See Chapter 10: "Sports and Recreation" for more toboggan information. (Waukesha County)

The Other Kind of Bowling

Lawn bowling, a gracious game like shuffleboard on grass, has been played in Lake Park for nearly a century. The Lake Park Lawn Bowling Club maintains a green near the Lake Park Bistro off of East Newberry Boulevard, a green large enough to handle half a dozen or more games at once. The lawn is perfectly manicured, perfectly flat, and perfectly level, like a Cartesian golf green, and is assiduously maintained, mowed, and rolled smooth by club members.

Players, traditionally dressed in white, roll a target ball to one end of the green. Then each throws four wooden balls, called bowls, at the target—trying to get closest to it and to knock opponent's bowls out of the way. Sound simple? Well, there's a hitch. The bowls are not perfectly spherical. Instead, one side is milled down on a lathe, making the other side heavier and throwing off the bowl's center of gravity. This imbalance allows skilled players to roll the bowls in a curved path, sneaking in behind their opponent's throw.

Stop at the Lake Park Lawn Bowling Club any Saturday or Sunday during summer for an introductory lesson, first shot at the game, or just to watch.

MCKINLEY BEACH
1750 N. Lincoln Memorial Dr.
Milwaukee

The county's newest beach, McKinley was built just north of the municipal marina to provide a low-key alternative to the popular and crowded Bradford Beach a short distance up the shore. Constructed inside a crescent-shaped breakwall, McKinley Beach is a great place to wet your toes in Lake Michigan on nice days without fighting your way through crowds. A lifeguard keeps watch at this small beach, and when you're done swimming, you can take a walk on adjacent Government Pier (see Chapter 5: "Sights and Attractions"). (East Side)

MITCHELL AIRPORT PARK
S. Whitnall Ave. and
S. Clement St.
Milwaukee

Located at the end of Mitchell International Airport's north-south runway, this park is a throwback to the days when air travel signified the most thrilling sorts of possibility. And it is still thrilling to sit in this park and watch the big planes take off right over your head. Any lunch hour will find people eating sandwiches to the rumble of jet engines. If you have some time to kill before your flight, there are worse places to kill it. (South Side)

MITCHELL PARK
W. Pierce and S. 27th Sts.
Milwaukee
414/649-9800 (Domes)

Mitchell Park, located along the north bank of the Menomonee Valley, is the premier green area of the near south side. Its most remarkable feature is its indoor botanical gardens (see Chapter 5: "Sights and Attractions"), but the rest of Mitchell Park is splendid, too, with a sunken garden, gorgeous mature trees, and walkways winding along the river bluff. The park is at its best during the Cinco de Mayo festival held there each May, when Milwaukee's Hispanic residents—and everyone else—celebrate the Mexican national holiday with food, music, and dancing. (South Side)

PÈRE MARQUETTE PARK
N. Old World Third and
W. State Sts.
Milwaukee

It was on this site that Father Jacques Marquette, the first European to visit the area, camped while exploring the western shore of Lake Michigan. Today the downtown park is home to the Riverwalk, the Milwaukee County Historical Center, and the Midwest Express Landing pavilion. Père Marquette Park is also the site of major political rallies; recent speakers have included President

All of the hybrids smell sweet at the annual Milwaukee Journal-Sentinel Rose Festival, held at the Boerner Botanical Garden each June. More than 50,000 blossoms grace 500 rose species in a dazzling display of color and scent, attracting flower lovers from around the Midwest.

Clinton and former German chancellor Helmut Kohl. Surrounded by delis and restaurants, Marquette Park is a great place for a picnic lunch on the banks of the river. (Downtown)

RIVERSIDE URBAN ENVIRONMENTAL CENTER
Riverside Park
N. Oakland Ave. and E. Newberry Blvd.
Milwaukee
414/964-8505

A decade ago, Riverside Park was a neglected wasteland of weeds and broken glass. At that time, a group of neighbors banded together to repair the damage. They cleaned up the garbage, shored up the eroding bluff along the Milwaukee River, and built a living environmental laboratory for the neighborhood. Now Riverside Park is a focus for strollers, off-road cyclists, and amateur biologists. The Riverside Urban Environmental Center offers educational programs for adults and children year-round—from bird-watching canoe trips during the autumn migration to mushroom hikes in spring. (East Side)

SCHLITZ AUDUBON CENTER
1111 E. Brown Deer Rd.
Bayside
414/352-2880

The largest tract of undeveloped lakeshore land in Milwaukee County, Schlitz Audubon Center is a nature preserve and environmental-education facility affiliated with the National Audubon Society. The center's 225 acres include six distinct environments sheltering an enormous variety of plant and animal life: lakeshore, bluff and ravine, woodland, open field, ponds, river and floodplain. There are six miles of hiking, snowshoeing, and skiing trails, one trail designed for people with disabilities, and a 60-foot observation tower that is open year-round. Tue–Sun 9–5. Adults $4, ages 2 to 12 $2. ♿ (East Side)

SOUTH SHORE PARK
S. Superior and E. Estes Sts.
Milwaukee

The pride of Bayview, South Shore Park is the most pleasant lakeshore park in the city of Milwaukee—a ribbon of green grass and golden sand that attracts boaters, picnickers, swimmers, and sunbathers throughout the summer. A pavilion, built around the turn of the century at water's edge, hosts public events and private receptions. As an added bonus, South Shore Park's bathing beach is the only one in the city inside the long South Harbor breakwall, which means that the water is often a degree or two warmer than elsewhere. (South Side)

Veteran's Park Lagoon, p. 130

DCD/David LaHaye

You've heard of dial-a-poem and dial-a-prayer, but in Milwaukee you can call the Nature Now hot line. A project of the Schlitz Audubon Center, the hot line features information on local nature issues. Find out what northern trees do in winter or what hawks eat during the spring migration. Messages change weekly; call 414/352-8833.

VETERAN'S PARK
800 N. Lincoln Memorial Dr.
Milwaukee

A couple of decades ago, "there was no there there." A huge landfill project to reclaim space from Lake Michigan, Veteran's Park was created practically out of thin air. The park, just north of the Milwaukee Art Museum, is a great way to get close to the lake when you're downtown. It provides a lovely area for stolling, eating lunch as the waves lap against the breakwall, and contemplating the county Vietnam veterans' memorial, a noble series of granite columns. (Downtown)

VILLA TERRACE RENAISSANCE GARDEN
Villa Terrace Decorative Arts Museum
2220 N. Terrace Ave.
Milwaukee
414/271-3656

The gardens of this Italianate blufftop villa, with a commanding view of Lake Michigan, had become dishevelled before the Friends of Villa Terrace undertook a major project to restore them in 1998. Falling down the steep bluff, the Villa Terrace gardens are organized like a formal garden of the Italian Renaissance: Shapes, colors, and textures are viewed as an artist's palette, and order is sought among the branches and leaves. The ongoing restoration should be complete by the end of 1999. Wed–Sun 12–5. Adults $2. (East Side)

WEHR NATURE CENTER
Whitnall Park
9701 W. College Ave.
Franklin
414/425-8550

The Wehr Nature Center covers more than 200 acres of hilly countryside. It features five miles of trails organized into short loops—none is longer than a mile or so—through woodland, oak savanna, prairie wetland, and lake environments. The wildflower-filled prairie areas undergo controlled burning every few years (lightning strikes would have done the job in the past) to prevent them from being taken over by forest. Wehr offers fun educational programs for kids and adults almost every day of the week. Open sunrise to sunset year-round. Admission: free. (South Side)

WHITNALL PARK ARBORETUM
5879 S. 92 St.
Hales Corners
414/425-1132

Occupying a thousand acres contiguous with the Boerner Botanical Gardens, the Whitnall Park Arboretum contains thousands of shade and ornamental trees, remarkable for their size, variety, and age. Picnickers can spread their blankets beneath the largest remaining American elm, and strollers can walk among oaks and maples dating from before 1750. More than 250 types of crab apple trees erupt in blossoms in May, as do an equal number of varieties of lilacs and many kinds of nut trees. Stop at the Boerner Botanical Garden information building for arboretum maps. (South Side)

9
SHOPPING

At one time, shopping in Milwaukee meant getting on the train and heading to Chicago for the day. But no more. While the citizens of Brewtown might make an annual holiday trip to the Miracle Mile for the sheer glamor of it all, there are more than enough interesting, even fascinating, stores of every kind right here.

In all honesty, Milwaukee is not known, nor will it ever be known, for its concentration of classy boutiques or high-end clothiers or ritzy, glitzy designer outlets. What it should be known for is its concentration of great, quirky *shopping.*

That quirkiness stems from three factors: Milwaukee's Old World neighborhoods that simply cannot survive without their local butcher and baker, the increasing concentration of artisans (and the arty types who buy their wares) who make the city home, and the fact that Milwaukee loves a bargain. Try to compliment a Milwaukeean on his or her shoes, hat, or couch, and the response will be: "Thanks, I got it at fill in the blank *during their floor-sample clearance!"*

In Milwaukee, you can flit from continental patisserie to artist-made furniture store to religious-supply discount house all in the same neighborhood. Of course, the city is surrounded by shopping malls, with all the big national clothing, houseware, and doodad chains. But even the malls have certain Milwaukee appeal in their smaller stores.

SHOPPING DISTRICTS

Old World Third Street

The "Old World" designation in this five-block downtown street's name refers to the thoroughfare's concentration of pristine 19th-century commercial buildings. Once Milwaukee's grandest shopping area, North Third Street is now home to an assortment of specialty food stores, restaurants, historic landmarks, and eccentric shops. It's very Milwaukee.

DONGES HAT AND GLOVE
1001 N. Old World Third St.
Milwaukee
414/273-9964

The Donges hat store has sold headgear, gloves, and scarves from this location since the beginning of time: fedoras, bowlers, porkpies, hats with earflaps, and hats without. Some of the sales clerks—eons old—have haberdashed Milwaukee heads for generations. The service is almost too personal: These guys get into your head to determine what should go on top of it. (Downtown)

MADER'S TOWER GALLERY
1037 N. Old World Third St.
Milwaukee
414/271-1911

The sentimental realism that finds its ultimate expression in Hummel figurines finds its ultimate outlet at Mader's Tower Gallery. The gallery features an astonishing array of collectibles, knickknacks, and imported geegaws, much of which recalls a day when Milwaukee was one of the world's largest German cities. Dusting must be a lifetime occupation at this museumlike store. (Downtown)

THE SPICE HOUSE
1031 N. Old World Third St.
Milwaukee
414/272-0977

Any cook will tell you that praises sung by the likes of John Thorne and Julia Child are high praises indeed. Well, they both shop (by mail) at the Spice House. Fresh spices, ground on the spot, are all this store sells: a dozen varieties of black pepper, multiple cinnamons, herbs, salts, custom blends, and more. The smell that greets you when you open the front door is worth the trip all by itself. (Downtown)

USINGER'S SAUSAGE
1030 N. Old World Third St.
Milwaukee
414/276-9100

Milwaukee's most famous butcher, Usinger's has been making sausage on Third Street for more than a century. This factory outlet store, with murals of gnomes stuffing sausage, delights visitors—including presidents and other dignitaries. If you want a taste of real Milwaukee, pick up a *sommersausage, weisswurst,* or gift assortment. There are 75 varieties from which to choose. (Downtown)

Historic Third Ward

Reclaimed by artists, colonized by renovators, the Third Ward's once-dilapidated 19th-century warehouses are now condos, and the neighborhood is the very definition of urban chic in Milwaukee. Galleries, boutiques, upscale antique stores, salons, theaters, and restaurants line Broadway, Water, and Chicago Streets a few blocks from the heart of downtown.

BROADWAY PAPER
181 N. Broadway
Milwaukee
414/277-7699

Wrapping paper, writing paper, gift boxes, hat boxes, handmade paper, paper plates and napkins, imported and domestic, recycled and virgin: If it's made of wood fiber, you'll find it at this trendy treasure of a shop. Cream City Ribbon, a manufacturer of cotton ribbon for department store gift wrappers nationwide, sells an almost impossible variety of products here as well. (Downtown)

ECCOLA
273 N. Broadway
Milwaukee
414/273-3727

Is your bedroom boring? Your dining room dull? Spice up your home life with a visit to Eccola. The dizzying array of funky furnishings, decor, and accoutrements—picture frames and mirrors, lamps and end tables, wine racks and coasters, even jewelry—will jazz up any room and add a spark to living space. No tacky sentimentality here, just cool stuff. (Downtown)

EDEN
241 N. Broadway
Milwaukee
414/291-9314

If all you want is a dozen yellow roses, don't come to Eden, which bills itself as an "alternative florist." The artists here create hip, funky, and shockingly beautiful flower arrangements, with a particular eye for unusual greens and unexpected textures. Eden also carries original paintings by local artists and *objets d'art* that bespeak a sort of urban millennial cool. (Downtown)

LINDA RICHMAN JEWELRY
Katie Gingrass Gallery
241 N. Broadway
Milwaukee
414/289-0886

Linda Richman Jewelry Gallery carries the work of local and national contemporary artists. The display cases are a sight to behold—from wispy to ponderous, these rings, earrings, necklaces, and other adornments take forms you probably haven't seen before. While some of the work is very pricey, a remarkable number of pieces aren't out of the ballpark by any means. (Downtown)

MILWAUKEE ANTIQUE CENTER
341 N. Milwaukee St.
Milwaukee
414/276-0605

Of the several antiques malls in the Third Ward, this is, in general, the most approachable and affordable. Dozens of dealers—some carefully organized, some ajumble—spread out over four floors make the MAC a mecca for rainy-day browsers. Furniture, textiles, clothing and hats, jewelry, books and records, dishes and glassware, and all kinds of whatnots await the intrepid shopper. (Downtown)

RUBIN'S FURNITURE
224 E. Chicago St.
Milwaukee
414/278-8100

Do you want a sofa that wouldn't have looked out of place in the Jetson's house? Rubin's has it, along with funky footstools, slightly outré towel bars, and hip household accessories. With a flip, fin-de-siècle style that picks up where Memphis-Milano left off, Rubin's has furniture for every room in the house, along with a no-pressure sales environment. (Downtown)

Historic Brady Street

Half old Italian neighborhood shopping district and half counterculture, Brady Street is synonymous with both parmasianno reggiano and studded leather. Brady Street—and the neighborhood within its sway—is rapidly gentrifying. Its boutiques, international restaurants, and coffeehouses serve the upscale residents of Prospect Avenue's Gold Coast high rises as well as hipsters with pierced noses.

CHANGIN' TIMES
923 E. Brady St.
Milwaukee
414/271-7473
The name might harken back to the 1960s—it used to be a head shop—but nowadays this boutique is all '90s. It's definitely oriented toward young people. T-shirts (some emblazoned with sayings that might make you blush), jewelry for the studded set, accessories in a variety of materials (vinyl, anyone?), and a great selection of lug-soled footwear put Changin' Times off the middle-class radar screen and smack in the middle of hipster-world. (East Side)

CLOSET CLASSICS
1531 N. Farwell Ave.
Milwaukee
414/271-1950
Whoever coined the expression "what goes around comes around" was certainly thinking about fashion. Brady Street is crowded with hip-hugging bell-bottoms these days, just like it was in 1979, and Closet Classics is one of the best places to find them. This great resale shop is jammed with paisley and denim, proving that if there's nothing new under the sun, used is just fine. (East Side)

GLORIOSO'S SPECIALTY FOODS
1020 E. Brady St.
Milwaukee
414/272-1311
Glorioso's is tiny and cramped and right out of a movie. A huge cheese selection, incredible butcher counter, fantastic deli—try the pickled cherry peppers stuffed with prosciutto and provolone—pastas, imported coffee, cookies, nuts, truffles, the area's largest selection of olive oil, and a service-oriented staff make Glorioso's a treat for anybody who likes to eat. And you know you do. (East Side)

TRIVIA

The Florence Eiseman Company has produced fine children's apparel for decades. Known for quality fabrics, innovative cuts, and decorative appliques, Eiseman clothes are dandy in both senses of the word. While its clothes are sold in specialty children's boutiques, the company also has spring and fall warehouse sales with decent discounts. Call 414/272-3222 to find out when the next sale is scheduled.

MANHYIA HOME GALLERY
1316 E. Brady St.
Milwaukee
414/272-5055
Pronounced "mon-CHEE-ya," this home-decorating store adds an interesting component to Brady Street's eclectic mix. The store's owners make frequent trips to Africa, looking for housewares, decorative items, artwork, and furniture. Many interesting carved wood and cast-metal *objets d'art* are found here, as well as substantial items like tables and chairs, mirrors, and intricate textile work. (East Side)

MR. SHOE
1533 N. Farwell Ave.
Milwaukee
414/277-0660
Purveyor of the hippest, trendiest, and all-out coolest footwear in the city, Mr. Shoe sells wild platforms, chunky-soled loafers, plastic mules, and more. This store caters primarily to young women making the scene—extreme heels, animal prints, thigh-high vinyl—but also carries women's styles that are slightly less *outré* and men's shoes as well. (East Side)

THREE DOG BAKERY
1229 E. Brady St.
Milwaukee
414/278-7297
It had to happen: baked goods for beagles, pastries for pugs, shortbread for shepherds. Yep, it's a bakery for dogs, featuring birthday cakes, cookies, and plain old (homemade) dog biscuits in a variety of flavors. If you have a dog, you know the occasional super-treat is hard to resist. (East Side)

Whitefish Bay

Whitefish Bay is home to a mix of small shops, ski outfitters, oriental rug dealers, clothing boutiques, and coffeehouses. An older, quiet North Shore suburb of solid homes, Whitefish Bay features the sorts of stores in which a Martha Stewart might find something interesting—which is to say, gracious stores.

GIRAFFE
527 E. Silver Spring Dr.
Whitefish Bay
414/332-8900
Giraffe is the ideal place to find a wedding gift for a cousin who, at age 40, is getting married for the first time. She already has life's necessities, but she doesn't have all the frills. Giraffe will fill in the blanks with high-quality housewares (pewter cups, crystal candlesticks, imported decanters, stainless-steel letter openers), lovely paper products, and nice cards. (East Side)

JUST KIDDING
318 E. Silver Spring Dr.
Whitefish Bay
414/962-2524
jkid@execpc.com
Just Kidding has found a great niche. Specializing in fun and funky children's clothes, the store also has a kids' barbershop. So, while kids are getting those precious locks lopped, Mom and Dad can browse for cool clothes, toys, and gifts. The sale racks at Just Kidding are always worth a look. (East Side)

ZITA OF MILWAUKEE
211 E. Silver Spring Dr.
Whitefish Bay

Author signing at Book Bay

414/332-0126
Milwaukee is low key, but you wouldn't know it walking into Zita, the city's source for high-end women's designer fashions. The collection starts at Chanel, and from there, well, the sky's the limit. Zita's formal, bridal, and business attire is just the thing for a Womens' Club luncheon, 35th-floor board meeting, cocktails at the country club, charity ball at the Milwaukee Athletic Club, or dinner at Grenadier's. (East Side)

BOOKSTORES AND NEWSSTANDS

AFTERWORDS
2710 N. Murray St.
Milwaukee
414/963-9089
Afterwords is the city's premier gay and lesbian bookstore, focusing on literature, art, gender studies, sociology, and more, as well as magazines and newspapers from around the country. Afterwords also features a comfortable espresso bar that is very conducive to reading. (East Side)

BOOK BAY
407 E. Silver Spring Dr.
Whitefish Bay
414/962-3444
Strictly for kids, Bookbay carries literature for children of all ages—picture books for newborns, storybooks for toddlers, easy readers for young children, and right on up the line. So if your kids want to read early and read often, Bookbay is your source. (East Side)

CUDAHY NEWS AND HOBBY
4758 S. Packard Ave.
Cudahy
414/769-1500
If the magazine exists, it is to be found at Cudahy News. Magazines about cars, sports, fashion, politics, fishing, and photography, journals about art, literature, and social science. Every magazine imaginable is here—and dozens that you could never have dreamed up. (South Side)

HARRY W. SCHWARTZ BOOKS
17145 W. Blue Mound Rd.
Brookfield
262/797-6140
When the big chains started a turf war in Milwaukee a few years ago, Schwartz Books, far and away the city's favorite locally owned bookstores, dug in to fight the good fight. With four large and friendly stores throughout the metropolitan area, Schwartz is simply the spot to buy books in Milwaukee. You'll also find fantastic bargains on the remaindered books tables. (Waukesha County)

PEOPLE'S BOOKS
2122 E. Locust St.
Milwaukee
414/962-0575
As its name might suggest, People's Books specializes in literature from the left-hand side of the spectrum. Fiction and poetry, history and the social sciences, the arts and belles lettres, and hard-to-find books are well represented. Don't look for best-sellers, just some of the best books. (East Side)

WOODLAND PATTERN
720 E. Locust St.
Milwaukee
414/263-5001
Woodland Pattern is the most remarkable non-mainstream bookstore in Wisconsin. For two decades, this Riverwest bookseller has specialized

Worth the Trip

Some Wisconsin products are so good that people are willing to drive miles out of their way to get them. Racine, 30 miles south of Milwaukee, is famous for kringle, *a rich Danish coffee cake. Kringle comes with a variety of fruit fillings, but absolute tops is rhubarb, only available in spring. A great exponent of kringle kulture is* **O&H Bakery**, *1841 Douglas Avenue, Racine. They ship nationwide: call 800/227-6665.*

An hour north of Milwaukee, Sheboygan is home of the best bratwurst in the state. Local butcher shops square off in an annual sausage competition, and the winner in recent years has been **Miesfeld's Market**, *1922 North 15th Street, 920/452-1214.*

While in Sheboygan County, stop at the **Gibbsville Cheese Factory** *(County Highway OO, State Highway 32, Gibbsville, 920/564-3242). Its sharp cheddar is among the very best anywhere. Prices are low, and the factory ships anywhere.*

 **TIP** Come summer, farmer's markets pop up around Milwaukee. The biggest is the West Allis Farmer's Market (W. National Ave. at S. 66th St.), which opens at one o'clock on Tuesday, Thursday, and Saturday, and draws fruit, flower, and vegetable growers from around the state. Other markets run downtown Saturday morning at Cathedral Square and Wednesday on Zeidler Union Square.

in the work of small presses, and its stock is particularly deep in fiction, cultural studies, and, above all, poetry. Carrying journals, chapbooks, and self-published works from around the country and the world, Woodland Pattern is a poetry treasure trove. (North Side)

OTHER STORES OF NOTE

ATOMIC RECORDS
1813 E. Locust St.
Milwaukee
414/332-3663

Proudly proclaiming "we were alternative before alternative was alternative," Atomic is the least-average record store in town. It stocks independent labels, posters and T shirts, and a large selection of used CDs. The staff listens to plenty of music and is more than willing to help you get what you want. (East Side)

DISCOUNT LIQUOR
5031 W. Oklahoma Ave.
Milwaukee
414/545-2175

Discount Liquor is the British Museum of liquor stores, a grocery store–sized building with aisle after aisle of every conceivable imported and domestic variety of beer, wine, and booze. The staff has a deep knowledge of their trade, and, best of all, the prices are 15 percent lower than anywhere else. From microbrews to cold half-barrels, this is the place. (South Side)

EUROPEAN SAUSAGE
1985 S. Muskego Ave.
Milwaukee
414/384-7320

Tucked in an out-of-the-way neighborhood in the heart of the south side, European Sausage is a tiny butcher shop making some of the best sausage in the city. The butchers are Polish, with accents and a touch with the spices borne of decades of experience. For connoisseurs of kielbasa, European sausage is a temple worthy of pilgrimage. (South Side)

FLIPVILLE RECORDS
1936 N. Farwell Ave.
Milwaukee
414/272-1131

Vinyl's not dead. Flipville is the city's source for record collectors, with a mind-boggling selection in all musical styles. Is your collection missing that rare record on which Faron Young sings theme songs from TV Westerns? You'll find it at Flipville. The store stocks vintage toys as well, with a special emphasis on

> ## Used Book Bonanza
>
> **Blake Books**: Quiet and well organized (714 N. Milwaukee St., 414/272-1000)
>
> **Book Seller**: Located in the Central Library, this great shop stocks hardcovers, paperbacks, records, and other materials that have been removed from library circulation. (814 W. Wisconsin Ave. 414/286-2142)
>
> **Constant Reader**: First editions and signed books (1627 E. Irving Place, 414/291-0452)
>
> **Downtown Books**: Big selection, adequately organized (327 E. Wisconsin Ave., 414/276-5330)
>
> **Renaissance Books**: The sprawling downtown location on four floors (834 N. Plankinton St., 414/271-6850) requires a tour guide. A second location in Mitchell International is the best airport bookstore ever (414/747-4526).

Mexican pro-wrestling figurines. (East Side)

GEORGE WATTS AND SONS
761 N. Jefferson St.
Milwaukee
414/291-5120
www.georgewatts.com

George Watts is the dean of the ritzy shops along Jefferson Street. Carrying crystal, china, and silver, along with high-end cookware, Watts has been outfitting the homes of Milwaukee's upper crust for more than a century. Names like Haviland, Tiffany, Baccarat, and Waterford are common, as are customers in Chanel suits. (Downtown)

GOLDI
4114 N. Oakland Ave.
Shorewood
414/961-9200

Goldi is one of the chief purveyors of that east-side look. Selling clothes, shoes, and accessories that are fresh, a little funky, and decidedly undowdy, Goldi's Soho-sophisticate approach to clothing appeals to women who are over 15 and under 50 at heart. Cool stuff—not kids' stuff—from small designers and producers. (East Side)

HOUSE OF HARLEY DAVIDSON
6221 W. Layton Ave.
Greenfield
414/282-2211

Where better than Milwaukee to buy your hog. The city's oldest Harley dealer has loads of new and used bikes to ogle and acres of gleaming chrome. If you were born to be wild but can't afford the hardware (and who can?), House of Harley Davidson still makes for fun browsing, with motorcycle accessories, clothing, and leather. (South Side)

JAZZMAN
4114 N. Oakland Ave.
Shorewood
414/967-0603
The male counterpart of Goldi, Jazzman not only shares a building with the women's clothing boutique but also has a kindred attitude. Casual, downtown, and funky are the watchwords, with shirts, sweaters, pants, shoes, and accessories that would be at home in a Walker's Point loft or at a Third Ward gallery opening. Kenneth Cole, Johnny Cotton, and like names are found on the racks. (East Side)

LAACKE AND JOYS
1433 N. Water St.
Milwaukee
414/271-7878
Locally operated since 1844 (!), Laacke and Joys is Milwaukee's original outdoor-sports outfitter. Camping, backpacking, paddling, and Nordic and Alpine skiing equipment is all stocked with remarkable depth in this huge store. So if the outdoors is calling you—or you just want to dress as though it is—this store along the Milwaukee River should be your first stop. (Downtown)

LINCOLN ART POTTERY
636 W. Lincoln Ave.
Milwaukee
414/643-1101
Working in the tradition of Arts and Crafts potters, the Lincoln Art Pottery produces hand-thrown pots, dishes, mugs, platters, vases, and decorative items that have that 1930s flair. With lustrous glazes and workmanlike forms, the ceramics made at this storefront potter don't blow with the winds of fashion, but rather remain true to a solid historical vision. (South Side)

MANHATTAN TEXTILES
10505 W. North Ave.
Wauwatosa
414/774-5858
The Bergdorf-Goodman of fabric shops, Manhattan Textiles carries cloth that is nothing short of splendid: designer fabrics, hard-to-find fabrics, fabrics of extremely high quality and unusual design. This is the best place is town to find fabric for reupholstering furniture, building a wedding gown, or any other sewing project that must transcend the ordinary. (West Side)

MILWAUKEE ART MUSEUM SHOP
750 N. Lincoln Memorial Dr.
Milwaukee
414/224-3210
This bookstore and gift shop showcases all kinds of arty goods for kids and adults. With stationary, postcards, trinkets, jewelry, toys and games, even clothes, the MAM shop will bring out the creative urge in gift givers. Exhibition catalogs, art books, and calendars are stocked in quantity. Satellite shops may be found in Brookfield at 18900 West Bluemound Road and at Mitchell International Airport. (Downtown)

MILWAUKEE MAP SERVICE
959 N. Mayfair Rd.
Wauwatosa

414/774-1300
If you're lost, plot a course for Milwaukee Map Service. With a selection that is among the largest in the country, Milwaukee Map carries regional and local road maps for most parts of the world, globes, atlases, topographic maps, survey maps, nautical charts, national park maps, star charts, and more. You can get there from here. (West Side)

MR. SPORTS
11018 N. Port Washington Rd.
Mequon
262/241-5750
Packer Backers, the Brew Crew, and sports fans of all kinds can find mementos of famous moments at Mr. Sports. Billed as Wisconsin's foremost sports memorabilia dealer, Mr. Sports carries autographed items, jerseys used by the stars, caps, balls, and significant hockey pucks. If someone in your family would die for a cheesehead hat worn by Brett Favre, this is the place to find it. (North Side)

NAPOLEON'S
3948 N. Maryland Ave.
Shorewood
414/962-6730
Napoleon's is a boy's toy and hobby store. Thousands of toy soldiers—from the Trojan War to Desert Storm—line the shelves, and boys (and men who are boys inside) can spend hours planning backyard Waterloos. The store also carries military games, along with classics like chess and backgammon. (East Side)

NORTHERN CHOCOLATE
2036 N. Martin Luther King Dr., Milwaukee
414/372-1885
Excellent chocolate alone is not what makes Northern Chocolate so special. A one-man operation, the chocolatier at Northern collects antique European chocolate molds. He produces bunnies drinking beer, Santa Clauses, Jacks and Jills, and other whimsical and delicate chocolate statues. Northern Chocolate has very limited hours, so call ahead. Note:

Mader's Tower Gallery, p. 133

Greater Milwaukee Conv. and Visitors Bureau

The chocolatier is an idiosyncratic fellow and master of his domain. Among his convictions is a strong antipathy to fur; if you're wearing any, expect to have the door slammed in your face. (North Side)

OWL IMPORTS
7546 W. GREENFIELD AVE., WEST ALLIS
414/453-0404

Boasting the largest display of clocks in Wisconsin, Owl Imports is a place you want to avoid on the hour. The chiming, ding-donging, and cuckoo-ing is enough to drive you crazy. With more that 1,500 hundred clocks, Owl Imports will keep you timely, and if that's not enough, Owl displays more than 2,000 beer steins, hundreds of music boxes, and much more. (South Side)

ROGER STEVENS MENSWEAR
428 E. Wisconsin Ave.
Milwaukee
414/277-9010

The name Roger Stevens is synonymous with men's clothing that is conservative, tailored, and of extremely high quality—impeccable, in other words, in both taste and construction. Clothes bought at Roger Stevens will be found in corner offices overlooking the lake, boardrooms, courtrooms, and dining rooms of the exclusive University, Athletic, Yacht, and Milwaukee Clubs. (Downtown)

T. H. STEMPER COMPANY
1125 E. Potter St.
Milwaukee
414/744-3610

Ever wonder where priests buy their albs? In Milwaukee, Stemper is the source for church goods and reli-

Village Bazaar

gious items of all kinds. It's the largest and most complete religious-goods showroom in the state. Statuary, baptismal fonts, glow-in-the-dark rosaries, dozens of varieties of candles, gifts galore, and vestments are all on display, and there's even a consignment center selling used church equipment. (South Side)

VILLAGE BAZAAR
2201 N. Farwell Ave.
Milwaukee
414/224-9675

The smell of sandalwood permeates this Northpoint jewelry and home-decor boutique. Specializing in art and artifacts from Saharan Africa and the Middle East, Bazaar's buyers have great eyes for the delicate and unique. Earrings, bracelets, musical instruments, statuary, textiles, and more are to be found, along with the area's best selection of amber jewelry. (East Side)

W. WALTHERS
5619 W. Florist Ave.

Milwaukee
414/461-1050
All aboard! W. Walthers is the world's largest supplier of model train equipment. The company's Milwaukee showroom stocks 72,000 items from 400 manufacturers—from to-scale Milwaukee Road engines to power supplies to miniature trees to line the tracks. (North Side)

DEPARTMENT STORES

BOSTON STORE
331 W. Wisconsin Ave.
Milwaukee
414/347-4141
www.carsons.com
Making a new commitment to quality, all of the Boston Stores have been fully remodeled and upgraded. The stores' product lines have taken an upscale leap as well, with clothing by name designers, excellent furniture, many of the classier cosmetic lines, and the sorts of service one expects from a nice deparment store. Boston Store anchors seven malls throughout the metro area. (Downtown)

GOLDMANN'S
930 W. Mitchell St.
Milwaukee
414/645-9100
Goldmann's, the last remaining department store of a bygone era, can best be described as idiosyncratic. It's the best place in town to find hi-test women's underwear in unusually sturdy styles and sizes (trusses, say, or macro-girdles), novelty lamps, and weird knickknacks. (See sidebar on page 147.) Goldmann's fabric section is also formidable, and the candy counter is great. (South Side)

KOHL'S DEPARTMENT STORE
9060 N. Green Bay Rd.
Brown Deer
414/355-6611
One of the country's hottest department-store chains, Milwaukee-based Kohl's is rapidly expanding throughout the East and Midwest. A moderately priced, everyday kind of store, Kohl's carries casual clothing, linens, shoes, small electronics, jewelry, and watches. Locations throughout Milwaukee. (North Side)

MARSHALL FIELD'S
Mayfair Mall
Wauwatosa
414/471-3700
Field's bears the torch as Milwaukee's highest class department store. In addition to quality ready-to-wear clothing lines like DKNY and Eileen Fischer, Field's also carries high-end housewares, quality rugs, furniture, name-brand cosmetics, jewelry—the whole shebang. Expect to be pampered, at least a little, at Marshall Field's. (West Side)

YOUNKER'S
Southridge Mall
5300 S. 76th St.
Greendale
414/421-6601
Younker's, once perceived as only a notch or two above Kohl's, has really improved its image in the last couple of years. You won't find the biggest name designer wear here, but you will find quality clothes and housewares at reasonable prices. It's middle of the road, but Younker's offers enough service, selection,

Grand Avenue Retail Center

and quality to anchor Milwaukee's largest mall. (South Side)

SHOPPING MALLS

BAYSHORE MALL
5900 N. Port Washington Rd.
Glendale
414/963-8780
The only indoor shopping center on the North Shore, Bayshore Mall houses a mix of stores, big and small, many of which are not found elsewhere in the area. Anchored by Sears and an upscale, recently remodeled Boston Store, Bayshore is notable for Zany Brainy—the mother of all toy stores—hip urban fashions for men and women at Ma Jolie, and a Barnes and Noble bookstore. (East Side)

BROOKFIELD SQUARE MALL
95 N. Moorland Rd.
Brookfield
262/797-7245
Brookfield Square is a retail focus for the entire western half of the metro area. Brookfield Square is a comfortable, large-ish, and fully average suburban mall. All the big chain stores are here—The Gap, Victoria's Secret, The Limited—and rumors of a Bloomingdale's entering the region are unfounded. (Waukesha County)

EAST TOWNE SQUARE
1505 W. Mequon Rd.
Mequon
This tiny mall has no anchors, no department stores, no run-of-the-mill—just a handful of specialty boutiques. High-end women's apparel is represented by Valentina, First Resort, and Faye's. Landmark Luggage sells fancy leather goods, and Benedon features jewelry that can only be described as exquisite. East Towne Square, like its nouveau-riche suburb, is a little snooty. (North Side)

GRAND AVENUE
275 W. Wisconsin Ave.
Milwaukee
414/224-0655

Grand Avenue, covering four city blocks downtown, suffers from a split personality. By day, the mall is habituated by besuited businesspeople, but by evening it becomes a hip-hop hangout for kids in baggy pants. It features a lovely Boston Store, Eddie Bauer, and Banana Republic on one hand and lots of athletic-shoe stores on the other. Notable stores include Premaman (a European kid's clothing store), Jay Jacobs, and The Limited. Connected to hotels, office towers, and the convention center by skywalk, Grand Avenue remains the focus of much downtown retail activity. (Downtown)

MAYFAIR MALL
2500 N. Mayfair Rd.
Wauwatosa
414/771-1300
Mayfair is Milwaukee's upscale mall—the one with all the "exceptional" stores—with Marshall Field's and Boston Store anchoring. The mall's vast interior includes Pottery Barn, Abercrombie and Fitch, Anne Taylor, Williams-Sonoma, Coach, and much more. With a large food court and a googolplex cinema, Mayfair is a destination in itself. (West Side)

NORTHRIDGE SHOPPING CENTER
7700 W. Brown Deer Rd.
Milwaukee
414/354-1804
While the northwest side has grown rapidly, it has not become as affluent as speculators hoped. Northridge, built to support the upper middle class that never really arrived, isn't bad, it just can't attract the best stores. It has a Younker's, a JCPenney, and more than 100 smaller shops, but if you don't live in the area, Northridge is not particularly attractive. (North Side)

SOUTHRIDGE MALL
5300 S. 76th St.
Greendale
414/421-1102
The workhorse of Milwaukee shop-

Mayfair Mall

> ## Odd Shopping
>
> *Goldman's Department Store on Mitchell Street stocks a huge selection of, er, unusual items:*
> 1. *Smiley Face latch-hook pillow sham kits*
> 2. *Dresser scarves*
> 3. *Whoopee cushions*
> 4. *Log-rolling shoes*
> 5. *Close Encounters of the Third Kind word search books*
> 6. *Plastic lace by the yard*
> 7. *Beer mugs with attached bicycle bells*
> 8. *Alarm clocks shaped like gold ingots*
> 9. *Rhinestone-studded pantyhose*
> 10. *Bab-O Cleanser*

ping centers, Southridge is like a city unto itself. It's a workaday sort of mall, without the glitz of Mayfair or the urban tinge of Grand Avenue. Anchored by Boston Store, Kohl's, Sears, JCPenney, and Younker's, and with nearly 150 stores in between, Southridge is where you shop for what you need, not necessarily for what you want. (South Side)

OUTLET STORES

KOSS FACTORY OUTLET STORE
4129 N. Port Washington Rd.
Glendale
414/964-5000
Koss began making headphones for the military during the Second World War, and now the company is one of the world's largest suppliers of stereophones and compact speakers. The goods are prized by recording-studio technicians as well as knowledgeable consumers. You'll find great discounts on stereophones, lightweight portable stereo systems, and high-def speakers for home computer systems. (East Side)

MITCHELL HANDBAGS AND LUGGAGE
226 N. Water St.
Milwaukee
414/272-5942
Once a manufacturer for Coach and other fine handbag companies, Mitchell Leather now sells directly to department stores. The company's outlet store offers portfolios, handbags, and the finest briefcases you have ever seen. Nothing quite perfect in the store? Tour the factory, pick your tanned leather, and custom order a bag—all at significant savings. (Downtown)

10

SPORTS AND RECREATION

Welcome, sports fans! Welcome to cheesehead country! Milwaukee, true to its blue-collar roots, is a sports town of occasionally raving-lunatic proportions. When the Green Bay Packers won the Super Bowl in 1997, the partying on North Water Street—the hooting and the hollering—went on uninterrupted for 48 hours.

At least that's what it seemed like. The point is, Milwaukeeans love their Bucks, their Brewers, their Admirals, and "their" Green Bay Packers. They love them even when those teams seem particularly unlovable, as the Brewers baseball team has been in the last few seasons. If you visit any of the city's myriad sports bars on Football Sunday—and every tavern in town is a sports bar on Football Sunday—or hang out with the shirtless, beer-soaked bleacher creatures at a Brewers game, you'll get a firsthand look at this adoration. (Don't worry if that's not your scene: County Stadium has alcohol-free Family Sections, too.)

And when Milwaukeeans aren't spectating, they're playing. The metro area offers opportunities to participate in every sport you can imagine and some, like curling, that you probably can't imagine. Whether you want to climb rock walls, take a hike in the woods, roll a lawn bowl, roll a bowling ball, serve an ace, drop a putt, or drop a line for a big salmon on the big lake, Milwaukee provides no end of options.

PROFESSIONAL SPORTS

Auto Racing

MILWAUKEE MILE
Wisconsin State Fair Park
7722 W. Greenfield Ave.
West Allis
414/453-8277
www.milmile.com/races
The "legendary oval." The "fastest mile in racing." Call it what you will, if you're a race fan you already know about the Milwaukee Mile. It's the country's oldest operating major speedway—the first races were held in 1903—and hosts the CART Indy cars on the weekend after the Indianapolis 500 for a 200-mile, full-throttle extravaganza. Other NASCAR car and truck races and stock car competitions are held here throughout the summer. This is where the big boys gun their engines. (West Side)

ROAD AMERICA
N7390 Hwy. 67
Elkhart Lake
920/892-4576
www.roadamerica.com
Race fans are more than willing to make the pilgrimage to Road America—even though it's located 60 miles north of Milwaukee. The only permanent road-racing track on the continent, Road America's four-mile track twists and turns through the rolling hills of the Kettle-Moraine countryside. It's as though these professional racers, the biggest names in the business, are running at top speed along country lanes—far more exciting than an oval race. There's even a Skip Barber racing school here, so you can get behind the wheel and put the pedal to the metal.

Baseball

MILWAUKEE BREWERS BASEBALL CLUB
Milwaukee County Stadium
201 S. 46th St.
Milwaukee
414/933-9000
www.milwaukeebrewers.com
The parking lot fills with tailgaters hours before the first pitch is tossed out, and the smell of grilling bratwurst wafts over the Menonomee River Valley long after the last out is recorded. Milwaukee loves its Brew Crew. Moving to the National League in 1998, the Brewers have created great rivalries with the Chicago Cubs and St. Louis Cardinals. Miller Park—the city's new stadium with retractable dome, set to open its doors in 2000—should give fans a lot to cheer about in the new millennium. Tickets are always available on game day. Tickets: $5–$22. (West Side)

Basketball

MILWAUKEE BUCKS
Bradley Center
1001 N. Fourth St.
Milwaukee
414/227-0500
www.bucks.com
Though the 1998–99 season was marred by a lockout (and nationwide fan indifference), the Milwaukee Bucks seem to be perched on the edge of greatness. Hopefully, they're ready to fall over the brink. The talent—Glenn Robinson, Ray Allen—is there, and with new coach George Karl the team may be able to make a run at the title. The Bradley Center fills up on game days (particularly when the Bulls are in town), and the

SPORTS AND RECREATION

atmosphere is one of basketball party. Tickets: $13–$35, with half-price bonus nights throughout the season. (Downtown)

Football

MILWAUKEE MUSTANGS
Bradley Center
1001 N. Fourth St.
Milwaukee
414/272-1555
www.milwaukeemustangs.com
When the Green Bay Packers pack it up in December (or rather January, these days), Wisconsinites still yearn for the bone-crushing blows, fleet interceptions, and think-on-your-feet pass plays of professional football. Enter the Milwaukee Mustangs of the arena football league. Played indoors from April to August, arena football, with its short field, high scores, and incredibly fast pace, has been wowing fans for more than five years. Admission: $7–$34. (Downtown)

Ice Hockey

MILWAUKEE ADMIRALS
Bradley Center
1001 N. Fourth St.
Milwaukee
414/227-0550
www.milwaukeeadmirals.com
For sheer adrenalin-pumping excitement, nothing beats a good hockey game: the thunderous cross checks, the blazing slapshots. The Admirals, Milwaukee's International Hockey League franchise, have been lacing up their ice skates here for nearly three decades. The team is affiliated with the Nashville Predators of the NHL. With affordable admission, more than 40 home games a year, and hot contests against division rivals the Chicago Wolves, professional hockey in Milwaukee is, as they say, a "smashing good time." Tickets: $5–$18. (Downtown)

Soccer

MILWAUKEE RAMPAGE
Uihlein Soccer Park
7101 W. Good Hope Rd.
Milwaukee
414/358-2655
Outdoor professional soccer with the Rampage means great family sports entertainment at great prices. Playing teams from all over the country, the Rampage does its trick at the Uihlein Soccer Park, an extravagant set of fields that is also home of the Milwaukee Kickers Soccer Club. Sure, the games are low scoring, but the fun is in the play, and these guys have a few tricks up their sleeves. Tickets: $6–$8. (North Side)

MILWAUKEE WAVE
Bradley Center
1001 N. Fourth St.
Milwaukee
414/241-7500
www.wavesoccer.com
It's faster than lightning, it's high-scoring, and it's a lot of fun. Professional indoor soccer with the Milwaukee Wave is one of the most popular sports tickets in town. The team, has been playing here since 1984. In 1997–98, the team finally defeated archrivals the St. Louis Ambush to capture the league championship in what has since been dubbed a "Title Wave." This team is good, the crowds are rambunctious, and, these days, everybody tends to leave happy. Tickets: $10–$14. (Downtown)

Milwaukee Bucks basketball, p. 149

Volleyball

MILLER LITE PRO BEACH VOLLEYBALL TOUR
Bradford Beach
2400 N. Lincoln Memorial Dr.
Milwaukee
Usually associated more with California and the Pacific Ocean than Milwaukee's Lake Michigan beaches, professional beach volleyball, sponsored by Miller Brewing, comes to Bradford Beach every July. The golden boys and girls of the tour spend a long weekend digging, setting, and slamming before hundreds of fans. Miller sets up a beer tent (naturally), and most everybody takes off their shirts to catch a few rays. (East Side)

AMATEUR SPORTS

BADGER HOCKEY SHOWDOWN
Bradley Center
1001 N. Fourth St.
Milwaukee
414/227-0700
This annual ice hockey invitational draws college hockey fans from across the country. The University of Wisconsin Badgers and three other teams compete over a December weekend for top honors in this event. The winner often ends up earning the NCAA title later in the season. (Downtown)

MARQUETTE UNIVERSITY BASKETBALL
Bradley Center
1001 N. Fourth St.
Milwaukee
414/288-7447
Marquette University has been a basketball powerhouse since the Al McGuire days of the late 1970s. Now the Golden Eagles (the school's Warriors name was changed in 1995) are perpetual contenders in the annual NCAA tournament. The Marquette women's team, which also entertains high hopes every season, plays at the Wisconsin Center Arena, located at 500 West Kilbourn Avenue. Tickets: $8–$24. (Downtown)

MARQUETTE UNIVERSITY SOCCER
Valley Fields
1818 W. Canal St.
Milwaukee
414/288-7447
The Marquette men's and women's soccer teams, playing at their new facility in the Menomonee River Valley across I-94 from the university, have particularly strong rivalries with the University of Wisconsin-Milwaukee Panthers and the UW Badgers, who travel here from Madison. The Golden Eagles have been contenders in

NCAA competition in the last several seasons. (Downtown)

PETTIT NATIONAL ICE CENTER
500 S. 84th St.
Milwaukee
414/266-0100
www.thepettit.com
The Pettit Center is the country's only indoor 400-meter oval, and one of few sites anywhere to consistently host competitions featuring the world's fastest ice skaters. Home of the U.S. Olympic Speed-skating Team, whose members regularly train here, the Pettit Center hosts national and international competitions like the U.S. All-around Speed-skating Championships, held in December 1998. (See also Chapter 5: "Sights and Attractions.") Admission prices vary. (West Side)

UNIVERSITY OF WISCONSIN-MILWAUKEE SOCCER
Engelmann Field
3200 block of N. Cramer St.
Milwaukee
414/229-5886
The Panthers men's and women's soccer teams tackle the competition in fall and spring at the university's Engelmann Field, located at the corner of North Cramer and East Hartford Streets. The games are relatively sparsely attended but don't lack for excitement. A couple of graduating seniors go pro every few years, signing with teams like the Milwaukee Wave. (East Side)

WAUWATOSA CURLING CLUB
Hart Park
7300 Chestnut St.
Wauwatosa
414/453-2875

Curling is sort of like frozen lawn bowling, and its popularity is primarily centered around the Great Lakes in both the United States and Canada. In competition, players slide a 40-pound stone-with-handle toward a target down the ice. Teammates with brooms sweep madly ahead of the stone to achieve maximum glide, and their competitors do the same, trying to bump them out of the way. The WCC is the home of curling in Milwaukee, and it hosts regional, national, and even international tournaments. You can watch or try for yourself. (West Side)

RECREATION

Bicycle Trails

BROWN DEER VELODROME
Brown Deer Park
7835 N. Green Bay Rd.
Milwaukee
414/352-7502
Not a bike trail but rather a bicycle track, the velodrome in Brown Deer Park is used by local cycling clubs for races. Don't expect to find the sort of steeply walled stadium that you've seen on TV during the Olympics. The Brown Deer Velodrome is more an outdoor track with inclined curves at the corners. Still, not having to brake into turns allows cyclists to work up an unholy head of steam. (North Side)

GLACIAL DRUMLIN STATE TRAIL
262/646-3025
Wisconsin completed many of the country's first Rails-to-Trails conversions, turning disused railroad rights of way into hike and bike thoroughfares. The Glacial Drumlin Trail runs

47 miles, from the city of Waukesha nearly to Madison. Along the way it passes through glacially mediated countryside, a number of small towns, and a couple of state parks. The grade is mostly level, there are some lovely bridges, and much of the trail is paved, making it a good choice

Hit the Trail

If you're a gearhead with a love of single-track riding or you just want to take a nice walk in the woods, check out these hot spots:

- *__John Muir Trails__. Located in the southern unit of the Kettle-Moraine State Forest near the town of La Grange, the John Muir Trails are the most popular—and best maintained—spot for mountain biking in southeastern Wisconsin. Extremely hilly and passing through many kinds of environments, the trails cover more than 20 miles of forest, prairie, kettles, and sandhills. Another trail complex across the road is open to foot traffic only and is loved by hikers, bird-watchers, and cross-country skiers. Trail fee required; stop at the state forest visitors-center on Highway 59, two miles west of the village of Eagle, 262/594-2135.*

- *__Milwaukee River Trails__. Both the east and west banks of the Milwaukee River are home to trails used—not quite officially—for extreme single-track biking. West river trails start where the river crosses East North Avenue and continue north to Kern Park and beyond. The east river trail begins in Riverside Park (some parts of the park are closed to biking due to erosion) and continues north to Lincoln Park. Note, these trails are also used by dog walkers, birders, and hikers, and they are very narrow—so be careful when riding fast.*

- *__Menomonee River Trail__. The city's newest hike and bike trail runs along the south bank of the Menomonee River from Milwaukee County Stadium east to South 26th Street. Another stretch continues east to South 13th Street. Used by anglers and walkers as well as cyclists, the trail features odd juxtapositions of decaying industry and blooming nature: rusting viaduct superstructures compete with tall river grasses and dense new tree growth.*

Milwaukee County Parks are home to 16 public golf courses—from par-three courses to championship links that host PGA competition. The county offers a special discount card for frequent golfers that provides quite a considerable savings if you're strolling the fairways more than once or twice a season.

You can make tee-time reservations at the county's better courses—Brown Deer, Currie Park, Whitnall, and several others—by calling the golf reservation hotline at 414/643-4653.

for recreational cyclists and families who want to take a little ride in the country. Access points are found in Waukesha, Wales, and Dousman. Nominal trail fees may be remitted at stations along the route. (Waukesha County)

LAKE COUNTRY RECREATION TRAIL
Another Rails-to-Trails conversion, this Waukesha County trail follows an old Milwaukee Interurban Railway route. The trailhead for the eight-mile long path is found at I-94 and County Highway T, just east of the enormous Country Inn Hotel. Surfaced in crushed stone, as are many such trails, the Lake Country Trail winds its way through the numerous inland lakes of central Waukesha, ending in the town of Delafield. A bike ride, jog, or hike on this level trail is a great way to see the countryside. (Waukesha County)

OAK LEAF TRAIL
414/257-6100
The Oak Leaf trail is a 90-mile bike route that circles the entire county. Its most popular and safest segment, for both commuters and recreational bikers out for a spin, is the lakefront loop. Running from Juneau Park downtown through Veteran's, McKinley, and Lake Parks, the loop is entirely off-road. Another stretch runs from downtown Milwaukee along the Milwaukee River on an abandoned railroad bed up through Estabrook Park. This segment is entirely below street grade and crosses no roadways, making for particularly enjoyable biking. The trail is heavily used by cyclists, dog walkers, runners, and in-line skaters, so be on your toes. (East Side)

Boating

GRANT PARK BOAT LAUNCH
2400 Oak Creek Pkwy.
South Milwaukee
414/762-8417
Located at the mouth of Oak Creek, this boat launch on the far southern end of the county lets you access good fishing and boating without having to negotiate the outer and inner harbors. A launch fee is charged at all Milwaukee County facilities. (South Side)

MCKINLEY BOAT LAUNCH
1750 N. Lincoln Memorial Dr.
Milwaukee
414/273-5244
Located at the county's huge public marina complex and adjacent to Government Pier, this launch is remark-

ably user-friendly for a busy facility. Launching your power- or sailboat here will allow you access to the most popular parts of the lakefront and great fishing. (East Side)

MILWAUKEE RIVER BOAT LAUNCH
700 block of S. Water St.
Milwaukee
The benefits of this public launch are twofold: great views and the ability to easily cruise the river downtown. Launching into the river just upstream of the harbor mouth, boaters get to see the skyline from an otherwise unreachable point while sailing out through the inner harbor. The riverfront downtown, meanwhile, beckons with riverside restaurants and taverns and plenty of docking space at entertainment facilities. (Downtown)

Bowling

AMF RED CARPET BOWLERO
11737 W. Burleigh St.
Wauwatosa

414/258-9000
If bowling were a religion (and for some Milwaukeeans it is), the AMF Red Carpet family of bowling centers would be its cathedrals and basilicas. The Bowlero is big and it's serious about bowling. Leagues, open bowling, bumper bowling, glow bowling, banquet rooms, billiard tables—heck, there's almost no reason to go home. Additional locations are found around town. (West Side)

HOLLER HOUSE
2042 W. Lincoln Ave.
Milwaukee
414/647-9284
Once upon a time, Milwaukee was dotted with small bowling alleys. Few of those Mom and Pop operations are running now, but you can still knock a few pins down at the Holler House Tavern. It's the city's oldest bowling alley (est. 1908) and claims to be the oldest operational alley in the country. Have a beer at the bar, then head to the basement where there are two lanes—fully un-automatic; kids set

Bradley Center

the pins up after you've rolled that strike! The Holler House speaks eloquently of an era when bowling was a social event on an intimate scale. (South Side)

KOZ'S MINI BOWL
2078 S. Seventh St.
Milwaukee
414/383-0560
Koz's is . . . well, Koz's has to be seen to be believed. It's an Up-North bar in the shadow of St. Josaphat's Basilica, with stuffed animals, ridiculously cheap tap beer, and, wonder of wonders, a set of mini-bowling lanes—like skittles or ninepins. Heft the palm-sized ball in your hand and let 'er rip toward the old wooden pins—the regulars can really grease that baby. Then (because this is Milwaukee, after all, and you shouldn't have to go without beer just because you're exercising) go get one of those 50-cent tappers between frames. (South Side)

ORIENTAL LANDMARK LANES
2220 N. Farwell Ave.
Milwaukee
414/278-8770
It's not the coolest bowling alley in town (that distinction is reserved for the Holler House), but Landmark Lanes in the Oriental complex is where cool people bowl around here. If regular open bowling isn't enough, try bumper bowling or blacklight bowling in a dark alley with a glow-in-the-dark ball. If that's not enough, there are pool tables and dart boards, three bars, a huge video arcade, and plenty of hipsters to ogle. (East Side)

VILLAGE BOWL
N86 W18330 Main St.,

Menomonee Falls
262/255-1580
Standard bowling center (26 lanes, automatic scoring) by day, headquarters for Rock 'n' Bowl after the leagues end on Friday and Saturday nights. Dim the lights, cue the loud music, get the beer flowing, and let the wild rumpus begin. When the pin with the blue stripe comes up in the headpin position, just roll a strike and the game is free. (North Side)

Fishing

JACK'S CHARTER SERVICE
McKinley Marina
1750 N. Lincoln Memorial Dr.
Milwaukee
414/482-2336
Captain Jack Remus has two big things going for him in the competitive sport charter fishing industry. First is a "no fish, no charge" policy: If you fail to land one legal fish, your deposit is refunded. Second, his boat holds the Wisconsin state record for largest Atlantic salmon. Combine that

Milwaukee Brewers, p. 149

© Joe Picciolo

with 18 years experience, and you're pretty much guaranteed a good fishing trip on Lake Michigan. Prices start at about $300 for a four-hour trip for four anglers. Mailing address: 2545 S. Delaware Ave., Milwaukee 53207. (East Side)

TAKE FIVE CHARTERS
McKinley Marina
1750 N. Lincoln Memorial Dr.
Milwaukee
414/871-FISH
Another charter boat out of McKinley Marina, Take Five's vessel is named the *Deborah Ann*. With all the latest fishing technology—electric downriggers, depth finders, deep-water temperature gauges, and hundreds of lures—Take Five will hook you up with a lunker chinook salmon, beautiful rainbow trout, or wily lake trout. Three-hour trips start at $145 for five or fewer persons. The boat is available for cruising the lake as well. Write to 10438 W. Herda Pl., Franklin WI 53132. (East Side)

Fitness Clubs

BRICKYARD GYM
2483 S. Kinnickinnic Ave.
Milwaukee
414/481-7113
Hardcore bodybuilding. Free weights. Bulging veins. Sweating, grunting men and women. If that's your scene, this is your place. (South Side)

IN MOTION
6870 N. Santa Monica Blvd.
Fox Point
414/352-6979
Billing itself as "Milwaukee's only fitness studio," In Motion is unique among area shape-up joints in that no contracts or memberships are required. In Motion offers all the latest and greatest workout fads: spinning, cardio-kickboxing, choreoweights, hip hop, power dance, and high-intensity yoga, which seems to be a contradiction in terms. (East Side)

Golf Courses

BROWN DEER GOLF COURSE
Brown Deer Park
7835 N. Green Bay Rd.
Milwaukee
414/352-8080
The premier public course in the area, Brown Deer hosts the Greater Milwaukee Open, an annual August stop on the PGA tour. (Tiger Woods played one of his first professional competitions here.) You'll encounter 18 holes, 6,716 yards, and a par of 71 that can eat up even experienced golfers. It's not cheap to play here, but it's worth it. Tee-time reservations should be made well in advance. (North Side)

CURRIE PARK GOLF COURSE
Currie Park
3535 N. Mayfair Rd.
Wauwatosa
414/453-7030
A nice course—set in the rolling hills on the northwest side of the city—Currie Park is designed to be challenging to experienced golfers but not utterly overwhelming to people who are newer to the sport. On the course grounds is the Currie Park Golf Dome, the county's indoor driving range, which opens in November and stays open through the winter. It's one of the few public spots to tee up when the snow is flying. (North Side)

INDOOR LINKS GOLF CENTER
1930 Bluemound Rd.
Waukesha
262/650-9155

It's January and your swing is getting rusty. Where do you go? Indoor Links, a virtual golf course (many courses, actually), will at least give you a facsimile of a golf game. Choose from 20 famous courses—like Pebble Beach or Mauna Kea—tee up at the first hole, and drive the ball toward the giant digital screen. A virtual ball then replaces yours and sails out onto the digital fairway. The technology is pretty sophisticated and a great cure for gloomy winter weather. (Waukesha County)

Northern Winter Fun

It's 20 below zero and the snow is piled up three feet deep? Well, that's no reason to stay indoors. Milwaukeeans take to the trails, the slopes, and the ice when winter descends.

Many sporting-goods stores rent cross-country skis by the day. If the snow is deep enough, a number of Milwaukee County Parks offer ski trails, including **Whitnall Park** and **Grant Park**.

Indoor skating rinks are one thing, but when the weather is crisp, county parks with lagoons make for great ice-skating and pick-up hockey games. **Lake Park**, **Veteran's Park**, **Kosciuszko Park**, **Humboldt Park**, and **Brown Deer Park** all have rinks.

Many area parks have great sledding hills. **Pulaski Park**, at 2701 South 16th Street, is one of the best, as is the area of the lakefront just east of the Northpoint Water Tower. Milwaukee County runs a terrifying toboggan slide at **Whitnall Park**. For a small fee, you can rent a toboggan and screech down a glacial moraine at breakneck speed.

Snowshoeing has become very popular in the last several years. Many area sports outfitters rent high-tech snowshoes, and when the snow is deep you can head to the **Schlitz Audubon Center** to hike the trails and lakeshore. (See Chapter 8: "Parks and Gardens.") **Pike Lake State Park**, about 35 miles north of Milwaukee on Highway 60 just east of Hartford, offers many miles of cross-country ski and snowshoeing trails. Call 414/644-5248 for information.

LAKE PARK GOLF COURSE
2800 N. Lake Dr.
Milwaukee
414/961-1763
This 18-hole, par-three course is squeezed into the south end of Lake Park. Great for beginning golfers or people who don't have the time for a major plan-ahead event, Lake Park's 1,100-yard course can't exactly be described as challenging, but it's close to downtown and impromptu tee times can often be accommodated. Club rental is available, too. (East Side)

WHITNALL PARK GOLF COURSE
5879 S. 92nd Street
Franklin
414/425-7931
One of the county's premiere courses, Whitnall Park is a spectacular setting for "a good walk spoiled." Designed to challenge low-handicap golfers, the course's rolling terrain and the winding Root River provide a pleasant backdrop for great golfing moments. And when you're done golfing, you can wander over to the Boerner Botanical Gardens to see some real greens. (South Side)

Horse Stables

MARY LYNN STABLES
1048 Lakefield Rd.
Grafton
414/377-0250
Catering to the "timid rider," Mary Lynn Stables is the perfect place for equestrian novices to enjoy a guided trail ride. Private and small group riding lessons are available, as is horse grooming and boarding and a series of summer riding-camp sessions. (North Side)

Milwaukee Mile, p. 149
© Dan Boyd

Ice-Skating Rinks

EBLE PARK ICE ARENA
19400 W. Bluemound Rd.
Brookfield
414/784-5155
Waukesha County built this lovely public ice arena to provide a home for the growing corps of youth hockey players and figure skaters in the area. It is the home of the Greater Milwaukee Figure Skating Club and numerous youth and adult hockey leagues. Open skating is scheduled daily year-round. Call for times. (Waukesha County)

PETTIT NATIONAL ICE CENTER
500 S. 84th St.
West Allis
414/266-0100
www.thepettit.com
Home rink of the U.S. Speed-skating Team and big enough to hold three 747s, the Pettit Center is one of the nation's major ice rinks. A 400-meter oval race course and two Olympic-size hockey and figure-skating rinks,

The Big Pond

There is much more to do on Lake Michigan than merely hit the beach. Many activities await summer-fun seekers in Veteran's, McKinley, Bradford, and Lake Parks, the greenbelt that stretches north of downtown Milwaukee on either side of North Lincoln Memorial Drive.

*If you are U.S. Sailing certified, it is sometimes possible to rent a 22-foot Ensign keelboat from the **Milwaukee Community Sailing Center**, the city's nonprofit learn-to-sail club. If you are unable to sail, the MCSC often provides sailboat rides out of McKinley Marina. Call 414/277-9094 for more information. You can also charter the Nor'wester, a 38-foot sloop built in 1926, for an afternoon on the lake. Prices start at $15 an hour per person. Call 414/939-3623 for information.*

*Sailboards, kayaks, canoes, and other personal watercraft are available for rent at McKinley Beach from Memorial Day through the beginning of autumn. Note: During much of the season, you'll need to rent a wetsuit if you're going to travel more than 100 or so yards from shore. Call the **Jet Ski Zone**, 414/630-5387, for more information.*

*Check out **High Rollers** (414/273-1343) in Veteran's Park to rent tandem bicycles, regular bikes, and in-line skates for tooling up and down the lakefront. With easy access to the Oak Leaf Trail and miles of gorgeous beach paths and piers to cruise, this is a great way to see the lakefront.*

*Many a schooner has found its final resting place on the bottom of Lake Michigan. If you're a scuba diver, there are dozens of wrecks off the Milwaukee shore just waiting to be explored. **Pirate's Cove Diving** organizes wreck dives year-round; call 414/482-1430.*

*Veteran's Park, projecting into Lake Michigan, is a great place to fly a kite. **Gift of Wings** (414/273-5483), a kite shop in the park at 1300 North Lincoln Memorial Drive, rents all kinds of kites by the hour. Kids and adults have a great time when these colorful, high-quality beauties lift off.*

 Call the Milwaukee County Pool and Beach Hotline to check on swimming conditions at the county's five Lake Michigan beaches. You'll get up-to-date information on air and water temperatures and the occasional beach closing (often due to high bacteria counts in the water when wind patterns are unfavorable). The number is 414/645-4806 or 414/961-6143.

a pro shop, skate repair and rental services, and a snack bar round out the facilities. Open skating sessions are held seven days a week, but times vary seasonally. Take a turn around the rink and you might find yourself side-by-side with Bonnie Blair—at least for a moment. Admission $4–$5, skate rental $2. (West Side)

WILSON PARK ICE ARENA
4001 S. 20th St.
Milwaukee
414/281-4610
In the pre–Bradley Center days, this Milwaukee County Park facility was home to the Milwaukee Admirals hockey team. Now, a lot of amateur and youth hockey is played here, and the arena is the practice ice of the amateur Badger Speed-skating Club. Open skating is available regularly, as are learn-to-skate programs for kids and adults. (South Side)

Roller-skating Rinks

SK8 U
10928 W. Oklahoma Ave.
West Allis
414/545-8444
It used to be named Wisconsin Skate University, in one of the better recreational puns around. But even with the streamlined moniker, SK8 U is still a great roller rink. Pop music blares, the lights flicker, and adolescents go around and around the polished wooden floor. Skate rentals available. (South Side)

Swimming Pools and Beaches

BRADFORD BEACH
2400 N. Lincoln Memorial Dr.
Milwaukee
414/962-8809
The city's main people-watching beach, Bradford is definitely the hang-out zone. (See also Chapter 8: "Parks and Gardens") As far as swimming goes, it's almost too crowded to get into the water on summer weekends, but at other times of the week the beach is a great place for a dip in Lake Michigan. Lifeguards are on duty during daylight hours in summer. (East Side)

GRANT PARK
100 Hawthorne Ave.
South Milwaukee
414/762-1550
The beach at Grant Park is lovely: big, clean, and with a majestic view of Lake Michigan. In many ways, it's the best beach in Milwaukee County, and though it's busy on hot July days, it is large enough to handle the pressure of many swimmers, sunbathers, and beach combers. See Chapter 8:

"Parks and Gardens" for more information on Lake Michigan beaches. (South Side)

NOYES POOL
8235 W. Good Hope Rd.
Milwaukee
414/353-1252
One of Milwaukee County's three year-round indoor swimming facilities, Noyes Pool is very, very well used. Open swimming is featured

Belay On!

Though Milwaukee isn't known for its chasms and canyons, the area has a couple of interesting places where rock climbers can practice their art.

*An indoor climbing wall is located at **REI**, the big sports outfitter, at its Brookfield location (13100 W. Capitol Dr., Brookfield, 262/783-6150). The store offers climbing clinics and classes year-round.*

*Also on the far west side, you'll find an indoor wall—complete with caves and overhangs—at **Adventure Rock** (21250 W. Capitol Dr., 262/790-6800). Call for a schedule of classes and open climbing sessions.*

*For an odd climbing experience in the middle of the city, rock hounds in the know head to the **Oak Leaf Trail**. This Rails-to-Trails conversion runs parallel to the lakefront on an abandoned railroad grade below street level. Many climbers practice on the vertical walls, made of huge limestone blocks, that form the street overpasses, and it's not unusual to find people suspended in harnesses twenty or more feet above the trail. The wall where East Lafayette Place crosses the trail is particularly popular, as it is the tallest and most difficult around.*

*Finally, for serious climbing near the Milwaukee area, it's worth the drive to **Devil's Lake State Park**. A geologic oddity for the region, the glacial lake features a sheer rock wall that climbs more than 150 feet up its western shore. The lake is very popular—partly because it's not too far from Madison—and after your climb you can hike the ridge or take a dip in the clean water. The park is located on U.S. 12, three miles south of Baraboo.*

 Fencing is a great sport (one that many people have never tried), requiring agility, speed, endurance, and skill. You can don a mask, draw your foil, and parry-thrust-parry to the touch at the Caliburn Fencing Club, which meets at the Plymouth Church Gym, 2717 East Hartford Avenue. Novices are welcome to give the sport a try on Wednesday at 6 p.m., Saturday at noon, and Sunday at 2. Call 414/281-1999 for more information.

daily, along with lap-swimming sessions, kids' swim, senior swim, and water exercise classes. Other indoor county pools are located at Moody Park (2200 W. Burleigh St.) on the north side and Pulaski Park on the south side (2701 S. 16th St.). (North Side)

WASHINGTON PARK POOL
4023 W. Galena St.
Milwaukee
414/344-5400
Milwaukee County operates 14 outdoor swimming pools throughout the metropolitan area. One of the largest, the Washington Park pool delights kids and adults (but mostly kids) throughout the hot summer. There are slides and diving boards and all the other amenities of an urban public pool. Other good pools are found in Jackson (South Side) and Hoyt (West Side) parks. (North Side)

Tennis Courts

HART PARK
7400 block of W. State St.
Wauwatosa
This City of Wauwatosa park has a bank of lighted tennis courts just south of West State Street, right in the heart of the village. Courts are often busy in the evenings and on weekends in summer—expect to wait a while at peak times. (West Side)

HUMBOLDT PARK
3000 S. Howell Ave.
Milwaukee
414/482-4270
Thirty-four Milwaukee County Parks contain tennis courts, most of which are kept in tip-top condition. Of those parks, 13 have courts with lights, allowing play well into the evening early and late in the season. The Humboldt Park courts, within a longish walk of the South Shore Yacht Club, are among the lighted and see less use than many other courts in town (South Side)

LOWELL PARK
Madison and Grandview Sts.
Waukesha
This City of Waukesha park, besides hosting one of the area's great toboggan runs for winter fun (see Chapter 8: "Parks and Gardens"), has a bank of the nicest public tennis courts in Waukesha County. Well-maintained and not too heavily used, the courts are lit on demand for evening use. You can put a quarter into the switch box and get 15 minutes of lights, not a bad deal when you're into that hotly contested third match at sunset. (Waukesha County)

MCKINLEY TENNIS COURTS
1700 block of N. Lincoln Memorial Dr.
Milwaukee
414/273-5224

The McKinley Courts, across Lincoln Memorial Drive from the McKinley Marina and Beach along Lake Michigan, are some of the best in town. These courts may be reserved (reservations are advised during peak times) for a fee of $3 at the marina office. The lights come on at dusk in summer and will be turned on with an evening reservation during good weather after Labor Day or before May 1. (East Side)

Wisconsin Conservatory of Music

11
PERFORMING ARTS

One of the biggest surprises in Milwaukee is the remarkable size and strength of its performing arts scene. Theater, opera, chamber and orchestral music groups, and dance companies abound, in numbers astounding for a city of this size. During the performing-arts season (roughly September through May), you should have no difficulty finding a performance that will elicit your interest—the difficulty is in choosing among the offerings.

Well, you may be thinking, that's a grand claim. Yet a glance at the Friday entertainment section of the daily newspaper will confirm it. There are dozens of fine-arts performing groups in Milwaukee. Part of the reason for this density is the United Performing Arts Fund, which helps many of the city's best-known—as well as many up-and-coming—theaters, dance ensembles, and orchestras fill out what would otherwise be fairly meager budgets. Raising tens of millions of dollars annually, UPAF is the most successful local arts funding agency in the country, and Milwaukeeans give more per capita than people in any other town.

Maybe it's because people need the lift that an opera or Shakespeare play gives them during the long and gloomy winters. Maybe it's just tradition. Whatever the motivation, the fact is that everyone, visitors and residents alike, benefit dramatically (get it?) from local support of the performing arts.

You can see the grandest of grand opera in high style at the Florentine. You can hear daring chamber music performed by internationally acclaimed Present Music. You can be overwhelmed by the African dance of Ko-Thi. You can see plays old and new at the Rep. You can, in other words, get out and get inspired.

THEATER

BOULEVARD ENSEMBLE THEATER
2250 S. Kinnickinnic Ave.
Milwaukee
414/744-5757

The Boulevard's tiny storefront theater, more than a decade old, can't hold more than a few dozen audience members. With such close quarters, the action is always life-sized. The Boulevard presents new plays (Shepherd, Mamet) and old (Moliere, Shaw), comedies and tragedies, along with the Alley Series of experimental one-act plays. A training ground for Milwaukee actors, the Boulevard Ensemble takes chances. The result, as often as not, is up close, personal, and intense. (South Side)

FIRST STAGE MILWAUKEE
Todd Wehr Theater
Marcus Center for the Performing Arts
929 N. Water St.
Milwaukee
414/273-7206

The city's premier children's theater company, First Stage productions are the place where kids' literature comes to life in full-scale, professional productions. Toddlers through 12-year-olds love these plays. (See Chapter 7: "Kids' Stuff" for more information.) (Downtown)

INERTIA ENSEMBLE
No phone

A loose collaboration between a handful of young actors and playwrights, Inertia Ensemble is sort of an abecedarian Theatre X (see page 168), staging original plays and dramatic readings. Although the results may be uneven, Inertia captures an organic excitement—born of a shoestring budget and uncertain talent—that no other company in town can boast. Staging (often surprisingly good) plays in coffeehouses, art galleries, and even beauty salons, Inertia Ensemble is a kick in the pants. They're not in the phone book, but watch for notices in the *Shepherd Express Metro*, the city's biggest weekly newspaper. (East Side)

MILWAUKEE CHAMBER THEATRE
Broadway Theater Center
158 N. Broadway
Milwaukee
414/291-7800
www.execpc.com/~mct

Listen closely: If there is a common thread in plays staged at the Milwaukee Chamber Theatre, it is the complicated and elastic nature of language—whether the dizzying

The Marcus Center for the Performing Arts is Milwaukee County's premiere arts venue, including the 2,400-seat Uihlein Hall and the smaller Wehr Theater and Vogel Hall. The center is the home of the Milwaukee Symphony Orchestra, the Milwaukee Ballet, and the Florentine Opera, and it provides a venue for touring Broadway shows and many other concerts and plays. Call the Marcus Center box office at 414/273-7206 or 800/472-4458 outside Milwaukee.

fountain of words issuing from the mouths of St. Joan and Major Barbara or the confusing doublespeak of a David Mamet professor. Very high quality, very intense, and very enjoyable, the MCT will not fail to please. The company's annual festival of G. B. Shaw plays is among Milwaukee's theater highlights. (Downtown)

MILWAUKEE REPERTORY THEATER
Theater District
108 E. Wells St.
Milwaukee
414/224-9490

The Rep is Milwaukee's largest and best-funded professional theater company, and the livelihood of many area actors. The Rep's Theater District building houses three theaters: the thrust-stage Powerhouse (built in an old riverside generating plant), the Stiemke Theater, a black box, and the Stackner Cabaret. Presenting more than a dozen plays each season—from Shakespeare to world premieres—the Rep rarely fails to delight. Plus, in their state-of-the-art theaters, all the seats are good. (Downtown)

NEXT ACT THEATER
414/278-7780

With no permanent home, Next Act is one of the city's most flexible—and exciting—professional theater companies. Staging contemporary off- and off-off-Broadway plays, and works written by artists-in-residence, Next Act makes do, typically, with minimal sets complemented by great acting. Recent venues for Next Act productions have included black-box theaters around town and the glorious Humphrey Scottish Rite Masonic Temple downtown. Call for information or write to P.O. Box 394, Milwaukee, WI 53201. (Downtown)

RENAISSANCE THEATERWORKS
414/273-0800
www.footlights.com/ren97.html

One of Milwaukee's smaller roving theater companies, Renaissance presents contemporary plays and staged

Pabst Theater, p. 174

The last few years have seen a tremendous rise in the popularity of grand opera, and Milwaukee's Florentine Opera Company has seen a remarkable increase in ticket demand. If you're interested in attending a Florentine show, buy tickets early, as productions often sell out. Call toll-free 800/472-4458 from outside Milwaukee for ticket information.

readings of classic works focusing on the feminine voice in drama. That voice, of course, has many timbres, and recently Renaissance has presented several well-received works by Jane Martins, along with readings of classics like *Iphegenia in Tauris* and *Medea*. Monday performances are pay-what-you-can.

THEATRE X
Broadway Theatre Center
158 N. Broadway
Milwaukee
414/278-0555

Theatre X has an international reputation for cutting-edge experimental drama. And don't be put off by the word experimental, either. It doesn't mean confusing, confrontational, or difficult. It does mean that Theatre X produces versions of classics and new plays (often original) that expand the notion of what a play can do. The productions are excellently acted, cleverly conceived, and always interesting. Willem Dafoe (the title character in *The Last Temptation of Christ)* is a former Theatre Xer. (Downtown)

MUSIC AND OPERA

ARTIST SERIES AT THE PABST
Pabst Theater
144 E. Wells St.
Milwaukee
414/286-8801

The Pabst is Milwaukee's grandest Victorian opera house, and nothing shows the place off better than the Artist Series, a group of chamber concerts by the world's great orchestras. Because the theater is not too large, chamber groups—numbering under 30 members—can fill the space with music. Recent concerts have featured the Vienna Chamber Orchestra under the direction of Phillipe Entremont and the Tallin Orchestra, which played the Arvo Pärt *Litany,* for which the group won a Grammy. (Downtown)

BEL CANTO CHORUS
1233 N. Mayfair Rd.
Wauwatosa (office)
414/476-6640
Bcanto@aol.com

The best known and among the largest of Milwaukee's vocal ensembles, the Bel Canto Chorus has been delighting audiences for more than half a century. Performing Baroque, classical, Romantic, and modern choral masterpieces, Bel Canto's choir members and soloists are known for their perfectionism. The chorus sings four concerts yearly; the holiday concerts, held in December, are particularly popular. (West Side)

EARLY MUSIC NOW
1630 E. Royall Pl.

Milwaukee (office)
414/225-3113
Founded just over a decade ago, as the early-music movement was beginning to take off, Early Music Now is currently reaping the benefits of a heightened interest in pre-Baroque chamber works in the form of a skyrocketing subscription base. A presenter, EMN stages up to a half-dozen concerts yearly—held in historic churches—by some of the world's finest early-music ensembles. Recent artists have included Fretwork, playing medieval English songs, and the acclaimed Anonymous 4.

ENSEMBLE MUSICAL OFFERING
818 E. Juneau Ave.
Milwaukee (office)
414/226-2224
Another early-music group, Musical Offering plays medieval, Renaissance, and early Baroque chamber music, usually performed on authentic period instruments. Seasons are typically organized around a theme—such as Renaissance music in Spain—and feature guest artists as well as the ensemble itself. Like Early Music Now, Ensemble Musical Offering presents its concerts in historic churches. (East Side)

FESTIVAL CITY SYMPHONY
4240 N. Ardmore Ave.
Milwaukee (office)
414/963-9067
With roots going back more than 70 years, the Festival City Symphony focuses on music for families. That means education and concerts geared for children—often informal, always informational, and genuinely fun. Holding Pajama Jamborees—hour-long classical concerts aimed at thrilling young children—and series for slightly older kids at the Pabst Theater and Alverno College, the Festival City Symphony is building tomorrow's music audiences. (East Side)

FINE ARTS QUARTET
Fine Arts Recital Hall
University of Wisconsin-Milwaukee
2400 E. Kenwood Blvd.
Milwaukee
414/229-4308
Called by the *New York Times* "truly one of the world's great ensembles," the Fine Arts Quartet is the resident ensemble of the School of the Arts at the University of Wisconsin-Milwaukee. The FAQ plays chamber music from past and present by the likes of Mendelssohn, Haydn, and Dvorak and brings in guest artists like Pinchas Zuckerman and the Borodin Quartet. Without a doubt the best chamber music in town, and among the best anywhere, Fine Arts Quartet concerts are nothing short of exhilarating. (East Side)

FLORENTINE OPERA COMPANY
Marcus Center for the Performing Arts
929 N. Water St.
Milwaukee
414/291-5700, 800/472-4458
www.florentineopera.org
Everything about every Florentine production can be summed up with one word: *grand*—as grand as grand opera gets. With huge sets, lavish costumes, the Milwaukee Symphony Orchestra, and some of the world's greatest singers, the Florentine presents three operas from the standard repertory each season. Erie Mills, Beverly Sills, Sherril

Check these ticket brokers if you can't get to a venue box office or if, heaven forbid, the event you want to see is sold out:
Connections Ticket Service: 414/540-1313 or 888/999-8497
Milwaukee World Festival (Summerfest): 414/273-2600
Ticket King: 414/273-6007
Ticket Master: 414/276-4545

Milnes, and Maria Spacagna have all sung with the Florentine, in operas like *Turandot, Magic Flute,* and *Barber of Seville.* Liebermann's *Dorian Gray* had its U.S. premier at the Florentine in February, 1999. & (Downtown)

MILWAUKEE CHAMBER ORCHESTRA
Schwan Hall
Wisconsin Lutheran College
8815 W. Wisconsin Ave.
Milwaukee
414/443-8802
The Milwaukee Chamber Orchestra is one of few regional chamber music groups made up entirely of professional musicians. Playing six or seven concerts each season, the MCO mixes and matches works for small orchestras, creating interesting themes and constrasts: Mozart and Stravinsky might share a program, for example. The orchestra is very good, and the annual concert showcasing the substantial talents of Frank Almond, rising star and principal violinist of the Milwaukee Symphony Orchestra, is invariably superb. & (West Side)

MILWAUKEE SYMPHONY ORCHESTRA
Marcus Center for the Performing Arts
929 N. Water St.
Milwaukee
414/291-7605
www.milwaukeesymphony.org
The Milwaukee Symphony Orchestra is on a roll—and not just a drum roll. Andreas Delfs, the orchestra's new conductor, lights both the musicians and the audience on fire, and his programs, while not shying away from the warhorses of the classical repertory, combine them with less-performed and new works as well. The finest musicians in the world perform regularly with the MSO, and the MSO Pops Orchestra is led by no less a musician than Doc Severinson. The MSO is, without a doubt, one of the country's finest symphonies. & (Downtown)

PRESENT MUSIC
1840 N. Farwell Ave.
Milwaukee (office)
414/271-0711
www.execpc.com/~newmusic
Acclaimed around the country, Present Music is perhaps Milwaukee's most important musical treasure. This professional orchestra plays the work of living composers and even commissions new pieces. Using timpani and tape loops, trumpets and trash-can lids, and all the instruments in between, Present Music performs the work of Kamran Ince, Michael Torke, Arvo Pärt, and other contemporary composers. Present Music concerts,

held in cathedrals and at the Milwaukee Art Museum, are invariably the talk of the town and must-hear events. (Downtown)

SKYLIGHT OPERA COMPANY
Broadway Theatre Center
158 N. Broadway
Milwaukee
414/291-7800
The Skylight's motto takes in the three I's: Intimate, Innovative, and In English. The intimacy is provided by the splendid Cabot Theater, a Baroque-style, three-tiered, curved-balcony beauty that seats 350 people in exquisite comfort. The innovation is found in the clever staging of operas, operettas, and even musicals—from Monteverdi to *Guys and Dolls*—performed by some of the country's most talented singers. And "In English" speaks for itself, as do these operas. An opera at the Skylight is a rare treat. ♿ (Downtown)

DANCE

DANCECIRCUS
3195 S. Superior St.
Milwaukee (office)
414/481-4324
Dancecircus, as its name suggests, is willing to take on more than the standard vocabulary of movement. Company founder Betty Salamun collaborates with musicians, writers, and dancers to create original works for the company. Performing on various stages throughout the city, from the Pabst Theater to Alverno College's Pittman Theater, Dancecircus presents three or four concerts every season. (South Side)

First Stage Milwaukee, p. 166

KO-THI DANCE COMPANY
342 N. Water St.
Milwaukee (office)
414/273-0676
A Ko-Thi dance concert is nothing short of transcendent—transforming, even. Working in the traditions of African and Caribbean dance, Ko-Thi seems to tap into the very forces of life itself. It is impossible to watch the dozen or so drummers and dozens of dancers—each in an individual ecstasy of movement—and not be swept away in that tidal wave of pounding rhythm. There is no equally visceral art experience with which to compare it. (Downtown)

MILWAUKEE BALLET
Marcus Center for the Performing Arts
929 N. Water St.
Milwaukee
414/643-7677
www.execpc.com/jjjurek/ mwballet
The Milwaukee Ballet is Dance Central for the city. A large and well-

funded company, the ballet is able to gracefully stage major dance concerts, with a full orchestra and all the other accoutrements that make ballet such a grand art form. You are as likely to see *Billy the Kid* as *Giselle* and *Nutcracker* around the holidays, and you'll see contemporary premieres in spring. Technically impeccable—surely the Milwaukee Ballet is in the country's top tier of dance companies—nearly every dance is dazzling. ♿ (Downtown)

TRINITY IRISH DANCERS
414/327-7250
With arms held stiffly at their sides and hair in curls, the Trinity Irish Dancers are serious about their ethnic art form. The rising popularity of Irish dance, fueled by several nationally touring companies, has put Trinity in the spotlight. They've performed throughout the country and in Europe, danced with the Milwaukee Ballet and on *Good Morning America*, and were named World Champions at a recent international competition in their home country across the ocean. A Trinity performance is awe inspiring both for the dancers' self-control (they are young girls, mostly) and their flying feet.

WILD SPACE DANCE COMPANY
820 E. Knapp St.
Milwaukee (office)
414/271-0307
Wild Space is perhaps the best established of Milwaukee's avant-garde dance companies. Performing three or four concerts every season on various stages around town—one performance took place in an empty swimming pool—Wild Space delineates the outer edges of dance. Don't expect tutus, but do expect remarkable physicality and athleticism, along with ingenious approaches to non-traditional ballet music, multimedia, the spoken word, and even comedic improvisation. (East Side)

CONCERT VENUES

BRADLEY CENTER
1001 N. Fourth St.
Milwaukee
414/227-0400
Primarily a sports arena, the Bradley Center does host blockbuster concerts—of the Neil Diamond, Janet Jackson, Bruce Springsteen variety—primarily during winter, when the outdoor Marcus Amphitheater is closed. The sound, typical of such arenas, leaves something to be desired, but

---

TRIVIA

The Festival of Milwaukee Dance provides a fantastic opportunity to see new work by more than a half-dozen of the area's contemporary dance companies in one place. Held over three days in March at Alverno College's Pittman Theater, the 1999 version of the event featured work by Wild Space, the Foothold Dance Collective, Ko-Thi, Dancecircus, and several other companies.

Ko-Thi Dance Company, p. 171

there is a certain exhilaration to swaying in time with 20,000 of your fellow fans. (See also Chapter 5: "Sights and Attractions") ♿ (Downtown)

MARCUS AMPHITHEATER
Maeir Festival Park (Summerfest)
200 N. Harbor Dr.
Milwaukee
414/273-2600
Rising like a big blue wave at the south end of the Summerfest grounds, Marcus Amphitheater is the city's pop-music mecca three seasons a year. Built on a landfill at the harbor mouth (the Hoan Bridge is suspended high above), the 24,000-seat theater has hosted the likes of Pearl Jam, Metallica, Kenny G, and everyone in between. The Summerfest headline acts play here, and lawn seats are free with admission to the festival for those who arrive early—very early. ♿ (Downtown)

MARCUS CENTER FOR THE PERFORMING ARTS
929 N. Water St.
Milwaukee
414/273-2787 (events line)
414/273-7206 (box office)
Home to the ballet, symphony, and Florentine Opera, the Marcus Center has recently undergone a major transformation. The exterior marble was replaced, and a new lobby and atrium were added, with two stories of glass facing busy Water Street. On concert nights, it is a pleasure to walk past and see the musically inclined filing into the hall. Uihlein Hall, the center's largest stage, was also completely remodeled, with new seats, miles of wood, new carpeting, and a computer-controlled amplification system. ♿ (Downtown)

MODJESKA THEATER
1134 W. Mitchell St.
Milwaukee
414/299-0021
An entertainment palace built in the Roaring Twenties—and named after a then-famous Polish actress—the

Modjeska has been a vaudeville stage and a second-run movie house. Now it's the home of an eclectic series of concerts, children's theater, and cultural events. Old and a little dilapidated, it is mostly notable these days for the off-beat bands that play here. (South Side)

PABST THEATER
144 E. Wells St.
Milwaukee
414/286-3663

The high-Victorian decoration of the Pabst Theater (see Chapter 5: "Sights and Attractions"), Milwaukee's grandest opera house, in no way detracts from the action on stage. Besides the Artist Series (see Music and Opera), the Pabst hosts the Hal Leonard Jazz Series, which brings most of the country's jazz greats to town. The Pabst also hosts numerous special concerts, recitals, dance shows, historical revues, and even pop music. A major interior renovation, which will add an elevator and windowed reception area, is underway. & (Downtown)

RIVERSIDE THEATER
116 W. Wisconsin Ave.
Milwaukee
414/224-3000 (box office)
414/390-1200 (info line)

Holding 2,500 seats, the Riverside Theater is one of the jewels of downtown Milwaukee and the city's largest historic venue. Once a vaudeville stage and opera house, the Riverside lacks the glamour of the Pabst Theater but is able to hold half-again as many concertgoers and is flexible enough to host pop

Top Ten Marcus Center Meals
by Shelley Taxman, programming director, Marcus Center for the Performing Arts

Try these fine downtown restaurants for a before-show meal or a cocktail and dessert after the curtain falls. All are within walking distance of the Marcus Center.

1. Café Vecchio Mondo
2. Eagan's
3. Metro Restaurant in the Hotel Metro
4. Elsa's on the Park
5. Water Street Brewery
6. Wells Street Station
7. Rock Bottom Brewery
8. The King and I
9. Karl Ratzsch's
10. Velvet Room

concerts, orchestras, comedy shows, and touring Broadway productions. ♿(Downtown)

SCHWAN HALL
Center for Arts and Performance
Wisconsin Lutheran College
8815 W. Wisconsin Ave.
Milwaukee
414/443-8801

Half a decade ago, tiny Wisconsin Lutheran College received the largest donation ever given to a private school in Wisconsin for the building of a state-of-the-art arts center. The result was the intimate, accessible, and acoustically phenomenal Schwan Hall. Happy are the music lovers who settle back into the wide and comfortable seats, and they are happier still when the first chord is struck. The sound in Schwan Hall is lively and rich. The Milwaukee Chamber Orchestra performs here, and the college brings in many musical groups throughout the year, from the Vienna Choir Boys to the National Opera Company. ♿ (West Side)

SUMMERFEST
N. Harbor Dr. at E. Michigan St.
Milwaukee
414/273-3378, 800/273-2860
www.summerfest.com

It's the event that made Milwaukee famous. For ten days surrounding the Fourth of July every summer, the city shuts down and nearly 1 million visitors descend on the lakefront for the world's largest pop-music festival. With a dozen stages showcasing hundreds of bands, comedians, and professional sports demonstrations—along with lots of food and gallons of beer—Summerfest rocks from morning till midnight. Blues, jazz, alternative rock, soul, rap, oldies, metal—everything has a place. There's a midway, a shopping area, children's activities, live broadcasts on VH1, walks along the beach and... well, on and on. ♿ (Downtown)

WISCONSIN CONSERVATORY OF MUSIC
1584 N. Prospect Ave.
Milwaukee
414/276-5760
www.wcmusic.org

Housed in a century-old bluff-top mansion, the Wisconsin Conservatory of Music is one of the state's primary music training grounds. Presenting more than 100 concerts yearly in its elegant recital hall, the conservatory features music by faculty, students, and guest artists. Music lovers visiting the city for even a short period are bound to find something going on—jazz, classical, and blues performances. Many shows are presented without charge. (East Side)

12

NIGHTLIFE

"What do you want to do tonight?"

"I don't know, what do you want to do?" Ever have that conversation? Of course you have, but you needn't have it again. Dancing, live music of all kinds, dinner theater, hopping martini bars, great little taverns in out-of-the-way corners of the city, cinemas from an era long past. These await you and more when the moon shines down on Lake Michigan.

Two Milwaukee nightlife phenomena bear special mention, because no visit to the city is really complete without sampling them. The corner tavern is a Milwaukee institution that is, sadly, disappearing. Milwaukee still has more bars per capita than any city in the country, but there was a time when some neighborhoods had a cozy bar on every corner. For the Germans who settled Milwaukee in the mid-19th century, the tavern was not merely a place to drink, it was the social center of the neighborhood, a place to celebrate, debate politics, meet your neighbors. Many corner taps remain in Milwaukee. Many are worth an hour or two of your time.

The second local marvel is the polka tavern. For people elsewhere in the country, polka might as well be music from outer space. But in Milwaukee, polka is the real thing. Part of an entrenched midwestern folk idiom, bred of immigration, improvisation, and the development of the concertina, the tiny drama of the polka-dance party is played out across Wisconsin every weekend, with live music and whirling couples. Check out a polka bar, and you'll check into Polka Happiness, a state of mind in which everything is all right, at least while the band is playing.

DANCE CLUBS

EMERALD CITY
1101 N. Old World Third St.
Milwaukee
414/226-2489
Emerald City, an R&B/soul club, is a classy operation. A strict dress code is enforced (dress to the nines, as urbanely as possible, and you'll fit right in), cocktails flow, and crowds dance to live music on weekends. The place simply oozes urban sophistication. (Downtown)

LA CAGE
801 S. Second St.
Milwaukee
414/383-9330
The city's longest lived gay dance club, La Cage dishes it up and dishes it out. A couple of dance floors, four bars, specialty nights (country line dancing on Tuesday is a hoot, to say the least), giant video screens, and relentless extended-mix dance music make La Cage very happening indeed. It's a friendly place, too: all sexes and preferences are welcome. (South Side)

LA PLAYA
Pfister Hotel
424 E. Wisconsin Ave.
Milwaukee
414/273-8222
La Playa is utterly nonthreatening: The decor has not been updated for 20 years, the music—dance versions of top 40 hits—won't offend your parents, and all the latest crazes (can anybody say *lambada*?) are practiced with vigor. But dancing is secondary, because the club sits on top of a downtown high-rise with great nighttime views. (Downtown)

MAD PLANET
533 E. Center St.
Milwaukee
414/263-4555
The city's coolest "alternative" dance club, Mad Planet rocks the house. In the dark cavern of this club, beneath the flashing lights, jungle-techno-trip hop fans, pale-faced goths, and party-happy sorority sisters mix amicably. Weekly special theme nights (Disco Inferno, for example) tame the past. (North Side)

METROPOLIS
788 N. Jackson St.
Milwaukee
414/272-7550
It's downtown, the music is thumping, the drinks are well mixed, and the crowd is not menacing. Summertime promotions with independent radio station WMSE draw counter-culture types, but for the most part the crowd is young, urban, and working on professional. Metropolis features all-ages nights during the week. (Downtown)

JAZZ CLUBS

THE ESTATE
2423 N. Murray Ave.
Milwaukee
414/964-9923
With live music almost every night of the week, the Estate is a mainstay in Milwaukee's traditional jazz scene. Local musicians play here, as do out-of-town combos, and the small club is as comfortable as you can imagine. With low cover charges and good prices on drinks, everything about the Estate is very, very "cool." (East Side)

JAZZ OASIS
2379 N. Holton St.
Milwaukee
414/562-2040
An island of civility in a not particularly welcoming neighborhood, Jazz Oasis is the rock on which Milwaukee's jazz scene is built. Established local musicians play here, and up-and-comers find it the perfect place to cut their teeth. If there's life in Brew City jazz, it pulses at the Jazz Oasis. (North Side)

RED MILL
1005 S. Elm Grove Rd.
Elm Grove
262/782-8780
What the Jazz Oasis does for its rough-and-tumble north-side neighborhood the Red Mill does for the western suburbs: It's a blast of oxygen in a thin cultural atmosphere. The Red Mill will never be mistaken for a dive. The music—traditional, bop, and Dixieland—is often great. Local and national acts play here. (Waukesha County)

BLUES CLUBS

BIG DOG'S HOUSE OF BLUES
3062 S. 13th St.
Milwaukee
414/645-5013
A newcomer to the Milwuakee blues scene, Big Dog's has been making quite a splash with its commitment to the art form. It's a south-side tavern with its working-class roots showing, but jeez! The music is wailing. Local blues bands play here several nights weekly, the beer is cheap, and the crowd is boisterous. (South Side)

UP & UNDER PUB
1216 E. Brady St.
Milwaukee
414/276-2677
At the Up & Under, the blues are a way of life. This is the bar where touring musicians stop for a beer after finishing their sets in fancy theaters around town, then sit in with the band on stage. This is the bar where Milwaukee's best harmonica players wail before a packed house. This is the bar where 12 bars is enough. (East Side)

ROCK CLUBS

CACTUS CLUB
2496 S. Wentworth Ave.
Milwaukee
414/482-0160
A tavern with a small stage, the Cactus Club is pretty hip, featuring local alternative rock bands and obscure touring bands from around the area. Low key but not a dive, the Cactus Club has become a hot spot on the local music scene in the last couple of years. It has a great jukebox, on which you'll find Hank Williams and Dean Martin alongside Hüsker Dü. (South Side)

FILTER INN
434 S. Second St.
Milwaukee
414/223-4613
Milwaukee's newest rock club, the Filter Inn is located in a block of 19th-century taverns. Making a big impression with alternative music fans, the bar hosts bands playing bubblegum punk, triphop, and anything not likely to be heard on commercial radio. It's remarkably comfortable,

and the drinks are reasonably priced. (South Side)

THE GLOBE
2028 E. North Ave.
Milwaukee
414/276-2233
The Globe is everything a rock club is meant to be: a big, empty space with a bar at one end and a gigantic PA system to shake the building to its foundation. Expect local punk and alternative rock bands here, inexpensive beer, and ringing ears as you stumble onto the street after last call. Tattoos and leather are not optional. (East Side)

QUARTER'S ROCK PALACE
900 E. Center St.
Milwaukee
414/263-4140
"Palace" is strictly ironic, as Quarter's is a dive: tiny, forbidding from the outside, and making only minimal concessions to ambience. But Quarter's plays a vital role in Milwaukee's music scene by booking the least commercially viable bands imaginable. Off-beat techno, strange lounge acts, noise bands, queer hardcore, nothing is *verboten*. Cover charges are minimal, and beer is dirt cheap. (North Side)

Polka Happiness

Polka runs deep in the blood of Wisconsinites. It's the official state dance, and it's celebrated at taverns and festivals throughout the state all year long. The idea of Polka Happiness is this: Once the band kicks in to "Dorothy's Oberek," the "Owl Polka," or the "Little Vagabond Waltz," your troubles disappear.

Chicago Style, Steven's Point Style, Slovenian Style, Dutchman, or Finnish: There are many variations on the general oompah theme. Some emphasize horn runs, some emphasize accordian wizardry, some are electric, some are acoustic, and all are fun. But where to start? In 1998, in honor of Wisconsin's sesquicentennial, the Smithsonian Institution released Deep Polka, *a collection of midwestern dance music on its Folkways label. The CD features seven bands playing seven different styles, with extensive liner notes explaining their distinguishing features. The CD is available in record stores everywhere.*

When in Milwaukee, tune into WTKM, polka radio at 1540 AM and 104.9 FM on the northwest side of town, or listen to "Polka Parade" every Saturday morning and Sunday at noon on WYMS, 88.9 FM.

THE RAVE
2401 W. Wisconsin Ave.
Milwaukee
414/342-7283
Found in a spectacular old Eagle's Club in Avenues West, the Rave is actually two nightclubs. The cavernous ballroom hosts big touring rock and alternative bands, and the smaller Rave Bar hosts local groups. This is the main venue for mid-level MTV bands who couldn't sell out a Milwaukee amphitheater but would cram Shank Hall (see below). (Downtown)

SHANK HALL
1434 N. Farwell Ave.
Milwaukee
414/276-7288
Named for the fictitious Milwaukee nightclub in the classic "rockumentary" *This Is Spinal Tap*, Shank Hall doesn't define its niche too narrowly. The club features local alt rock bands, along with small-venue national touring groups: punk rock, blues, jazz greats, folk artists, and more. While the atmosphere is minimal, Shank Hall is a great place to catch bands before they hit the big-time. (East Side)

COUNTRY MUSIC CLUBS

SUE'S BAYVIEW BANDWAGON
2463 S. St. Clair Ave.
Milwaukee
414/486-1330
There's not a lot of live country music to be found in Milwaukee these days, but Sue's features country-rock, local alt-country, and rockabilly bands on Friday night—except the second Friday of the month, which (hey, this is Milwaukee) is polka night. There's often no cover charge, and the bands have little in common with what you hear on sappy "country" radio. (South Side)

OTHER MUSIC CLUBS

ART ALTENBURG'S CONCERTINA BAR
1920 S. 37th St.
Milwaukee
414/384-2570
If there is a shiny buckle on the Polka Belt—which runs from Albany to Bismarck—it is Art's Concertina Bar. Art Altenburg raises a paean to the buttonbox, with dozens of beautiful instruments behind the bar and polka bands several nights a week. Have a couple of drinks, then hit the dance floor. (South Side)

CLUB TRES HERMANOS
1332 W. Lincoln Ave.
Milwaukee
414/384-9050
A number of Milwaukee restaurants

Check the *Shepherd Express Metro*, Milwaukee's biggest weekly newspaper, for updated concert, theater, and nightclub listings. The paper is available free in news boxes downtown and at businesses throughout the metro area.

and nightclubs feature Latin music regularly, from mariachi to the macarena. Tres Hermanos is one of the best, with local and national salsa and merengue bands on weekends. The bands are hot, the dance floor is hot, and there is often no cover charge. (South Side)

THE COFFEEHOUSE
631 N. 19th St.
Milwaukee
414/299-9598

The Coffeehouse, found in the basement of Trinity Lutheran Church, is Milwaukee's premier folk music venue. The club has no liquor license, but when the singing starts, drinks are beside the point. Shows start early, usually around 7 or 8, and feature many of the area's best singer-songwriters and folk ensembles. (Downtown)

NASH'S IRISH CASTLE
1328 W. Lincoln Ave.
Milwaukee
414/643-9654

An Irish pub with old-time charm, Nash's features the full spectrum of Irish music, from guitar-strumming folksingers to Pogues-inspired Celtic free-for-alls. Most of the musicians tend toward the former end of the spectrum. The beer is darn good, too. (South Side)

PUBS AND BARS

AT RANDOM
2501 S. Delaware Ave.
Milwaukee
414/481-8030

At Random hasn't been altered since it was incarnated 40 years ago in an

Taylor's Bar

era of crooners and luau lounges. Don't expect beer or wine. Instead, dig into the world of the Missionary's Demise and the Strawberry Blonde. If you're up for it, the Flaming Tiki Love Bowl comes alight and with two straws. (South Side)

BOOBIE'S PLACE
502 W. Garfield Ave.
Milwaukee
414/263-3399

Anchor of the north side, Boobie's is always crowded but remains fairly mellow. It's a little short on interior ambience, but it compensates with big windows, a great staff, and plenty of beer. Live jazz and a busy dance floor round out a weekend at Boobie's. (North Side)

BRYANT'S COCKTAIL LOUNGE
1579 S. Ninth St.
Milwaukee
414/383-2620

Rumor has it that the first Brandy Alexander was poured at Bryant's, Cocktail Lounge, the land that time

Parking is difficult in the Northpoint neighborhood on Milwaukee's east side. Moviegoers attending screenings at the Oriental Cinema, the city's most opulent artsy theater, can park on the street, then have theater attendants keep the parking meters plugged. Just give the attendants a handful of change and directions to your car.

forgot, the ur-cocktail lounge. Once your eyes adjust to the preternatural darkness, sidle up to the upholstered bar or into one of the shallow booths, each with a waitress call button, and order a Manhattan, an old-fashioned, a Rob Roy . . . anything involving dark liquor and vermouth. (South Side)

GASTHAUS ZUR KRONE
839 S. Second St.
Milwaukee
414/647-1910
Zur Krone is an old German pub, and it's the real thing—not the product of a focus group trying to create the perfect tavern atmosphere. The old woodwork and bar have remained unchanged for decades, and there is a *feuchtes eck*, or "moist corner" for regulars, zither music on Sunday evening, and a gigantic selection of imported beer. (South Side)

GREAT NATIONAL SALOON
6833 W. National Ave.
West Allis
414/774-0042
The Great National's stained-glass windows (by artist Edward Mucha) are coveted, they say, by a curator from the Art Institute of Chicago. Fortunately, they're not for sale. The saloon serves good beer and good pub food in a classic tavern atmosphere. You need a beer, buddy? Then stop in here. (South Side)

HI HAT
1701 N. Arlington St.
Milwaukee
414/225-9330
Capitalizing on swing cool and the return of cocktail culture, Hi Hat is Brady Street's newest, greatest place. One of the most architecturally interesting taverns in town, Hi Hat is also among the hippest, with cool jazz and lounge music, fancy mixed drinks, a funky atmosphere, and a small but rather interesting menu. (East Side)

HOOLIGAN'S
2017 E. North Ave.
Milwaukee
414/273-5230
Hooligan's is the mother of all Northpoint taverns. Part neighborhood bar, part college hangout, part workingman's lunch spot (the bar food is outstanding), Hooligan's is all Milwaukee, all the time. This tavern features 30 or more microbrews on tap and TVs for watching the Packers game. Hooligan's is everything a bar should be. (East Side)

KELLEY'S BLEACHERS
5218 W. Bluemound Rd.
Milwaukee
414/258-9837
Who's got the most homers this year? Should we dump the first baseman? From April to September, come to

Kelley's Bleachers prepared to talk stats. Thanks to its location directly across from County Stadium, Kelley's Bleachers is the prime pub for Milwaukee Brewers fans. Order a beer and analyze the manager's every move. (West Side)

LUKE'S SPORTS SPECTACULAR
1225 N. Water St.
Milwaukee
414/223-3210

Milwaukee is a big sports town, and Luke's is the king daddy of sports bars. Anchoring the north end of the Water Street Entertainment District (see Tip on page 184), Luke's offers more than 50 televisions, so no corner of this formidable establishment is left unbathed in the blue glow of sports TV. (Downtown)

MAYFIELD'S PEACE AND LOVE
3315 N. Pierce St.
Milwaukee

Mayfield's is fly—superfly, that is. A 1940s-Modern lounge with a curving pale-wood bar, Mayfield's is a very mellow place indeed, with jazz and R&B on the sound system and a couple kinds of bottled beer and cocktails on the menu. At Mayfield's, peace and love reign in the heart of Riverwest. Mayfield's is open only on Friday night. (North Side)

MILWAUKEE GREAT NORTHERN
366 E. Stuart St.
Milwaukee
414/481-5480

You've seen this setting in the movies: The streamlined locomotive hurtles through the night while the debonair hero sips bourbon and soda amid polished chrome. The Milwaukee Great Northern is, without peer, the city's most wonderful secret cocktail lounge: three 1930s club cars serving drinks in quiet sophistication on Thursday, Friday, and Saturday. Unique? Yes. Hard to find? Yes. Worth the effort? Definitely. (South Side)

NOMAD WORLD PUB
1401 E. Brady St.
Milwaukee

Marcus Amphitheater, p. 187

414/224-8111
www.nomadpub.com
The most comfortable watering hole on the lower east side, the Nomad has big windows—unusual for a pub—dozens of imported and microbrewed beers, wines, liquor, occasional live music, and great coffee. The Nomad is relaxed, never too loud, never filled with drunken blockheads, and always fun. (East Side)

ORIENTAL LANDMARK
2220 N. Farwell Ave.
Milwaukee
414/278-8770
Is it a cinema, bowling alley, video arcade, or tavern? It's the Landmark, and it's all four. This cavernous basement space houses not one but three bars, each with its own character. Nightly drink specials, pool tables, dart boards, and a loud jukebox make the Landmark extremely popular with UWM students and young people from around the city. (East Side)

PIECES OF EIGHT
550 N. Harbor Dr.
Milwaukee
414/271-0597
Pieces of Eight, the only pier-side business on the lakefront, has some sort of ancient exemption from the stricture that the lakefront remain parkland. Pieces of Eight has a 1970s lounge feeling to it—a sort of Playboy club/sunken-living-room ambience that can be quite charming if you're in the mood. The view of downtown is great, the happy hour is adequate, and the patio seating is perfect on summer evenings. (Downtown)

THE SAFE HOUSE
799 N. Front St.
Milwaukee
414/271-2007
The secret tavern every visitor needs to discover, the Safe House has serious fun with its Cold War theme—a friendly haven for spies working undercover. The building's entrance is disguised, you must provide a password to enter through the secret doorway, there are myriad small rooms and cubbyholes throughout the bar, and you exit through a telephone booth. And hey, the drinks aren't bad. Come in from the cold. (Downtown)

TAYLOR'S BAR
795 N. Jefferson St.
Milwaukee
414/271-2855
Taylor's is the best of the tony Cathedral Square nightspots, maintaining a relaxed atmosphere but much swankier than a neighborhood tap.

North Water Street has become, in recent years, the center of downtown nightlife. A scad of bars, restaurants, and nightclubs populate the stretch between East Juneau Avenue and City Hall, just a block east of the Milwaukee River and within an easy walk of the Bradley Center, Marcus Center, Pabst Theater, and major hotels. Sports bars, brewpubs, cigar bars, and upscale lounges are found here, and on Friday and Saturday night the street is crowded with revelers.

It's a place to be seen, surely, so the better dressed you are the happier you'll feel. The architecture and interior design are Euro-chic, with warm colors, high wooden tables, and custom Dutch doors that open to the street. The drinks are top shelf, and Happy Hour hors d'oeuvres include sushi. (Downtown)

TONY'S TAVERN
412 S. Second St.
Milwaukee
414/273-6321
Tony's is an old neighborhood bar in Walker's Point, once the watering hole of Pfister-Vogel Tannery employees. The neighborhood has changed, with artists taking over the industrial loft spaces, so Tony's clientele now includes gritty artists, actors, and musicians. But the bar hasn't changed, not one iota: It's just a no-nonsense Milwaukee tavern. (South Side)

THE UPTOWNER
1032 E. Center St.
Milwaukee
414/372-3882
The Uptowner may be the quintessential Milwaukee tavern. The warm 19th-century woodwork, pressed-tin ceiling, grade-A jukebox, and unbelievably affordable prices make this tavern extremely popular with its Riverwest neighbors, many of whom are artists. On Saturday night, be forewarned, it's loud and smoky, and the young crowd is hammered. (North Side)

VON TRIER
2235 N. Farwell Ave.
Milwaukee
414/272-1775
Oozing Teutonic ambience, von Trier is a German beer garden without peer, complete with antler lamps, murals of grape stomping along the Rhein, a glorious oak bar, two-dozen tap beers, and the nicest outdoor seating in Northpoint. Drink a *weiss* beer sitting under the trees on a warm summer evening, and you'll be wishing your neighbors *ein Prosit* before you know what's happening. (East Side)

COMEDY CLUBS

COMEDY CAFE
615 E. Brady St.
Milwaukee
414/271-5653
This is Milwaukee's big-time comedy club, hosting national stand-up stars and TV comedians. It's also the best place in town to catch the people you'll see on Letterman next year. The nightclub atmosphere is not particularly noteworthy, but on the right night you'll laugh for sure. (East Side)

ComedySportz, p. 186

TRIVIA

Wisconsin's largest cinema recently opened at Mayfair Mall in Wauwatosa. The googolplex features 18 screens, stadium seating, and all the creature comforts imaginable.

COMEDYSPORTZ
126 N. Jefferson St.
Milwaukee
414/272-8888

Comedysportz is the antidote to everything that ails comedy: that barrage of dirty words, self-effacement, and coarse put-downs. Comedy-sportz is improvisational, clean (the whole family is welcome), quick-witted, physical, and genuinely hysterical. Two teams of actors improvise routines on instructions from the audience, changing gears in the wink of an eye and keeping everyone in stitches. (Downtown)

DINNER THEATER

BROADWAY BABY
5132 W. Mill Rd.
Milwaukee
414/358-2020

Eat a steak, sit back in your comfortable chair with cordial in hand, and prepare to be entertained. Broadway Baby Dinner Theater presents classic comedies, musical revues, and other light entertainment with professional actors. The food is adequate and so is the entertainment. It's like watching TV, but live. (North Side)

STACKNER CABARET
Milwaukee Center
108 E. Wells St.
Milwaukee
414/224-9490

The Stackner Cabaret is unique among the city's play venues. An actual cabaret, the Stackner features decent food, decent drinks, and top-notch musical entertainment. The revues staged here are fully professional, with witty writing and great music. Whether the focus is doo-wop music or holiday carols, shows at the Stackner are guaranteed to please. (Downtown)

MOVIE HOUSES

AVALON THEATER
2479 S. Kinnickinnic Ave.
Milwaukee
414/744-2451

An old movie palace in Bayview, the Avalon is remarkable for two reasons. First, it's still in operation as a neighborhood cinema, showing second-run movies at discounted prices. Second, the theater's ceiling still twinkles with the glow of hundreds of stars, a milky way of tiny lights far above your head as the movie plays. (South Side)

BUDGET CINEMA SOUTH
4475 S. 108th St.
Greenfield
414/529-4050

On the pocketbook-conscious far southwest side, no one would dream of paying $7 to see a movie ("$7! Are you nuts?"). Hence this suburban multiplex showing all second-run films—those that came out last month—for as little as $1.75. If you missed a film the first time around, you can catch it here, and spend the savings on a popcorn upgrade. (South Side)

**MARCUS CINEMAS—
MENOMONEE FALLS
W18 N9393 Premier Ln.
Menomonee Falls
262/502-9070**

The Milwaukee-based Marcus Corporation is remodeling all its cinemas, adding stadium seating, better sound systems, and automated ticket counters. The Marcus-Menomonee Falls was among the first completed, and if you haven't experienced stadium seats—plush, wide, and steeply pitched to avoid obstructed views—you'll find them marvelous. There are even love seats! (North Side)

**ORIENTAL THEATER
2230 N. Farwell Ave.
Milwaukee
414/276-8711**

They don't build 'em like this anymore. From the giant Buddha sculptures (with glowing belly buttons) that guard the staircase to the lighted minarets that grace the exterior, the Oriental is second to none in architectural detail. With independent and art-house films on three screens, the program isn't bad either. Plus, you can get an espresso before the show. (East Side)

**TIMES CINEMA
5906 W. Vliet St.
Milwaukee
414/453-2436**

The Times, an old-faithful type of movie theater in Washington Heights, does Milwaukee a great public service by showing only classic films (changing weekly). The programmers at the Times are intelligent and inspired. You'll see film noir, screwball comedies, spaghetti Westerns, and epics—and admission is only $4.50. (West Side)

13

DAY TRIPS FROM MILWAUKEE

Day Trip: The East Shore

Distance from Milwaukee: 25–50 miles

People who have never seen the Great Lakes have a difficult time understanding just how, well, *great* they are—how tremendously large, how oceanic and majestic. Lake Michigan is more than 200 miles long and has shoreline in four states. A day trip north up the shore from Milwaukee will take you through charming harbor towns, across beautiful farmland, to the lip of steep bluffs, and to unique sites and attractions. Your trip can vary in length, depending on available time.

Only 25 miles from Milwaukee, **Port Washington** (or Port, as the locals call it) has become a bedroom community for the city. But the explosion of subdivisions on the edge of town has had little effect on the village's delightful harborfront area, perfect for languid strolls past sailboats, a lighthouse, and little shops and restaurants on Lake Street. The delicate spire of **St. Mary's Church**, high on a bluff over the harbor, watches over the village. The **Pebble House** visitors center—built of tiny lake stones—is on the National Register of Historic Sites; stop in for information on local events.

Port Washington is a great place to charter a fishing boat, and during the town's **Fish Day**, held the third Saturday of July, the place really loosens up. There's a parade, live music, craft vendors, and "the world's largest fish fry," a sight to behold for the tons of coleslaw slung!

If it's not Fish Day and you find yourself hungry, stop in at **Smith Bros. Fish Shanty** (at the corner of Grand and Lake), one of Wisconsin's best-known seafood restaurants. Or go a few blocks farther up the lakefront to

MILWAUKEE REGION

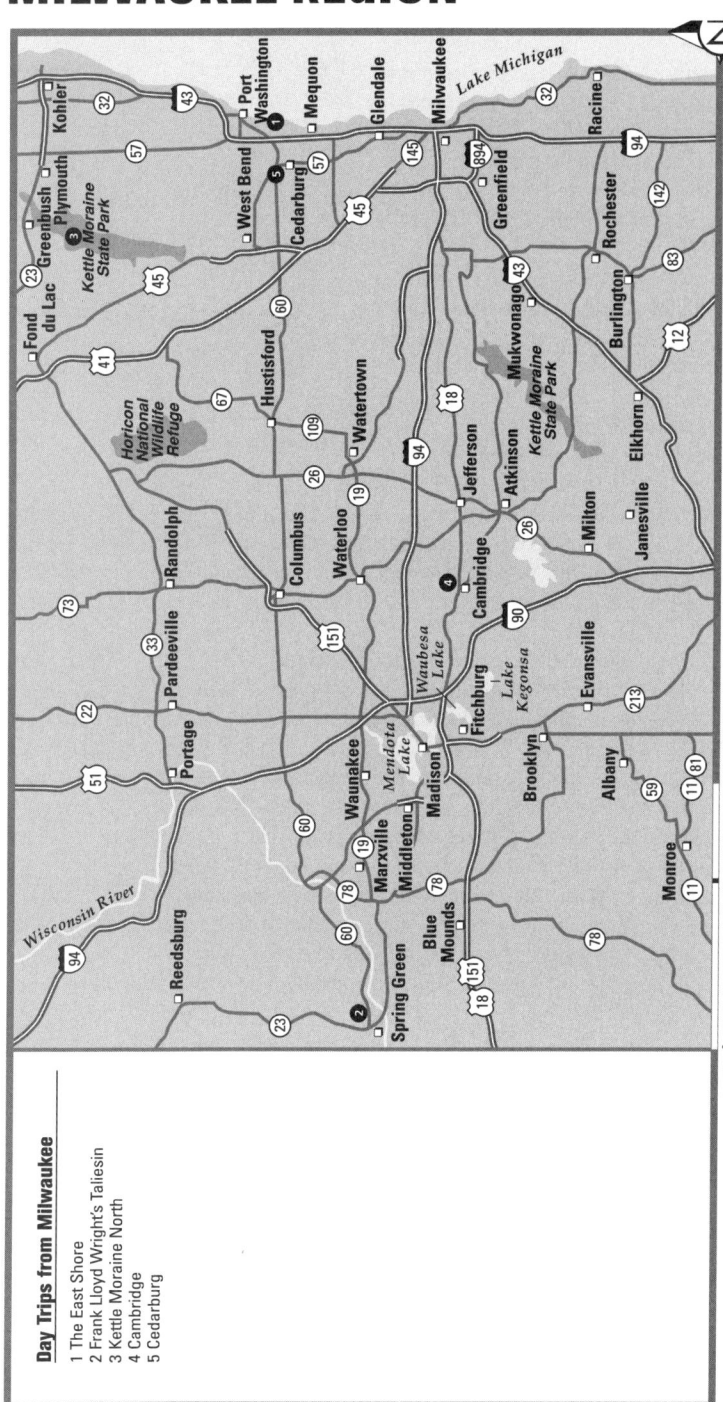

Day Trips from Milwaukee

1 The East Shore
2 Frank Lloyd Wright's Taliesin
3 Kettle Moraine North
4 Cambridge
5 Cedarburg

the **New Port Shores**, a supper club at the foot of Jackson Street. Finally, Port Washington is the home of **Allen-Edmonds Company**, maker of the world's finest men's shoes, favored by Fortune 500 execs and movie stars. The company has an outlet store at 201 East Seven Hills Road (262/284-7158).

The next stop to the north is **Sheboygan** and its neighbor town of **Kohler**. In Sheboygan, walk the **Riverfront Boardwalk,** with its collection of boutiques, and the **Lakefront Promenade** at the marina. There, the salvaged wreck of the *Lottie Cooper,* a schooner sunk during a storm in 1894, offers an excellent lesson in Great Lakes maritime history. Regular sailing regattas enliven the harbor all summer long. Up the hill, the **John Michael Kohler Arts Center** (608 New York Ave., 920/458-6144) is said to mount the finest contemporary art exhibitions in the state. Admission is free.

Cambridge Wood-fired Pottery, p. 194

Sate your appetite at the **Trattoria Stefano** (522 S. Eighth St., 920/452-8455), one of the best regional Italian restaurants in the state; reservations are recommended. Just south of downtown waits a restaurant experience of another sort. The **Charcoal Inn**, 1313 South Eighth Street, one of the world's great greasy spoons, has received the attention of the *New York Times* and *Bon Appetit* for its bratwurst patty (the meat without the casing), cooked over an indoor charcoal grill. Try the patty with onion rings and a malt, then take your cholesterol medication.

Take a walk on the beach at the **Kohler-Andrae State Parks** at the south edge of town. The parks are home to the largest sand dunes on Lake Michigan's western shore. **Indian Mound Park** (5000 S. Ninth St.) is home to 20 animal and geometric effigy mounds, built by woodland Indians about 1,300 years ago.

A few miles to the west lies the village of Kohler, which has two big attractions: the **Kohler Company** and the **American Club**, the only five-diamond resort in the Midwest. The Kohler Company, of course, is the world's largest manufacturer of high-end plumbing equipment. Tours of the enormous Kohler factory are available free of charge by making reservations a day in advance. Call 920/457-3699. The **Design Center** (Highland Dr., 920/457-3699) showcases the company's beautiful fixtures in dozens of bathrooms and kitchens created by the nation's leading interior designers and in "the Great Wall of China," a three-story mountain of toilets.

The American Club was first built to house immigrant factory workers.

It now houses travelers looking for elegance and pampering. With 236 class-A rooms, seven restaurants—including the prestigious **Immigrant Room** and casual **Horse and Plow**—three spectacular golf courses (Blackwolf Run hosted the 1998 LPGA Championship and ate up the pros), a tennis and swimming facility, spa, wildlife preserve, and the gracious **Shops at Woodlake**, the American Club is really out of this world. Call 920/457-8000 for information.

If the five-diamond accommodations of the American Club aren't your style, Sheboygan offers many hotels, motels, and B&Bs. Try the **Holiday Inn Express** (920/451-8700), the **Budgetel** (920/457-2321), or the **Lake View Mansion Bed and Breakfast** (920/457-5253), which features fireplaces, balconies looking over the bluff, and off-season discounts.

Getting There from Milwaukee: Take I-43 north from downtown to Highway 23 east to Sheboygan or west to Kohler.

Day Trip: Frank Lloyd Wright's Taliesin

Distance from Milwaukee: 110 miles

Many argue that Frank Lloyd Wright is the only American artist of international significance. Of the many Wright-designed buildings in Wisconsin, none offers more insight into the mind of the controversial architect than Taliesin, his home, studio, and workshop in Spring Green. Nestled in the spectacular hill country southwest of Madison—untouched by the glaciers that scraped and molded the rest of the state—Spring Green is the holy shrine of architecture pilgrimages. For anyone even marginally interested in Wright's work, the trip to Taliesin is eye-opening. In addition, the road to Taliesin is littered with interesting pit stops—some Wright-related and some not.

Spring Green, the home turf of the Wright family for generations, is located about 30 miles west of Madison on the sand banks of the lower Wisconsin River. After many years of traveling, FLW wrote of the area that "there is nothing anywhere better than this." His relationship to the rolling countryside is the basis for his peculiar emphasis on the coexistence of the built and natural environments.

Start your visit at the **Frank Lloyd Wright Visitor Center**, on the south bank of the river at the intersection of Highway 23 and County Highway C. This former restaurant, designed by Taliesin Associates (Wright's firm), houses a bookstore, information center, café, and ticket office. Choose a tour—from the $8 hour-long walking tour of the grounds to a full four-hour interior and exterior estate tour for $50—then head across the road to Taliesin itself.

Taliesin (pronounced tal-ee-ESS-in) is Welsh for "Shining Brow." The grounds contain a number of buildings designed by Wright, including the **Wyoming Valley Elementary School**, the firm's **Hillside Studio**, and the whimsical **Romeo and Juliet Windmill**. Taliesin itself, Wright's beloved home, was the stage on which much of his life's drama was played out (including the grisly murder of his first wife). Much of Wright's Prairie School philosophy was worked out here, and the house's horizontal masses, shallow-pitched red roofs, rambling limestone exterior, and cantilevered walkways—along with the Wright-designed furniture and textiles that adorn its interior—speak volumes about the architect's goals and ambitions. Taliesin is a remarkable and unforgettable home. Tours are given daily May through October and off-season by appointment. Call 608/588-7900 for tour information or log on to www.TaliesinPreservation.org.

The attractions of Spring Green don't end at Taliesin. The town is home to the **American Players' Theater**, a nationally known outdoor classic theater, whose productions of Shakespeare, Moliere, and others draw drama enthusiasts from Milwaukee, Madison, and Chicago.

A few miles south of town stands the storied **House on the Rock**, a tourist trap that simply boggles the mind. The house itself is unorthodox to say the least. Perched on an outcropping, it is a multilevel, nook-and-cranny-filled building erected in the 1950s and 1960s. A cross between a Hugh Hefner acid trip and a surrealist conversion van, the house features crazy windows, shag carpeting, and extreme bachelor-pad amenities (built-in champagne coolers and chafing dishes). In addition, the original owner was a compulsive collector of trinkets, and he built a series of attached warehouses to store his goods. The house tour winds through several miles of carousels, scrimshaw, mechanical banks, stuffed animals, glassware, and much more than can be described. Thousands upon thousands of people visit the House on the Rock each year, but you are advised to enter at your own risk.

Returning via **Madison**, you'll have a chance to explore the state capital. Built on an isthmus between two large inland lakes, Madison is one of Wisconsin's more attractive cities. Among its attractions are the capitol building in the center of the isthmus and **State Street**, where university hip meets capital chic in a great amalgamation of bookstores, clothing boutiques, restaurants, and specialty shops. Visit the **Madison Art Center** (211 State St.) to see outstanding contemporary art exhibitions. A great meal can be found at the **Opera House Café**, a Euro-bistro located at 117 Martin Luther King Boulevard, one block south of the capitol dome.

In Madison, Frank Lloyd Wright enthusiasts will want to see the **First Unitarian Church** and the

Wisconsin State Capitol in Madison

Monona Terrace Convention Center. Monona Terrace was designed by Wright many decades ago, but it wasn't built until 1997. Projecting into Lake Monona at the foot of Martin Luther King Boulevard, the center features Wright's flying-saucer design, characteristic of the end of his career, as does Annunciation Church in Milwaukee (see Chapter 5: "Sights and Attractions").

Getting There from Milwaukee: Take I-94 west to Madison and I-90 east to Highway 12/18 west (the Madison Beltway). On the south side of Madison, take Highway 14 west to Spring Green. Returning to Madison, take Highway 151 north into downtown and the state capitol area.

Day Trip: Kettle Moraine North

Distance from Milwaukee: 50 miles

Having pushed mountains of soil and rock ahead of them, when the glaciers receded after the last ice age they left their indelible mark on southeastern Wisconsin in the form of a terminal moraine. A line of tall hills, running more than 100 miles from southwest to northeast, marks the glaciers' utmost extension. Only 30 miles from Milwaukee, the moraine landscape abounds in geological oddities such as kames (perfectly conical hills), kettles, (inverted conical ponds), and eskers (long twisting ridges that mark the paths of ancient rivers in the ice).

The glaciers also left a legacy to the state's early European settlers: rich topsoil, perfect for farming. The northern unit of the **Kettle-Moraine State Forest** and the towns surrounding it preserve a good portion of Wisconsin's geologic, natural, and ethnic heritage in a series of recreational areas and historic sites. If you're looking to take a walk in the woods (or a bike ride, ski trip, or snowshoe hike) or through quaint rural towns, it's all to be found a short drive from Milwaukee.

At the northern end of the state forest stands **Old Wade House State Historic Park**. Located in the village of Greenbush on Highway 23, the Wade House was once a stage stop—and a tiny dot of civilization in the wilderness—on the plank road between Sheboygan and Fond du Lac. The village has been painstakingly restored. The old inn, blacksmith's shop, and carriage house (full of antique horse carriages) are open for tours May through October.

At the Wade House you will find the beginning of the **Kettle-Moraine Scenic Drive**, a series of well-marked county roads that run the length of the Kettle-Moraine State Forest. As you drive south, you'll come across a series of well-marked trailheads. The **Greenbush Trails** and **New Fane Trails** offer mountain bikers and hikers many miles of winding trails through several interesting environments, including wetlands and prairie. The **Parnell Tower Trails** include a huge observation tower; the view from the top is breathtaking. A stop at the **Ice Age Visitor's Center**—on State Highway 67 just south of Dundee—yields information on local geology, recreations areas, and special events. Free maps are available, and the site has a self-guided nature trail. Stop at **Long Lake** for a swim and a picnic (the lake has a campground, too).

Winding south through the state forest, you'll eventually end up in the city of **West Bend**, located at the intersection of Highway 33 and the Milwaukee River. Stop for a bite at the **St. Somewhere Café** on Main Street, a pleasant coffeehouse that features excellent soups, or the upscale **Inn on Courthouse Square**, across from the **Historical Museum**. The **West Bend Art Museum** (300 S. Sixth St.) houses an enormous historical painting by German-American academic painter Carl von Marr (really enormous: a special room was built for it). Finally, West Bend is home to **Amity Leather**, the country's premier wallet maker, and the **West Bend Company**, manufacturers of home appliances. Both businesses have outlet stores in the city at 400 Washington Street.

Getting There from Milwaukee: Take I-43 north to Highway 57 north (at Port Washington) to Plymouth, then go west on Highway 23 to Greenbush. Go south on Kettle-Moraine Scenic Drive to West Bend and south on U.S. 45 to Milwaukee.

Day Trip: Cambridge

Distance from Milwaukee: 65 miles

A journey to Cambridge may be the perfect day trip from Milwaukee: It is just far enough, the landscape is just different enough, and the shopping and dining are more than good enough to make the city a bona fide getaway. Set in the lake country southeast of Madison, Cambridge is a popular destination for travelers, who come to visit the town's pottery works, antique stores, and artisans' shops.

Your trip to Cambridge should begin at **Rowe Pottery Works**, the ceramists that put the town on the art and shopping map. Rowe is famous for its stoneware dishes, candlesticks, pots, and other items bearing lovely and highly distinctive salt glaze—deep-blue overpainting on a nubbly stone-gray base. You can see the potters in action and browse the extensive shop for hours (you'll find all kinds of decorative items in addition to pottery).

With Rowe well established and well known among ceramics collectors, other potteries began to establish operations in town, making Cambridge a sort of artisan's mecca. Among the most notable is **Cambridge Wood-fired Pottery**, at 355 Highway 18 (608/423-4507). Smaller than Rowe, CWP offers spectacular stoneware. Its dinnerware, in warm browns, is particularly notable.

When you've had enough of slips, casts, and greenware, take a walk through the streets of Cambridge, past the many lovely Victorian homes. You'll end up at the **Cambridge Antique Mall**, located in a white clapboard church on the town square. With two-dozen dealers, this antiques

Taliesin living room, p. 191

wonderland has good selections of the implements of rural living and, perhaps because of the town's proximity to the great state university, a surprising selection of old books.

If all this shopping makes you hungry, look no further than the incredible **Clay Market Café**. Easily one of the most creative and interesting—not to mention delicious—restaurants in Wisconsin, the Clay Market Café practices eclectic cooking with a deft touch, never reaching too far from established principles, but never giving in to easy solutions either. A changing menu of pastas (tortellini with wild mushrooms and bell peppers) and entrées (grilled chicken breast stuffed with pesto) will please any palate. The café has the best children's menu around and a relaxed but not slouching atmosphere. If these delights don't tempt you, the **Cambridge Pub** is directly across the street, serving good tavern food like burgers and beer.

Getting There from Milwaukee: Take I-94 west to Highway 26. Go south to Jefferson, then west to Cambridge on Highway 18.

Day Trip: Cedarburg

Distance from Milwaukee: 20 miles

Cedarburg is just one of those towns—as attractive and charming and, yes, quaint as a village can be, without the cloying fakery of a Disneyland model. This town of stone and brick Victorian houses on the banks of Cedar Creek is close enough to Milwaukee that you can spend the better part of a day here without having to hurry back to make cocktail hour. It's close enough to be considered a suburb, yet Cedarburg has retained its individuality with sensitive restorations, a slew of unique boutiques and antique shops, and interesting little restaurants.

The center of attraction in Cedarburg is the **Cedar Creek Settlement**, located where Washington Avenue meets the creek. A group of shops and restaurants in a spectacularly renovated stone woolen mill—built during the Civil War to make clothing for Union troops—the settlement alone offers a day's worth of browsing. The emphasis here is on artsy, and the Settlement's cup runneth over with jewelry, ceramics, and housewares. The Settlement also has a number of antique dealers, the **Cedarburg Winery**, and funky boutiques like **Gaby's**, which carries all kinds of chic casual wear.

If you're hungry, one of Cedarburg's best-known restaurants is in the Settlement. The **Cream and Crepe Café** serves light entrée and dessert crepes, sandwiches, and soups. To the south, on Washington Avenue, you'll find plenty of charming pubs, diners, restaurants, and, of course, more shops.

Getting There from Milwaukee: *Take I-43 north to County Highway C. Go west to Highway 57, then north into the village.*

APPENDIX: CITY·SMART BASICS

EMERGENCY PHONE NUMBERS

Police, Fire, Ambulance
911

Milwaukee County Sheriff
414/278-4700

Wisconsin State Patrol Emergency
414/785-4710

Wisconsin State Patrol
Non-emergency
414/785-4700

Suicide Prevention Hotline
414/257-7222

Poison Center
800/815-8855

U.S. Coast Guard
414/747-7180

MAJOR HOSPITALS

Children's Hospital
9000 W. Wisconsin Ave.
414/266-2000

Elmbrook Memorial Hospital
19333 W. North Ave.
262/785-2000

Froedert Memorial Lutheran Hospital
9200 W. Wisconsin Ave.
414/259-3000

St. Joseph's Hospital
5000 W. Chambers St.
414/447-2000

St. Luke's Medical Center
2900 W. Oklahoma Ave.
414/649-6000

St. Mary's Hospital
2323 N. Lake Dr.
414/291-1000

Sinai Samaritan Medical Center
945 N. 12th St.
414/219-2000

VA Medical Center
5000 W. National Ave.
414/384-2000

RECORDED INFORMATION

Time
414/844-1414

Local Weather
414/936-1212

Air Quality (Ozone) Alert
414/263-8582

Road Conditions
800/762-2947

VISITOR INFORMATION

Greater Milwaukee Visitors and Convention Bureau
800/554-1448

Metro Milwaukee Chamber of Commerce
414/287-4100

CITY TOURS

American Sightseeing International
414/282-6465

Gray Line
414/271-0996

Historic Milwaukee Walking Tours
414/277-7795

POST OFFICES

Main Branch
345 W. St. Paul Ave.
414/270-2000

Airport Branch (24-hour service)
5500 S. Howell Ave.
414/481-4032

PUBLIC TRANSIT

Amtrak
800/USA-RAIL

Milwaukee County Transit System
414/344-6711

Waukesha Metro Transit
262/524-3636

CAR RENTAL

Avis
800/831-2847

Budget
800/527-077

Dollar
800/800-4000

Hertz
800/645-3131

Mayfair
414/489-6600

National
800/227-7368

Thrifty
800/367-2277

MULTICULTURAL RESOURCES

African American Chamber of Commerce
414/871-5838

American Indian Chamber of Commerce
414/383-7531

Hispanic Chamber of Commerce
414/643-6963

OTHER COMMUNITY ORGANIZATIONS

AIDS Resource Center-Wisconsin
414/273-1991

Centro de la Communidad Unida
414/649-4404

Gay People's Union
414/562-7010

Interchange (Older Adults)
414/276-0988

Mental Health Association
414/276-3122

Milwaukee Center for Independence
(People with Disabilities)
414/272-1344

Milwaukee Islamic Dawah Center
414/462-1998

Milwaukee Jewish Federation
414/390-5700

Milwaukee Women's Center
414/272-6199

CHILD-CARE REFERRAL

Childcare Finders Plus
414/425-2550

Community Coordinated Child Care
414/562-2676

NEWSPAPERS

Business Journal
414/278-7788

Catholic Herald
414/769-3500

Hmong News Journal
414/355-6419

Irish American Post
414/273-8132

Milwaukee Community Journal
(African American weekly)
414/265-5300

Milwaukee Courier
(African American weekly)
414/449-4860

Milwaukee Journal-Sentinel
414/224-2000

Milwaukee Labor Press
414/771-7070

The Onion (satire)
414/272-1372

Shepherd Express Metro (alternative press)
414/276-2222

Spanish Journal
414/271-5683

Wisconsin Jewish Chronicle
414/271-5888

Wisconsin Light (gay and lesbian)
414/372-2773

MAGAZINES

Computer User
414/641-9421

Exclusively Yours
414/271-4270

In Step (gay and lesbian)
414/278-7840

Metroparent
414/259-1884

Milwaukee Magazine
414/273-1101

Northshore Lifestyle
414/375-5100

BOOKSTORES

Audobon Court Books, Ltd.
383 W. Brown Deer Rd.
414/351-9140

B. Dalton
Northridge Shopping Center
7700 W. Brown Deer Rd.
414/354-1240
Southridge Shopping Center
5300 S. 76th St.
414/423-1810

Barnes & Noble
16220 W. Blue Mound Rd.
414/782-1514
4935 S. 76th. St.
414/281-8222
Bay Shore Mall
5900 N. Port Washington Rd.
414/967-0007

Books & Company
1039 Summit Ave.
Oconomowoc
414/567-0106

Harry W. Schwartz Bookshops
2551 N. Downer Ave.
414/332-1181
4093 N. Oakland Ave.
414/963-3111
Loehmann's Plaza
17145 W. Blue Mound Rd.
414/797-6140
Pavilions
10976 N. Port Washington Rd.
414/241-6220

The Little Read Book
7603 W. State St.
414/774-BOOK

Scribner's
2500 N. Mayfair Rd.
414/453-3305

Waldenbooks
Northridge Shopping Center
7700 W. Brown Deer Rd.
414/354-0510
Southridge Shopping Center
5300 S. 76th St.
414/421-4290
Brookfield Square
95 N. Moorland Rd.
414/921-6298
Grand Avenue Mall
275 W. Wisconsin Ave.
414/224-9400

AM RADIO STATIONS

WAUK 1510, sports
WEMP 1250, oldies
WISN 1130, talk
WJYI 1340, Christian
WMCS 1290, soul
WOKY 920, big band
WTMJ 620, news
WTKM 1540, polka

FM RADIO STATIONS

WAMG 103.7, easy listening
WFMR 98.3, classical
WHAD 90.7, Wisconsin Public Radio
WJZI 93.3, smooth jazz
WKKV 100.7, urban contemporary
WKLH 96.5, classic rock
WKTI 94.5, Top 40
WLTQ 97.3, easy listening
WLUM 102.1, rock
WLZR 102.9, hard rock
WMIL 106.1, country
WMSE 91.7, really alternative
WMYX 99.1, Top 40
WPNT 106.9, adult new rock
WTKM 104.9, polka
WUWM 89.7, National Public Radio
WVCY 107.7, Christian
WYMS 88.9, jazz/ethnic
WZTR 95.7, oldies

TELEVISION STATIONS

UNI 46, Latin American
WCGV 24, independent
WDJT 58, CBS
WISN 12, ABC
WITI 6, FOX
WMVS 10, PBS
WMVT 36, PBS
WTMJ 4, NBC
WVCY 30, Christian
WVTV 18, WB

INDEX

accommodations, 27–50
air travel, 24–25
Allen Bradley clock tower, 93, 101
America's Black Holocaust Museum, 108
American Geographical Society Collection, 88–89
American System Built Homes, 95
Annunciation Greek Orthodox Church, 92
Apple Works, 114–115
Art Street Window, 112

bakeries, 63
bars, 181–185
bed-and-breakfasts, 45
Betty Brinn Children's Museum, 109–110, 116
Betty Brinn Children's Room, 116, 121
bicycling, 23–24, 152, 154
Boat House, 89
boating, 154–155
Boener Botanical Gardens, 124
bookstores, 137–139, 140
bowling, 155–156
Bradley Center, 81, 172
Bradley Sculpture Garden, 106
breweries, 98
"Bridge War," 11
Brooks Stevens Automotive Museum, 110

The Calling, 81
Cambridge, 194–195
Candycane Lane, 95
Captain Frederick Pabst Mansion, 81
Cathedral Square, 124
Cedarburg, 195–196
Charles Allis Art Museum, 106
city tours, 102–104
classical music, 168–171
Clown Hall of Fame, 81
coffeehouses, 69

comedy clubs, 185–186
dance clubs, 177
dance companies, 171–172
department stores, 144
Discovery World Museum, 108, 116
Downtown Ambassadors, 18
driving, 22–23

economy, 14–15
Exploration Station, 117

Family Sundays, 117
fencing, 163
Festival of Milwaukee Dance, 172
fish fries, 73
fishing, 156–157
fitness clubs, 157
Florence Eiseman Company, 135
Frederick Bogk House, 89
Froemming Park Observatory, 95
frozen custard, 66

Germania Building, 82
Gertie the Duck, 92
Goldman's Department Store, 144, 147
golf courses, 154, 157–159
Grain Exchange Building, 82
Greendale, 3

Haggerty Museum of Art, 107
Harley-Davidson Factory Tours, 92–93
Heirloom Doll Museum, 101
hiking trails, 153
Historic Brady Street, 89, 91, 135–136
Historic Third Ward, 82, 133–135
history, 4–8
Holy Hill, 93
horseback riding, 159
housing, 15–16
Humphrey Imax Dome Theater, 84

ice-skating, 159, 161
Inova, 107

Jeremiah Curtin House, 95–96

Kettle Moraine North, 193–194
Kilbourntown House, 91

Lady Elgin, 24
Lake Michigan, 160, 188, 190–191
Lapham Peak, 126
lawn bowling, 127
Lowell Damon House, 99

malls, 145–147
Manfred Olsen Planetarium, 91
Marcus Amphitheater, 173
Marcus Center for the Performing Arts, 166, 173, 174
Midwest Express Center, 84
Milwaukee Art Museum, 107
Milwaukee Ballet, 171–172
Milwaukee Brewers, 149
Milwaukee Bucks, 149
Milwaukee City Hall, 84–85
Milwaukee County Courthouse, 85
Milwaukee County Historical Center, 109
Milwaukee County Stadium, 99
Milwaukee County Zoo, 99–100
Milwaukee Journal Sentinel, 85
Milwaukee Journal Sentinel Rose Festival, 128
Milwaukee Public Library, 85
Milwaukee Public Museum, 109
Milwaukee Riverwalk, 85–86, 87, 103
Milwaukee Symphony Orchestra, 170
Milwaukee Visitors Information Center, 86
Mitchell Park, 96, 128
Modjeska Theater, 173–174
movie houses, 186–187
Museum Center, 106
museums, 105–110
music clubs, 177–181

Nature Now hot line, 130
Newhall House Hotel, 39
nightlife, 176–187
North Harbor Breakwall, 91
Northpoint Lighthouse, 91–92
Northpoint Watertower, 92
Notre Dame Convent, 101–102

Old Falls Village, 93
Old St. Mary's Catholic Church, 86
Old World Third Street, 133
Old World Wisconsin, 102
opera, 169, 171
outlet stores, 147

Pabst Theater, 86
parks, 123–131
Pettit National Ice Center, 100, 122, 152, 159
polka music, 179
population, 8–9, 12
Potawatomi Bingo Casino, 86–87
Pryor Street Well, 96
public art, 113
public transportation, 19–21

restaurants, 51–79
Riverside Theater, 174–175
Riverside Urban Environmental Center, 115, 129
rock climbing, 162
roller-skating, 161

St. Joan of Arc Chapel, 87
St. Josaphat Basilica, 97
St. Sava Serbian Orthodox Cathedral, 97
Schlitz Audubon Center, 115, 129
schools, 16
Schwan Hall, 175
Shepherd Express Metro, 180
shopping, 118–120, 132–147
skywalks, 82
sports, 148–164
Stackner Heritage Farm, 115

Summerfest, 175
swimming, 161–163

Taliesin, 191–193
tennis, 163–164
theater, 117–118, 166–168
Timber Wolf Farm, 97
Tripoli Shrine Temple, 100–101

Urban Fishing Program, 115–116

Villa Terrace Decorative Arts Museum, 107–108
Villa Terrace Renaissance Garden, 130

weather, 9–10
Weather Flame, 88, 102
Wehr Nature Center, 130
West Allis Farmer's Market, 139
Whitefish Bay, 136–137
Whitnall Park Arboretum, 130–131
Wisconsin Conservatory of Music, 175
Wisconsin Gas Building, 88, 102
Wisconsin Lake Schooner Association, 88
Wisconsin State Fair Park, 101
Wright, Frank Lloyd, 88, 191–193

You'll Feel like a Local When You Travel with Guides from John Muir Publications

CiTY·SMaRT™ GUIDEBOOKS

Pick one for your favorite city: *Albuquerque, Anchorage, Austin, Calgary, Charlotte, Chicago, Cincinnati, Cleveland, Denver, Indianapolis, Kansas City, Memphis, Milwaukee, Minneapolis/St. Paul, Nashville, Pittsburgh, Portland, Richmond, Salt Lake City, San Antonio, St. Louis, Tampa/St. Petersburg, Tucson*

Guides for kids 6 to 10 years old about what to do, where to go, and how to have fun in: *Atlanta, Austin, Boston, Chicago, Cleveland, Denver, Indianapolis, Kansas City, Miami, Milwaukee, Minneapolis/St. Paul, Nashville, Portland, San Francisco, Seattle, Washington D.C.*

TRAVEL✦SMART®

Trip planners with select recommendations to: *Alaska, American Southwest, Carolinas, Colorado, Deep South, Eastern Canada, Florida Gulf Coast, Hawaii, Illinois/Indiana, Kentucky/Tennessee, Maryland/Delaware, Michigan, Minnesota/Wisconsin, Montana/Wyoming/Idaho, New England, New Mexico, New York State, Northern California, Ohio, Pacific Northwest, Pennsylvania/New Jersey, South Florida and the Keys, Southern California, Texas, Utah, Virginias, Western Canada*

Rick Steves' GUIDES

See *Europe Through the Back Door* and take along guides to: *France, Belgium & the Netherlands; Germany, Austria & Switzerland; Great Britain & Ireland; Italy; Russia & the Baltics; Scandinavia; Spain & Portugal; London; Paris;* or the *Best of Europe*

ADVENTURES IN NATURE

Plan your next adventure in: *Alaska, Belize, Caribbean, Costa Rica, Guatemala, Honduras, Mexico*

JMP travel guides are available at your favorite bookstores. For a FREE catalog or to place a mail order, call: 800-888-7504.

John Muir Publications P.O. Box 613 • Santa Fe, NM 87504

Cater to Your Interests on Your Next Vacation

**The 100 Best Small Art Towns in America
3rd edition**
Discover Creative Communities, Fresh Air, and Affordable Living
U.S. $16.95, Canada $24.95

**The Big Book of Adventure Travel
2nd edition**
Profiles more than 400 great escapes to all corners of the world
U.S. $17.95, Canada $25.50

Cross-Country Ski Vacations
A Guide to the Best Resorts, Lodges, and Groomed Trails in North America
U.S. $15.95, Canada $22.50

Gene Kilgore's Ranch Vacations, 5th edition
The Complete Guide to Guest Resorts, Fly-Fishing, and Cross-Country Skiing Ranches
U.S. $22.95, Canada $35.50

Indian America, 4th edition
A traveler's companion to more than 300 Indian tribes in the United States
U.S. $18.95, Canada $26.75

Saddle Up!
A Guide to Planning the Perfect Horseback Vacation
U.S. $14.95, Canada $20.95

Watch It Made in the U.S.A., 2nd edition
A Visitor's Guide to the Companies That Make Your Favorite Products
U.S. $17.95, Canada $25.50

The World Awaits
A Comprehensive Guide to Extended Backpack Travel
U.S. $16.95, Canada $23.95

**JMP travel guides are available at your favorite bookstores.
For a FREE catalog or to place a mail order, call: 800-888-7504.**

John Muir Publications • P.O. Box 613 • Santa Fe, NM 87504

ABOUT THE AUTHOR

Nathan Guequierre was born in Milwaukee and raised in Detroit. In 1987, he returned to Milwaukee and became staff writer for the Milwaukee Art Museum. He also copyedited and contributed to *Art Muscle*, a Milwaukee art magazine. He is currently an art critic for the *Shepherd Express Metro*, a weekly Milwaukee newspaper. His creative writing has appeared in journals around the country. His art criticism has appeared in exhibit catalogs, the *Wisconsin Academy Review*, and other publications. Nathan is married to Jean Roberts Guequierre, a painter. They have one child, Felix.

JOHN MUIR PUBLICATIONS and its City•Smart Guidebook authors are dedicated to building community awareness within City•Smart cities. We are proud to work with Literacy Services of Wisconsin as we publish this guide to Milwaukee.

Since 1965, **Literacy Services of Wisconsin** has offered free tutoring in adult basic education, GED/high school equivalency exam preparation, and English as a Second Language. Our Laubach Center hosts more than 600 hours of tutoring and small group classes each week. As an independent nonprofit organization, Literacy Services relies on a dedicated core of volunteer tutors and the contributions of hundreds of community donors.

For more information contact:
Literacy Services of Wisconsin
2724 W. Wells St.
Milwaukee, WI 53208
414/344-5878
www.execpc.com/~literacy